Musical Masterpieces

Jean-Jacques Soleil
and
Guy Lelong

Chambers

EDINBURGH   NEW YORK   TORONTO

Published 1991 by W & R Chambers Ltd,
43–45 Annandale Street, Edinburgh EH7 4AZ
95 Madison Avenue, New York N.Y. 10016

First published in France as *Les oeuvres-clés de la musique*
© Bordas, Paris, 1988
© English text edition W & R Chambers 1991

Library of Congress Cataloging-in-Publication Data applied for

ISBN 0550 17004 9

Cover design Blue Peach Design Consultants Ltd
Typeset in England by Butler & Tanner
Printed in England by Clays Ltd, St Ives, plc

Acknowledgements

Translated from the French by Imogen Brian

Adapted for the English edition by Alan Dury
Hugh MacDiarmid

Chambers Compact Reference Series Editor   Min Lee

Illustration credits

Page

iv   Nicholas Tournier, Le Concert: ph. Hubert Josse
223   © J. Aubert-Photogram

Front cover (symphony orchestra) Chuck Kuhn © The Image Bank
Spine (Beethoven, painting by Karl von Dtieler) © Roger–Viollet

Other titles in
Chambers Compact Reference

Catastrophes and Disasters
Crimes and Criminals
50 Years of Rock Music
Great Inventions Through History
Great Modern Inventions
Great Scientific Discoveries
Masters of Jazz
Movie Classics
Mythology
The Occult
Religious Leaders
Sacred Writings of World Religions
Saints
Space Exploration

To be published in 1993

Great Cities of the World
Movie Stars
Operas
World Folklore

Nicholas Tournier, *Le Concert*

Contents

Composers and their works

Introduction

This book examines, at roughly the rate of one work per page, 215 instrumental music compositions, each one worthy of being considered a masterpiece in this field. The works covered in this book have all determined, by their importance, a context which they have helped (as we will explain further) either to characterize or to transform.

What need is there to give an account of these masterpieces? The aim is to facilitate, through the creation of an understanding of the workings of these masterpieces, a renewed aesthetic pleasure. For, unlike a speech too often analysed, the emotion that one feels on listening to a piece of music is not diminished by the explanations provided. On the contrary, our pleasure is increased by our analytical understanding. Without being sufficiently supported, all pleasure has a tendency to become deadened. Analysis also has the advantage of putting first impressions in a new perspective.

The *aesthetic emotion* released by *critical listening* is, in a sense, the final objective of this book. But before coming to that, it is first necessary to explain the reasons for our choices and the presentation methods used.

A deliberated choice

The historical division

Of all the works examined here opus 6 by Corelli is the oldest, since at least some of the six Concerti Grossi which make up the piece were played as early as 1682. *Responses*, by Pierre Boulez, written three centuries later, is the most recent musical score. While four major periods of the history of instrumental music are represented (baroque, classicism, romanticism, and modern), no works from the Middle Ages or the Renaissance have been examined. This 'exclusion' is by no means arbitrary, and can be justified solely by the pre-eminence of vocal music during these two periods and by the fact that purely instrumental medieval pieces are extremely rare, and all Renaissance instrumental music (transcriptions,

dances and free pieces) is based, in its writing, on vocal music. Furthermore, despite some exceptions and some precursory signs (pieces for the lute such as those by John Dowland, pieces for the virginal by William Byrd, pieces for the organ by Antonio de Cabezon, etc) it was only in the seventeenth century that instrumental music really began to break away from its functional role (transcriptions, voice and dance accompaniments) and gain the status of pure music, with its own specific forms (suites, sonatas, concertos).

However, Corelli was not, in fact, the first baroque musician, but as he contributed so greatly to the definition, indeed to the invention, of several forms of this period and as he was one of the very rare composers (and certainly the first) to have written exclusively for instruments, we turn to him to mark the chronological starting point of this collection of works. At the other end of the scale this assessment of instrumental masterpieces needed to take into account, if not the most recent developments in musical research, at least the undeniable contributions of the generation of composers born in the 1920s, from Pierre Boulez to Iannis Xenakis.

Major works, prominent works

Within the defined limits, what works should be selected?

A preliminary grouping put together the works that we would call 'obligatory', those for whom a general consensus has gradually emerged to recognize their exceptional intrinsic value. In these works, formally complex and rich with constantly renewed auditory approaches, are found the irreplaceable moments of historic process and cultural givens of Occidental music. From '*The Art of Fugue*' by Bach to '*The Rite of Spring*' by Stravinsky examples abound: *Concertos for piano and orchestra* by Mozart, *String quartet* by Haydn, *Eroica symphony* by Beethoven, *Études and Preludes* by Chopin, *La mer* by Debussy, etc.

In contrast with these major scores, a second grouping puts together those works which can simply be described as 'prominent'. These works differ from the 'major' works in that the history of music would not have been greatly altered by their absence. Nevertheless, as these are the undeniable testimony to particular characteristics of their eras, the collective memory has retained them and it is therefore legitimate to include some of them here. This is why there are, on the pages to follow, some works which are exemplary of a genre (Tchaikovsky's ballets), others remarkable for their challenging aspects (*Parade* by Erik Satie) or by their flaunted mood (Rossini's overtures) or because they have become the special totem of their composer (Paul Dukas' *The Sorcerer's Apprentice*). Yet another work may be included because it is a hit due to its virtuoso repertoire (Grieg or Rachmaninov's concertos) or because it has acquired a quasi-sociological value (Johann Strauss' *Blue Danube*).

Yet, the distinction between these two groupings is not as clear-cut as it may seem, and in fact there exist all the possible intermediary combinations, which would allow a merely prominent work to become one which, in giving constant evidence of a particular characteristic of its era, is in fact major. In other words, these two divisions are less those of two mutually exclusive groups than of two poles of attraction between which the works in question are qualitatively distributed. Although the choice of works, with regard for some kind of consensus, is dependent on a degree of objectivity, there is a bias towards the first pole, that of the major works, to the detriment of the second which has been reduced to its bare minimum.

The advantage of innovation

By giving preference to the works which have resulted in considerable transformations in the history of music, we have prized innovation. The selection made from the realm of French music is particularly revealing. For while three of the four symphonies written by Berlioz are included, and Debussy has been given ten works and Ravel seven, Franck, Fauré, and Roussel

are only represented by two of their works, and Bizet, Chabrier, Chausson, Honegger, Lalo, Milhaud, Saint-Saëns by only one each.

It is also this principle that led us to favour the second school of Vienna over its contemporary, the French group of six, as is evident in that the three Viennese composers (Schönberg, Berg and Webern) figure here with fourteen works, while the French group has only two (Milhaud and Honegger, with the exception of the piece by Poulenc, which is primarily vocal). During this time music gave evidence of an entirely different scope in Vienna than in Paris, one which has, moreover, amply justified its subsequent evolution.

A Double Classification

Having chosen the works, how should they be classified?

Dictionaries generally maintain an alphabetical order and music histories a chronological, national and stylistic classification. But this book is neither a dictionary nor a history of music, nor an anthology (it is really more of an analytical repertoire of works). It therefore makes more sense to endow it with a classification of its own.

A plural chronology

It was finally decided to make a classification by *musical categories*. This name reveals only that the works have been arranged according to their membership in a class (ballets, concertos, quartets, etc.), even though the categories themselves cannot be defined with the same degree of precision.

The categories we have determined correspond to five major divisions: the writing process (chorales, fugues, variations), the set forms (sonatas and classical symphonies), instrumental formations (quartet, trio...), the basic genres (études, symphonic poems...), and finally the free-form pieces. Under this last heading we have included both the very unrestrained forms (*rhapsodies* are characterized by their use of national elements) and forms which are defined in terms of the categories that they do not quite, but almost, fit into (romantic *fantasias* for example, can be seen as a kind of lapsed sonata).

But as musical works do not all obey the norms established beforehand and as, from the end of the nineteenth century, they have tended more and more to create their own structures, a final section has been given to those works which do not fit into any of the previously established categories.

In other words, the book is divided into as many sections as distinctions have been determined, and within each category the works are arranged in a chronological[1] order. This order shows the evolution of each category insofar as, in the case of the symphony, it has given rise to a large number of works.

Each section is introduced by a text which presents the category under consideration, its processes of establishment (origins and time of first appearance), its transformations, its eventual cession and often its unexpected reappearances. Also cited in this text is a big enough number of works to allow the reader to better understand the choices made.

The justification for this double classification based both on category and chronology, is firstly that it confers on the book a rhythm (certain sections, like *Ballades* or

[1] This order is based on the date of the works, which ostensibly easy to establish, actually poses almost unsolvable problems. For each work, in general, three dates were taken into account: that of the composition, that of the first production and that of its publication. A priori, the most pertinent date would seem to be that of the publication, but certain works (notably those by J. S. Bach) were sometimes published more than one hundred years after their composition, and it is obviously out of the question to insert a work by Bach between the works of Schumann and Liszt. The date of the first performance, which we turned to next, poses similar problems. We are thus left with the date of composition, but this is not always known, and the writing of the score (in the case of an opus belonging to a group of works) is sometimes spread out over so many years that no one appears more legitimate than any other. This is why the date beside the title of each of the works is only that which seemed to be the most representative — the details of the dating being, in any case, given in the historical references that accompany each work.

Toccatas, are very short, while others, like *Sonatas* or *Concertos* are very long). But, it is primarily because it seems infinitely more useful to show the precise transformations in a particular domain than to skim through instrumental music in its entirety, throughout its history and its diversity of styles. In brief, quality was preferred over quantity.

Difficulties of classification

With this classification system a difficulty arose. Some works turned out to belong to two distinct categories. This is the case of the twenty-four preludes and fugues of the *Well-tempered Klavier* by J. S. Bach and of the sonatas and partitas for solo violin by the same composer. But, as the two solutions were equally pertinent, the dilemma was resolved in favour of the general equilibrium of the book. This was also the case for several of the works written for a chamber formation, but belonging no less to another category, as is the situation with the *Lyric Suite* for string quartet by Berg or with Schönberg's *Transfigured Night*, a symphonic poem for a string sextet. In each case a decision was made based on the title of the work.

The effects of classification, even after the necessary adjustments have been made, can appear to favour certain composers to the detriment of others, and it is likely that a distribution by composer would have led to very different results. Thus Beethoven, whose mainly instrumental productions perfected all forms of classicism, is the composer most represented with twenty works, all of which are undeniably 'major'. But if the quantity of works attributed to Beethoven is indicative of the quality of the composer, this equation is far from being valid in each case, as, for example with Berlioz and Brahms. Only four works by the former are examined, and ten by the latter, but this distribution does not at all indicate the value of the musicians. The large numerical gap in this case is the result, firstly of Berlioz having written far less than Brahms did, and of the fact that Berlioz's works were mostly vocal, and finally of Brahms, the last great defender of classical forms, having attempted virtually all of them.

In other words, the number of works of a particular composer is only a vague indication of his intrinsic importance. For all the musicians who are poorly represented it was necessary to be particularly mindful that the works selected were characteristic of their composer and of the category to which they belonged.

The commentary

Having chosen and classified the works, how best to finally account for them? The principle is simple: a subtitle, brief and informative plus a short presentation presenting the principal idea of the work, followed by an analytical commentary developing this idea.

If the choice of works attests to only a relative objectivity and the classification system is even more subjective, the commentaries stem from an undeniable bias. Considering that the richer and more well-wrought a work is the more susceptible it is to analysis, and the more it is analysed the better it will be listened to, the main objec-

tive of these commentaries has been to explain how, precisely, these works were written and what it is that makes them so original. These brief analyses are responsible, in a sense, for providing the initial access to reading that we feel to be so important. For this reason, they have been kept fairly succinct and do not require any special knowledge on the part of the reader. In order that these commentaries should be presented in the clearest manner possible, all the technical terms used are listed in a glossary at the end of the book.

Each work is also accompanied by historical references (limited to giving some dates or to placing the work in a more general context) and by *additional information* in boxes in the text.

Acknowledgments

The authors would like to thank, for the help given to them throughout the creation of this book, Marc Choquer, Michel Gauthier, Patrice Hamel and Beatrice Jacobs.

Bagatelles

The word *bagatelle* (from the Italian *bagatella*, meaning 'an object of little value, a trifle') describes a short and lively composition of a frivolous nature, generally presented by its composer as a work of little importance. Most often written for the keyboard, bagatelles do not follow any precise rules. One of the first examples goes back to François Couperin who introduced it in his *Pieces for the Harpsichord* (*Bagatelles*, book II, tenth arrangement, 1717). In the second half of the 18th century compilations of short and varied pieces were unpretentiously given this title (*A Thousand and One Bagatelles* by J. Boivin, 1753; *Musikalische Bagatellen* by C. W. Maizier, 1797).

But it was not until Beethoven and his three collections of *Bagatelles for the Pianoforte*, opus 33, 119 and 126, that this form of music attained a high level of artistic value. The number of bagatelles produced up until the end of the 19th century is significant, but the works themselves of little interest. There is one exception which proves the rule: *Bagatelle without Tonality* by Franz Liszt, written in 1885 but only discovered in 1956. The first work to dispense almost entirely with tonality (25 years before Schönberg), this prophetic piece goes beyond the free form of the bagatelle, while still maintaining its brevity and liveliness.

In the 20th century, the *Fourteen Bagatelles* for the piano, opus 6 by Béla Bartók, correspond equally well to the definition of the genre. But in the *Six Bagatelles for String Quartet*, opus 9, by Anton Webern, one of the major works of the century, the title no longer relates to anything more than the brevity of a barely restricted form.

Beethoven, Ludwig van

Six bagatelles for piano, 1825

Opus 126

Beethoven the miniaturist

Largely misunderstood, the Six Bagatelles *opus 126 were the last important work by the composer for the piano.*

Unlike the second collection, opus 119, where the eleven pieces were put together only for the edition, the *Six Bagatelles* opus 126 were conceived of as a series. They, therefore, do not have the disparate nature of the preceding collection and their succession is even organized according to an alternation of slow and fast pieces. The many studies left behind in his sketchbooks bear witness to the importance Beethoven attached to this last series, which he considered the best-executed of the three.

Historical references

Beethoven's contemporaries failed to understand the importance of these miniatures written in the margins of the *Diabelli Variations* and of the *Ninth Symphony*. One editor even refused to publish the miniatures of opus 119, and Beethoven composed opus 126 in answer to his critics.

Webern, Anton

Six bagatelles for string quartet, 1913

Opus 9

Minuscule revolutions *(Jean Ricardou)*

The three minutes of arranged sound of Webern's opus 9 contain more music than many longer works.

These *Six Bagatelles* strike one by their sonorous seduction, more than for their brevity, the result of a complex writing effort which tends to distribute statistically the heights, durations and intensities. The work does not contain any suggestions of melody nor stable rhythm, and its intensity varies constantly. It thus establishes a new perception of music, for listeners must adjust their hearing, not at the level of the classical theme, but at the level of the note or the sound and must even take into account the role of silence.

Historical references

Composed in 1913 after a depressing period, these *Bagatelles* were first performed at the Donaueschingen Festival in 1919 by the Amar Quartet.

Ballades

Instrumental *ballades* first appeared around the middle of the 19th century. The ballade is a free form whose character, which may be epic, lyrical and sometimes even narrative, is also found in the romantic German vocal ballade (originated at the end of the 18th century). The composers liken this latter form to the stanzaic lied made up of a poem with an often legendary subject and a piano (Loewe, Schumann) or choral orchestra (Mendelssohn) accompaniment.

Brahms, in his *Ballade*, opus 10, No. 1 in D minor, brings to light an old Scottish poem (the ballad of Edward the Parricide) while Chopin (although the fact is uncertain and has yet to be proved) seems to have transferred his musical phrases on to the verse of his friend, the poet Adam Mickiwicz. Other ballades are the products of pure music.

Chopin, Frédéric

Ballade for piano No. 1, 1836

G minor, opus 23

For the romantic piano

The four Ballades *were written several years apart and therefore do not form a cycle; they fit in to the romantic musical movement as the archetypal ballade for the piano.*

Schumann, referring to the *Ballade* no. 1 in G minor, said, 'I thought it was brilliant'. Even today it is regarded by some as one of the most beautiful pieces ever written for the piano. Whether or not Adam Mickiwicz's poem *Konrad Wallenrod* is its literary source, this eminently lyrical work is in no way like the programme music, from which the other three *Ballades* also remain quite distinct. Divided into three sections (the characteristic formula of the four *Ballades*), it begins with a *largo* followed by a *moderato*, and ends with a *presto con fuoco*. Its musical worth, which is intrinsic in the contrast between calmness and violence, emphasis and attenuation of the pathos, is also linked to the use of dissonant chords, which were judged to be too bold by most of Chopin's contemporaries.

Historical references

When Chopin was composing his first *Ballade* in Paris in 1836, he was in love with a childhood friend, Maria Wodinska. He asked for her hand in marriage during the summer of that year, but Maria's mother, the countess Wodinska, insisted that the engagement remain a secret. Once the Wodinska family had returned to Poland, which they had left at the time of the Varsovie insurrection (1830–31), Chopin waited for his matrimonial hopes to be confirmed, but in vain. The engagement was eventually broken in 1837.

The other ballades

One of Mickiwicz's poems, *The Lake of Willis*, might have inspired the composer's 2nd *Ballade* in F major opus 38 (1840), whilst the 3rd, in B flat major opus 47 (1841) takes up the poetic theme of water that is found both in Mickiwicz (*The Water Sprite*) and in Heine (*Lorelei*). Compared to the *Ballade* in G minor, these two pieces seem less outstanding. With the 4th *Ballade* in F minor opus 52 (1843) on the other hand, Chopin created a beautifully harmonious piece for piano, overflowing with melodic invention, where what Alfred Cortot called the 'precursory tones of impressionism' can be found. Undoubtedly here 'Chopin suggests, supposes, insinuates, captivates, persuades; he hardly ever affirms. And we listen to his thought all the better for its being somewhat hesitant' (André Gide).

A famous couple
At the time of the composition of the *Ballades* Nos. 2, 3 and 4 (1839 to 1843), the author of the *Polonaises* was living with George Sand, spending the Winter and Spring in Paris and the Summer and Autumn in Nohant. This was a happy period in his life.

Ballets

Usually composed for the piano and intended to accompany dance or mime, the development of ballet music has paralleled that of opera and choreography.

Ballet is directly descended from the court festivals of the Italian Renaissance. When Catherine de Medici became Queen of France she introduced there the banquet entertainments of her native Italy. The ballet of the French Court, a combination of dancing, singing and instrumental music, became one of royalty's favourite pastimes. Under the regency of Catherine de Medici and during the reign of Henry IV, it assumed a dramatic aspect which it lost under Louis XIII in favour of the farcical-ballet (Billehaut's *Dowager*, 1626). Under Louis XIV, Lully brought in his own Court ballets (*Alcidiane*, 1658) which were comedy-ballets written in collaboration with Molière (libretto) and Beauchamp (dance). The orchestra already occupied an important place: concerts, serenades, etc (*Le Bourgeois Gentilhomme*, 1670). Soon after, Lully inaugurated the genre of tragedy-ballet which adapted the recitative from Italian to French and integrated dance into the action, while increasing the opportunities to listen to music (*Cadmus and Hermione*, 1673). With Colasse (1649–1709) and Campra (1660–1744) a new genre emerged: the opera-ballet (*L'Europe galante*, 1692 by Campra) brought to its glory by Rameau who was responsible for considerable advances in harmonic writing in the 18th century (*Les Indes Galantes*, 1735). Gradually, erudite music brought to the heart of ballet a synthesis with classical dance, which Jean Georges Noverre (1727–1810), promoter of action ballet, reformed by abolishing heeled shoes, wigs and crinolines.

At the beginning of the 19th century the collaboration between the young Beethoven and the choreographer Salvatore Vigano (1769–1821) ended in a failure (*The Creatures of Prometheus*, 1810). From 1830 to 1840 romantic choreography, with the use of toe-shoes for an aerial dance and the wearing of a tutu of white muslin, radically transformed the technique of classical ballet; but the major composers of the 19th century, Schubert, Liszt, Brahms, Berlioz, Wagner, Chopin and Schumann disregarded this genre. The Wagnerian conception of lyric art entailed the suppression of ballet inserted into opera. Between 1840 and 1870 romantic ballet music consisted of no more than agreeable melodic support intended to create atmosphere (*Giselle* by Adolphe Adam; *Coppélia* by Léo Delibes). Not long after 1870, Tchaikovsky, in part influenced by the style of his first symphonies, wrote ballet music for the choreographer Marius Petipa (1818–1910) which contained incontestable musical qualities, while still effectively sustaining the dramatic action: *Swan Lake* (1876), *The Sleeping Beauty* (1889), *Nutcracker* (1892). Twenty years later, Sergei Diaghilev's *Ballets Russes*, created in 1909, began a revolutionary period in the history of ballet. Hereafter, ballet was based on a subtle proportioning of different artistic disciplines; it almost always left room for innovative instrumental music that was not reducible to music intended only for dance (*Jeux* by Debussy, *The Rite of Spring* by Stravinsky, etc.)

Tchaikovsky, Piotr Ilyich

Nutcracker, ballet in 2 acts and 3 scenes, 1892

Opus 71

A choreographic diktat

Of Tchaikovsky's three ballets, all choreographed by Petipa, Nutcracker is, by virtue of its innovations, musically the most interesting.

Nutcracker, the third and last ballet by Tchaikovsky, is based on an imaginary story by Hoffman in the French version by Alexandre Dumas Sr *Nutcracker and the King of the Mice*. The work contains some of the most beautiful orchestral pages written by Tchaikovsky (1st scene) who knew, moreover, how to handle many scores with humour (the citing of popular songs like *Cadet-Rouselle*). Eight parts were extracted in the form of an orchestral *suite* (opus 71 a). Unfortunately, these were the most mediocre (Overture, March, Dance of the Sugarplum Fairy).

Historical references

In order to write the score to *Nutcracker* (begun during a trip to the United States, and finished in St Petersburg) Tchaikovsky had to follow precisely the detailed instructions of his very demanding choreographer, Marius Petipa. The work was first performed in St Petersburg on 29 December 1892. Previously, in *The Sleeping Beauty*, Petipa had imposed his technical demands on Tchaikovsky. This ballet, commissioned by the Marie theatre (August 1888) was performed for the public on 27 January 1890. The sets, costumes and dancers were very well received. But the music left audiences perplexed. This failure was, however, less absolute than that which occurred on the night of the first performance of *Swan Lake* at the Moscow Grand Theatre (4 March 1877). The work, almost entirely composed during a visit to Paris in 1876, was created around the choreography of Julius Reisinger. But it was Petipa's choreography which was to assure, eighteen years later (1895) its definitive and total success. Sadly, Tchaikovsky had died two years earlier.

The other ballets

The music for *Swan Lake* (1876, opus 20), the first of Tchaikovsky's ballets, did not satisfy the composer: he called it 'a fraud', expressing a very severe judgment of a brilliant instrumental score (introductions to the 1st and 2nd act, czardas, finale) and what was to become one of the most often performed of the entire repertoire of classical dance. Less well-known, *The Sleeping Beauty* (1889, opus 66) in three acts and a prologue, is taken from a fairytale by Perrault. This popular ballet is still performed by numerous troupes throughout the world.

Marius Petipa (1818–1910)

French dancer and choreographer, he emigrated to Russia in 1847. Named Master of ballet at the Imperial Theatre in St Petersberg (1858), he created there, throughout a long life, the Russian school of classical dance.

Stravinsky, Igor

Firebird, ballet for full orchestra in one act and two scenes, 1910

Towards *The Rite of Spring*

From Firebird, *primarily ballet music, Stravinsky drew an orchestral* Suite *which modernized the work.*

By revising, from 1911, the work whose 'glowing orchestration' (R. de Candé) made him instantly famous, Stravinsky managed to get rid of the parts of the original score of his choreographed tale which he owed to Rimsky-Korsakov, Dukas, Debussy and Ravel. It is the second part of the original version which makes up the essence of the *Suite*. Here one finds Kastchi's infernal dance theme whose intense rhythmic beat heralds *The Rite of Spring*.

Historical References

Commissioned by Diaghilev, Stravinsky's *Firebird* was first performed at the Paris Opera on the 25 June 1910. The libretto and the choreography were by Mikhail Fokine; sets and costumes by Alexandre Golovine.

Stravinsky, Igor

Petrushka, ballet in 1 act and 4 scenes, 1911

A stylized popular imagery (Michel Hofmann)

With Petrushka *Stravinsky wanted to write 'an orchestral work in which the piano would play the dominant role'.*

This work broke away from the post-romanticism to which *The Firebird* remained indebted. Its piano part, martellato and very dull in tone, contrasts with the impressionism of Debussy. Elliptical, blunt and very crude in tonal quality, the orchestra resorts, in the first scene, to citing a popular French refrain (*Elle avait une jambe de bois*). On the stage of a small marionette theatre the puppet Petrushka courts a lovely ballerina who prefers him to a finely-dressed Moor. The jealous Moor finally kills his rival whose ghost appears at the end.

Historical References

Diaghilev, captivated on hearing the sketches of this work, suggested to Stravinsky he make it into a ballet. Performed in Paris on 13 July 1911 by the Ballets Russes (choreographed by M. Fokine; sets and costumes by A. Benois), *Petrushka*, like *Firebird*, achieved considerable success.

Ravel, Maurice

Daphnis et Chloé, ballet in 1 act and 3 scenes, 1912

The orchestra as protagonist

Exhibiting unrivalled skill in instrumentation, Daphnis et Chloé *is one of the major symphonic works in French music of the 20th century.*

Determined to remain faithful to the image of ancient Greece depicted by French artists at the end of the 18th century, Ravel adapted the plot given to him by the choreographer of the Ballets Russes, Mikhail Fokine, without changing the essence of the plot: Daphnis and Chloé, young shepherds, discover love but all kinds of obstacles thwart their romance before they marry.

The ballet is made up of a series of dances without the symphonically constructed score becoming a slave to the dance. The composer uses language based on the key of A major which is both simple, in the reduced number of thematic elements used, and complex, in the skilful arrangement of these elements. An important orchestral effect is created by rarely-used instruments: alto flute in G, clarinet in E flat, celesta, etc. A mixed choir of four voices blends in at times, with closed mouths, to the sounds of the orchestra. The beauty of the work culminates in the famous sections 'Lever du jour' (beginning of the 3rd scene) and 'Bacchanale' (fino).

Historical References

Begun in 1909, *Daphnis* was the object of a long and difficult process (notably the admirable *Bacchanale*). Ravel worked on the piece for more than three years and Diaghilev, who had commissioned the work, became especially impatient when the composer used extracts from his unfinished ballet to write his first *Symphonic Suite* (played in concert on 2 April 1911).

At rehearsal, many members of the ballet company felt the music was impossible to dance to. But, with the difficulties overcome, the first production took place in Paris on 8 June 1912 at Châtelet (choreographed by Mikhail Fokine, sets and costumes by Leon Bakst). Nijinski was Daphnis, Tamara Karsavina Chloé. Pierre Monteux conducted. But Diaghilev had put the *Prélude à l'après-midi d'un faune* by Debussy on the same programme and the choreography of *Faune*, having created a scandal, deprived *Daphnis* of any chance of success.

In 1913, Ravel published a second *Symphonic Suite* taken from *Daphnis et Chloé* (*lever du jour, Pantomime, Bacchanale*). This is the one we hear most often today.

Many works, notably an opera-ballet by J. B. de Boismortier and an operetta by J. Offenbach were inspired by the bucolic novel *The Pastoral love of Daphnis and Chloé* attributed to the Greek writer Longus (3rd–4th century AD)

Roussel, Albert

Le Festin de l'araignée (The Spider's Banquet), ballet-pantomime in 1 act, 1913

Opus 17

Starlike webs

The manoeuvres of a spider in its web act as the narrative thread in this orchestral evocation of insects transformed into star dancers at the time of a feast.

The rise of the curtain reveals a garden and, at its centre, an immense spider's web in which the immobile occupant lies in wait for its prey. Along come some ants trying to take possession of a rose petal, but their efforts are interrupted by the arrival of a butterfly. This new arrival, soon drawn towards the spider, allows itself to fall into the deadly web and the voracious insect begins a victory dance. After several episodes staging a battle between worms and praying mantises, followed by the brief lifespan of a mayfly, the spider is finally killed by one of the mantises. The ballet finishes with the funeral of the mayfly, the grandiose music which accompanies it finally giving way to the silence of the now deserted garden.

Composed around this plot by A. Gilbert de Voisins and based on the *Souvenirs Etym-ologiques* by Fabre, *Le Festin de l'araignée* is interesting primarily due to its timbre, made more precise by the orchestral complement used, which is fairly restricted (two woodwinds, horns, trumpets, percussion, harps and strings). The music from *Festin* only appears to be based on the 'impressionist' aesthetic that we hear in it at the beginning (Reynaldo Hahn spoke of 'voluntarily indistinct colours'), having favoured the linear design over the harmonic colour. thus certain themes, sometimes developed, are attributed to each of the insects, and the short pastoral which acts as prelude and epilogue of the piece sees its theme recalled throughout. Ultimately, *Le Festin de l'araignée* is characterized by a rhythmic innovativeness which clearly heralds the later Roussel, particularly in the rapid three-part time, both agile and energetic, which we invariably find in his mature symphonic works.

Historical references

Written in only three months (October to December 1912), the work was performed with great success on 3 April 1913, conducted by Gabriel Grovlez, with choreography by Léo Staats and sets and costumes by Maxime Dethomas. As Marc Pincherle notes, the constraints of time, setting and orchestral complement 'acted as the strongest of stimulants' to the point that the work quickly became Roussel's most popular piece.

The suite that was extracted from *Festin* (prelude, arrival of the ants, appearance, dance, death and funeral of the mayfly), despite its fame, suffers from having eliminated the most interesting passages of the work: the victory dance of the spider and the duel of the mantises.

Other ballets by Albert Roussel: *Bacchus et Ariane*, opus 43 (1930), *Aeneas*, opus 54 (1935).

Debussy, Claude

Jeux, ballet in 1 act, 1913

A musical mosaic

*The outcome of an orchestral quest
by Debussy,* Jeux, *originally
intended for dance, gradually
revealed itself to be a work crucial
to the evolution of modern music.*

A young man and two young girls are searching for a tennis ball they have lost, but the search turns out to be in vain. They soon turn to childish games which quickly become ambiguous until a ball thrown from we don't know where interrupts the improvised flirtation.

Debussy seems to have liked this scenario of 'tennis without a racket' by Nijinsky even though he later detested the choreography. The furtive and fickle games allowed him to write a deliberately unstable and fleeting musical score, creating 'an entanglement of motifs and structures that disappear and reappear in a sporadic and sometimes devious manner' (Jean Barraqué). Furthermore, the novelty of *Jeux* far exceeded its intended purpose as a 'poème dansé'. 'The constant evolution of the thematic ideas rules out all symmetry' (Pierre Boulez) and the very notion of a theme dissolves to give way to the arrangement of constantly varying motifs. The rhythmic flow of the piece comes from the way in which Debussy

'blurred the heavy regularity of the Occidental "clatter"', (Éveline Andréani). The work carried out on the timbre also responds to this technique of division: the motifs constantly pass from one instrument (or group of instruments) to another. In contrast to the classical orchestra where their importance is secondary to the harmonic and melodic levels, the rhythm, and certainly the timbre, have been liberated in *Jeux*, where they become components removed from musical discourse and turn the very concept of the orchestra upside down.

Historical references

Commissioned in 1912 by Sergei Diaghilev's Ballets Russes, *Jeux* was first performed on 15 May 1913 to Nijinsky's choreography with sets and costumes by Léon Bakst, with Pierre Monteux conducting. It left the public unmoved and was quickly eclipsed by the scandalous performance, 15 days later, of Stravinsky's *The Rite of Spring. Jeux* was regarded for a long time as the work of an aging man and the scattering into constantly changing short motifs taken to indicate a lack of melodic inspiration. But since 1950 the work has been played frequently, its value finally acknowledged.

Sergei Diaghilev (1872–1929)	Producer
Pierre Monteux (1875–1964)	Conductor
Vaslav Nijinsky (1890–1950)	Choreographer and dancer

Stravinsky, Igor

The Rite of Spring, ballet in 2 scenes, 1913

A formidable rhythmic construction

One of the most original works of the 20th century, The Rite of Spring *strongly affirms the aesthetic value of raw sound and the primordial function of rhythmic beat.*

Based on a fairly weak plot — the sacrifice of a young girl to the God of Spring in order to put the year under favourable auspices — *The Rite* is divided into two principle parts: 1) The adoration of the earth (8 sections), 2) the sacrifice (6 sections). The orchestral strength necessary for the execution of the piece is gigantic (no less than 8 horns in the colossal group of 38 wind instruments).

Called an 'exemplary moment of modernity' by Pierre Boulez, it cannot help but appear so because it is not reducible to a music intended only for dance, which is only a pretext for a score that can stand on its own. Except for *The Firebird*, Stravinsky has never severely modified his ballet music, which is played in concert without revisions. And it is certainly through the intermediary of the concert (some choreographic interpretations, like that of

Maurice Béjart in 1959, are the exceptions that prove the rule) and of the record, that *The Rite*, from its creation to the present has found its largest audience.

Loaded with a large 'potential for novelty' (Boulez), this work is original, not only because of its harsh melodic formulae or its transgression of harmonic laws than because of its unique use of rhythm. Contrary to the demands of Occidental tradition which, until the beginning of the 20th century, put melody and harmony before rhythm in the hierarchy of musical components, *The Rite* subordinates the first two to the third. This primacy of rhythm is particularly evident in the sections 'The Glory of the Elect' and the 'Sacred Dance'.

Historical references

The première *Rite*, composed for Diaghilev's Ballets Russes, took place on 29 May 1913 at the Champs Elysées Theatre in Paris. Pierre Monteux conducted. The choreography by Nijinsky and Stravinsky's music, which defied a good number of rules, created a memorable scandal.

In one of these curious about-faces by the public, which were not rare to witness, the performance of *The Rite* in concert, in Paris 1914, resulted in a storm of applause.

Satie, Erik

Parade, 'ballet réaliste' in 1 scene, 1917

A new approach

At the time of the creation of
Parade, *in collaboration with*
Cocteau, Satie was widely
considered to be a 'neo-dadaist',
avant-garde musician.

Parade belongs to the second period (1897–1918) of Satie's works, that of the humorous pieces for piano (*Three Pear-shaped Pieces*, 1903). Written in a spirit resembling that of the 'café-concert' music, it creates its effects through the frequent use of percussion and the sudden introduction of different noises (sirens, typewriters, lottery wheels).

Historical references

Developed by Satie, Cocteau (plot), Picasso (set and costumes), Massine (choreography) and Diaghilev, *Parade* had its world première on 18 May 1917 in Châtelet where it caused a scandal — and established Satie.

Milhaud, Darius

Le Boeuf sur le toit (The Ox on the Roof), Pantomime-ballet, 1919

Opus 58 a

Slumming it with South-American rhythms

This pantomime illustrates in a
striking way the aesthetic of the
Group of Six: the demystification of
the sublime, simplicity and irony.

Jean Cocteau devised and staged a pantomime-ballet to fit the music of *Boeuf*. This mixed personal melodies with some popular South-American tunes (tangos, maxixes). Heard regularly, between every tune, the first of these melodies gives the composition the form of a *rondo*. The humour and the frenzy of the work are seen mostly when the orchestra emphasizes forcefully the South-American themes (the title itself recalls a Brazilian refrain).

Historical references

Performed for the first time at the Comédie des Champs-Elysées on 21 February 1920, *Le Boeuf sur le toit* amused some and shocked others. Guy-Pierre Fauconnet created the costumes and masks, Raoul Dufy the sets.

Bartók, Béla

The Miraculous Mandarin, pantomime in one act, 1919

Opus 19

A dance of death

Despite a fairly weak libretto, this pantomime is one of Bartók's most outstanding scores, in terms of the writing, before the great works of his third period.

Along with the ballet *The Wooden Prince* (1914–16), *The Miraculous Mandarin* inaugurated Bartók's period of prominent compositions in which the folklore material became integrated with a clever polyphony, resulting in writing whose originality resides in the fusion (to the point where they are rendered indistinguishable) of rhythm with harmony. *The Mandarin* takes up the theme of lack of communication between man and woman, already seen in *Duke Bluebeard's Castle* (1911) and *The Wooden Prince*, but this time it is also associated with those of money, desire and death.

In a shady bar, a prostitute, forced by three penniless hoodlums, accosts first a bourgeois, and then a shy young man. The first, having no money on him, and the second, totally broke, get beaten up. Suddenly, a surprising 'client' appears; a Mandarin dressed in oriental costume. Aroused by a lascivious dance, the strange character rushes into pursuit of the young woman. He is caught by the three hoodlums, who rob him and attempt to kill him by smothering him. But nothing is able to kill the Mandarin who, kept alive by desire, will not die until this is satisfied.

Owing to the richness of the orchestral 'colour' and its unusual combinations of timbre and discords, there is no doubt that this grating drama, in which we also hear the wild clamour of a big metropolis, owes something to *Petrushka* and to *The Rite of Spring*. Certainly, *The Mandarin* is 'less new, less epic and more anecdotal than *The Rite*' (Pierre Citron); but with it Bartók displays stylistic mastery that will, in the future, make his aesthetic instantly recognizable.

Historical references

The successful stagings of *The Wooden Prince* in 1917 and *Duke Bluebeard's Castle* in 1918 made Bartók's name known to the public of Budapest, but the severe political problems at the time of the composition of *The Miraculous Mandarin* (1918 to 1919) prevented the piece from being performed then. Played for the first time in 1926 in Cologne, it caused a scandal. Banned in Budapest in 1931 and 1941, and shown in 1936 in an expurgated version, *The Mandarin* had to wait until 1956 before being regularly included in the repertoire of Hungarian national theatres. Bartók extracted from the piece a very beautiful *Piano Suite*.

Prokofiev, Serge

Romeo and Juliet, ballet in 4 acts and 9 scenes, 1938

Opus 64

Prokofiev from all angles

*After the 'accidental' ballets (*The Buffoon, *1921,* The Age of Steel, *1927), Prokofiev created, with* Romeo and Juliet, *his first 'Soviet' ballet devoted to a psychological drama.*

The requirements of the USSR at the end of the 1930s, in terms of ballet, were poles apart from the avant-garde aesthetic of Diaghilev, the creator of the Ballets Russes in Paris in 1907. His main interest was in staging, far from psychological and emotional situations, forceful and succinct productions. And it is certainly to this agenda that the aggressive music written by Prokofiev for the *Age of Steel*, a constructivist ballet in two acts, responded. Nonetheless, the modernity of this music seems today to be a bit forced, for Prokofiev was a classicist. He also conformed, apparently without harm, to the populist aesthetic called for by the USSR.

Romeo and Juliet was one of the first results of this conversion, as well as the first example of a new kind of ballet. In order to adapt to the choreographic conventions of the time, Prokofiev had to write a work of long duration, and to illustrate a very precise action and even the psychology of the characters. Effective music, sometimes a bit too effective, *Romeo and Juliet* redefines the 'action ballet' or choreographic drama, which simultaneously respects the 'laws of symphonic development, those of psychological and dramatic development and, finally, those of the evolution of theatrical action' (M. Hofmann).

A work of transition between the Occidental and Soviet phases of the composer, bringing together, therefore, of all their aspects, *Romeo and Juliet*, unlike the great ballets of the 20th century, is written specifically for dance. It also sets the groundwork for the music, written not long after, of Eisenstein's films.

Historical references

The death of Diaghilev in 1929 broke one of Prokofiev's main links with the West. In 1933 he returned permanently to the USSR, where he received important commissions. It was immediately after the production of *Peter and the Wolf* (1936) that Prokofiev began to work on *Romeo and Juliet* with the director Radlov. The work was first performed in 1938 in Brno, Czechoslovakia. The Soviet première took place in Leningrad on 11 January 1940.

Prokofiev extracted from *Romeo and Juliet* two Symphonic Suites in seven movements each (1936, 1937), and a third in 1946.

Instrumental chorales

The word *chorale* (from the Latin *choralis*; 'pertaining to a chorus') describes, firstly, a type of canticle that serves as the basis of the Lutheran liturgy. This assembly singing, generally in unison, spread rapidly from the beginning of the Reformation, as it was, for Luther, one of the foundations of the religious practice. The popular musical style of chorales, their distinctive structure, the ease with which they are sung, all contributed to their success. Since the beginning of the 16th century, composers like Schein, Praetorius, Franck and Hassler harmonized chorales for many voices, while still preserving their ease of execution. And those composed by Bach for his Cantatas also comply, two centuries later, to this principle.

As well as this vocal chorale, the writing of which had remained fairly simple, an instrumental chorale, for the organ, was developing and gradually became one of the most complex musical forms. The choice of the organ is readily explained. Firstly its role is uniquely utilitarian: it allows the vocal chorale to be accompanied. Also, in acquiring its own identity in becoming concertante, the instrument gradually developed what we call, in short, chorales for the organ. 'In short' because these instrumental chorales, besides the fact that they occur in fairly diverse forms, serve either to introduce the vocal chorale (*chorale prelude*) or to comment upon it during the interlude (*choral fantasia*). Chorales for the organ always exhibit the melody of a canticle, generally a familiar one, and accompany it in counterpoint, the sense of which is underlined by the rhythmic, harmonic and melodic elements. In brief, the chorales make up the sound commentary of a text.

The history of the chorale for the organ did not really start until the beginning of the 17th century, with musicians like J. P. Sweelinck (1562–1621). And it was D. Buxtehude (1637–1707) whose chorale preludes already used symbolic motifs, who first attempted to musically transcribe the text. Finally, J. Pachelbel (1653–1706) added the *partita de choral* and the *prélude fugué*.

But it was J. S. Bach (1685–1750) who, with more than 150 chorales for the organ, perfected the scoring. Simple canticle tunes, subjected to all the possible transformations (chorales in counterpoint, fugued, figured, in canon, with variations, in trio, harmonized and in choral fantasia), the majority of Bach's chorales 'derived their raison d'être from the technique of variation' (André Hodeir). The method most characteristic of Bach 'consists in the expression of the theme, accompanied in counterpoint, by the three other parts, in which the smallest modulation, the smallest rhythmic movement elucidates the implied text'. (Gilles Cantagrel).

The history of Lutheran organ chorales was completed with J. S. Bach, for no other new chorale form was developed after him, and his best students, J. L. Krebs and J. C. Kittel, were content to maintain the tradition.

From the 19th century, instrumental chorale was divided into two groups. The first group included works which were organ chorales in the strict sense of the term; the sound commentary of a text. Notable examples of this type were the *Choral Vorspiels* (Chorale preludes) by J. Brahms (1833–1897) and M. Reger (1873–1916). The second group contained works whose passages borrowed or cited some of the aspects of chorales. In this group we find, disseminated and concealed, if not chorales in a strict sense, at least allusions to this type of composition by musicians like Mendelssohn, Franck, Stravinsky, Berg, Honegger — and even in the last bars of *Intégrales* by Edgar Varèse.

Bach, Johann Sebastian

21 chorales of the catechism, for organ, 1739

BWV 669–689

A proliferous work

Extremely difficult, the 21 Chorales *testify to writing of great complexity. However, some of them count among Bach's most innovative works.*

Bach chose to illustrate, or rather to paraphrase, ten Lutheran chorale melodies in his 21 chorales. Nine of the canticles receive two musical commentaries; one of them is complex, written for the organ with a pedalboard, for 'experts'; the other, more simple and playable with hands only, for 'amateurs'. Each chorale also has two versions, one large and one small, played one after the other. One exception to this division: the chorale melody of *Gloria* has undergone three adaptations.

Musically, the *21 Chorales*, in their density, are typical of later Bach and some

The *21 Chorales of the Catechism* belong to the third volume of the Klavierübung (Klavier Exercise) published by J. S. Bach. This volume also contains four extraordinary Duets and one Prelude and fugue which frame the whole. This unexpected collection of liturgical pieces and concert extracts is perhaps the result of numerical symbolics founded on the number 3, the sign of the Trinity. (As evidence, the number of chorales, 21, is equal to 3x7, and the total number of pieces, 27 is 3^3.

of the 'great' chorales show an extreme innovativeness. Superimpositions of different structures, polyphonies of up to five voices, discords and polyrhythms are linked up by the 'extended textures, practically continuous, throughout their duration' (Pierre Boulez). So many elements do not facilitate the access to an already difficult collection, both for the listener and for the interpreter. Among the most innovative pieces are the three parts of *Grand Kyrie* BWV 669–671, the great adaptation of *Chorale of the 10 Commandments* BWV 678, the Lutheran *Credo* BWV 680 and, above all, the great *Our Father* BWV 682.

Historical references

The *21 Chorales*, published in 1739, constitute the crowning achievement of Bach in this very vast domain, as he composed more than 150 organ chorales, of which some were grouped into compilations. Besides the *Chorales of the Catechism*, he wrote the 45 chorales of the *Orgelbüchlein* (*Little Organ Book*) BWV 599–644 (1717), the 18 *Leipzig* chorales which formed an anthology, compiled by Bach himself of revisions of his earliest works, and, finally, the six Schübler chorales BWV 645–650 (1746), which were transcriptions for the organ of cantata excerpts. But the *Chorales of the Catechism* constitute the only series of the composer's maturity that we can date with certainty. To this collection we can also add the *Canonical variations of 'Von Himmel hoch'* BWV 769, composed in 1747, as they are also based on chorale melodies.

Concerti Grossi

The musical form of *concerto grosso* consists in the contrast of two unequal sonorous groups. The first, constituting solo instruments, is the *concertino*, or 'small concert'; the second, bringing together the full orchestra, is the *ripieno*, sometimes more simply called 'grosso'.

While this form seems to have been inaugurated in 1674 by the German Schmelzer, it was the Italian Gregori who was the first to use the title 'concerto grosso' in 1698. Yet Stradella (1644–82), Corelli (1653–1713), Muffat (1653–1704) and Torelli (1658–1709) were the principal initiators of this form, and Corelli is even considered to be its inventor for having been the first to perfectly master the form with *Twelve Concerti Grossi for Strings* opus 6, published in 1712.

In the beginning, the concerti grossi, such as those by Corelli, hovered between the old form of the Church Sonata, with its four movements 'slow-fast-slow-fast', and that of the series of French dances which contained most often a free plan of four to six movements. Under the influence, notably, of concertos for a solo instrument by Vivaldi, the concerto grosso adopted the preclassic division into three movements 'fast-slow-fast', and spread, in this form, throughout Europe.

In 1721, with his Brandenburg Concertos BWV 1046–1051, J. S. Bach renovated the form of concerto grosso, by the large variety which he exhibited in his choice of solo instruments which, before him, had been principally limited to strings. G. F. Handel, on the other hand, seemed to be more traditional, as his *Twelve concerti grossi* opus 6 published in 1739, went back to both the free plan and the string orchestra used by Corelli.

Independently of these characteristics, the form of concerto grosso, as Nikolaus Harnoncourt remarked, depends equally on the possibilities and conditions of execution. Furthermore, Corelli's concertos were played with a fairly considerable instrumental strength; and Handel's required, in order that the alternating play between *concertino* and *ripieno* worked well, a spatial separation of soloists. In other words: 'for many generations concerto grosso meant both a certain genre of instrumental music and the manner of execution that corresponded' (N. Harnoncourt).

From 1750 the concerto grosso gave way to the solo concerto, but the 19th-century formula of the triple or double concertos — for piano, violin and cello; or violin and cello — as tried by Beethoven or Brahms, was very probably derived from concerto grosso.

In the 20th century, the concerto grosso reappeared in the form of the orchestral concerto, where each instrument is capable of becoming soloist. The best received attempt of this type is, without a doubt, that of Béla Bartók (*Concerto for Orchestra*, 1943).

Corelli, Arcangelo

Twelve concerti grossi for two violins, cello and strings, 1682.

Opus 6

The birth of a new form

These twelve concertos made Corelli the inventor of concerto grosso. Others before him had set a small group of instruments against the orchestra, but Corelli was the first to systematize this principle.

This first major cycle of concerti grossi is striking in the variety of its construction and the multiplicity of its orchestral combinations.

If the first eight seem to be more Church Trios and Sonatas, and the last four to be chamber works, one must, above all, note that each is composed of four to six movements, the succession of which does not obey any clearly defined structure. This title evokes only the series of dances (prélude, Allemande, Jig, Saraband, Gavotte, Minuet) and their tempo can be fast, slow or moderate. Corelli's adoption of these varied arrangements, more than of the tripartite form 'fast-slow-fast', results without a doubt from the influence of dramatic

music. For this type of music is 'more fertile in vicissitudes than abstract symphony, and therefore less demanding of symmetry' (Marc Pincherle).

The diversity of the orchestral combinations comes firstly from the manner of distributing the interventions between the three solo instruments (the *concertino*) and the orchestral ensemble (the *ripieno*). The transition from one group to another is never the product of a mechanical alterations, but functions much more at the will of cleverly determined proportions. This diversity involves the treatment of the solo instruments, two violins and cello. A plurality of solutions is adopted: the two violins play the parts of equal interest, or one of them may become solo, sometimes the cello plays the main role.

Historical references

In 1712, twelve years after the publication of the *Twelve sonatas for violin and bass* opus 5, Corelli published his sixth and last opus which, like all the previous ones, comprised twelve pieces. But the beginning of their composition dates back to at least 1682, for contemporary musicians, such as G. Muffat swore he had heard them at that time. This evidence reinforces the theory that Corelli was the inventor of this form, as does the opinion expressed by the Venetian G. Reali, even before their publication, that Corelli's concertos would serve as models for future musicians.

> Of his twelve concertos, the eighth, *Concerto for Christmas Night* is considered the most beautiful, due in particular to its Pastoral finale.

Bach, Johann Sebastian

Brandenburg Concertos, 1721

BWV 1046 to BWV 1051

A synthesis of Vivaldi and Corelli

These six pieces for strings and wind instruments that Bach entitled Concerts avec plusieurs instruments *broke new ground with their diversity of instrumental colouring.*

Bach modelled his *Concerts avec plusieurs instruments* on the concerto grosso, an Italian musical form (Corelli, Torelli) which had spread throughout Europe at that time. This form, under the influence of Vivaldi's violin concertos, subsequently adopted the three movements (fast-slow-fast).

In the *Brandenburg Concerto* No.2 in F major, No.4 in G major and No.5 in D major, Bach respects the spirit of concerto grosso; we find in them a rivalry, a continuous opposition between the *concertino* and the *ripieno*. Few solo instruments intervene, with the exception of the admirable harpsichord part heard in the 5th Concerto, which heralds — mostly in the first movement — the keyboard concerto. The case is very different with the Brandenburg concertos No.1 in F major, No.3 in G major and No.6 in B flat major. In these works, one instrument or many small groups of instruments (for example the three violins, three violas and three cellos of No.3) separate from the orchestral mass to evolve on their own, conversing among themselves or with the ripieno.

But regardless of the way in which the instruments, grouped or not, converse, the *Brandenburg Concertos* attest to such an exceptional mastery in the handling of timbre that numerous musicologists think of them as one of the main sources of the classical symphonic structure. Bach, in writing them, took particular care over the viola parts (which are magnificent in the first and sixth concertos).

Historical references

Composed in Cöthen between 1718 and 1721 for the margrave of Brandenburg Christian Ludwig, the *Brandenburg Concertos* (almost finished at the time of the unexpected death of Bach's first wife, Maria-Barbara, in 1720), are full of the youthful fervour and liveliness that makes them heirs to the Italian Instrumental school; they number among the most dynamic pieces written by the composer who was then musical director for the Court of Prince Leopold d'Anhalt.

An opinion

The *Brandenburg Concertos* contain 'this extraordinary sense of a linear dimension which, at each stage of Bach's career, was the definitive mark, the indelible signature of the greatest musician who ever lived' (Glenn Gould).

'Concert' in the 18th century meant a conversation among various instruments.

Handel, George Frideric

Twelve concerti grossi for 2 violins, cello and strings, 1739

Opus 6

Baroque style lapsing into brio

Composed in only a month, Handel's
Twelve concerti grossi, *opus 6*
owe their improvised and
unpredictable nature to the speed with
which they were written.

The *Twelve Concerti Grossi*, written after a series of works intended for the stage or Church, marked Handel's return to a more limited orchestral complement and to pure music, although he admits to some slight variation, as the concerti grossi were originally conceived as music for the intervals of oratorios and operas.

In terms of the structure of these concertos, the formal plans in use offered three possibilities: the sequence 'slow, fast, slow' of the old church sonata, the modern concerto form of Vivaldi 'fast, slow, fast', and the French orchestral sequence (an overture followed by dance pieces). But Handel preferred 'to create his own sequence of movements for each of his concertos, combining his style with formal arrangements' (N. Harnoncourt). His concertos comprised between four and six movements each and are very similar to those by Corelli, so much so that they also

use a string orchestra. But this limitation of instrumental resources does not prevent the three solo instruments, the two violins and the cello, from establishing, outside the dialogues with the full orchestra, plays of sound remarkable in their variety or from merging with the orchestra to introduce exceptional tone colour. It is possible, according to Handel, to double the most virtuosic passages with wind instruments to reinforce their brilliance. A light dance movement at the end of each concerto wipes out this baroque surge of effects.

Historical references

Opus 6 was written between 29 September and 30 October 1739 and was published shortly afterwards. Handel was going through difficult financial times and he composed these concertos, modelled after Corelli in order to deal with his money problems. The Italian musician was enjoying undeniable popularity in England and Handel 'let himself be carried along by this wave of success' (J. Gallois). The choice of string orchestra, which made the work easier to play, also helped it sell more readily.

The other concertos

Handel also wrote a series of organ concertos opus 4 and 7, as well as six concerti grossi opus 3, often falsely called oboe concertos.

Solo concertos

An instrumental composition based on dialogue, or even opposition, (the Italian word *concerto* is derived from the Latin verb *concertare* which means to rival, but also to converse) between one or more instruments and the whole orchestra, the solo concerto evolved formally in parallel with the symphony, the symphonic poem, etc.

In the classical form, attributed to Mozart, it is split into three movements: the first a fast movement (*allegro*) in Sonata form, the second slow (*andante* or *adagio*) in the form of a lied or a theme and variations, and a third fast (*allegro*) most often in the form of a rondo.

By the time the concerto grosso disappeared (around 1760), the solo concerto became established. It had made a cautious appearance in musical history with Torelli (*concerto a uno violino che concerta solo*, 1698) and Albinoni (*Sinfonie e Concerti a cinque*, 1700).

But it was not really organized into three symmetrical movements ('fast-slow-fast') until the beginning of the 18th century (Vivaldi's *Concerto for one violin* from the '*Estro Armonico*', 1712). A new musical form was thus born by the intervention of the violin which, at least until 1770–85, remained the most frequently used solo instrument. Other solo instruments, even in Vivaldi's time, had been put to use in 'dialogue' with the orchestra: the cello (Vivaldi), the viola (Telemann, Vivaldi), the flute (Vivaldi), the oboe (Albinoni, Handel), the horn (Telemann) and the bassoon (Vivaldi).

The concerto for keyboard and orchestra was inaugurated by J. S. Bach (the eight *Concertos for harpsichord and strings*, BWV 1052–1059, between 1728 and 1735). An important pioneering role was subsequently played by two of Bach's sons; Carl-Philipp Emanuel (1714–88), composer of about fifty concertos and Johann Christian (1735–82) who composed his four concertos opus 7 (1770) with the firm intention of emphasizing the tones of an instrument invented around 1710 which was becoming more and more popular: the piano.

J. Haydn left behind a dozen keyboard concertos (organ and harpsichord), four for the violin, two designed for the cello and about ten for various instruments (horn, trumpet, flute, oboe, etc.), but he does not seem to have found the solo concerto to be a form in which he could wholeheartedly involve himself. Mozart, on the other hand, exploited the dramatic possibilities brilliantly. His piano concertos are considered by many to be models of perfection; he also excels in the composition of concertos for violin and orchestra (*Concertos No.3 in G major* K.216 and *No.5 in A major* K.219) and imposes his know-how in the technically-difficult domain of concerto for wind instruments (*Concerto for Bassoon and Orchestra in B flat major* K.191; *Flute Concerto in G* K.313, *Oboe Concerto in C* K.314, *Horn Concerto No.2 in E flat major* K.417; *Clarinet Concerto in A major* K.622).

Before bringing the genre to its maximum potential (*Concerto in E flat major* 'Emperor', opus 73), Beethoven transformed and softened the orchestral and pianistic construction of Mozart (*Concerto No.4 in G major* opus 58). He only composed one violin concerto (in D major opus 61), the kind of concerto which afterwards, with the exception of some authentic (Mendelssohn, Brahms) or spectacular (Tchaikovsky) successes, fell more and more into disuse. The masters of the 19th century seemed to concede more importance to the cello concerto, as seen in Schumann (*Concerto in A minor* opus 129), Lalo (*Concerto in D minor*), Saint-Saëns (*Concertos* opus 33 and 119), Brahms (*Concerto for violin, cello and orchestra in A minor* opus 102) and Dvořák (*Concerto in B minor* opus 104).

But this century, with the advent of the modern piano, a taste for contrasting tone, the often exaggerated virtuoso role of the soloist, is above all the century of piano and orchestra concertos intended to convey all kinds of bursts of subjective expression: Schumann (*Concerto in A minor* opus 54), Chopin (*Concertos in E minor* opus 11 and in *F minor* opus 21), Liszt (*Concerto No.1 in E flat major, No.2 in A major*), Brahms (*Concerto No.1 in D minor* opus 15, *No.2 in B flat major* opus 83), Tchaikovsky (*Concerto No.1 in B flat minor* opus 23, *No.2 in G major* opus 44), Grieg (*Concerto in A minor* opus 16); and not forgetting Weber (2 concertos), Mendelssohn (2 concertos) and Saint-Saëns (5 concertos).

In the 20th century, the solo concerto survived in its tripartite form (concertos for piano and orchestra by Ravel, Rachmaninov, Stravinsky, Prokofiev, Poulenc, Jolivet) before giving way to more innovative pieces, whether or not labelled 'concerto', which in fact only vaguely follow the concertante principle: *Chamber Concerto* by Alban Berg, *Concerto for nine instruments* by Webern, *Double Concerto for piano, harpsichord and two chamber ensembles* by Elliott Carter, *Domaines for clarinet and instrumental ensemble* by Pierre Boulez, *Tout un monde lointain* (for cello and orchestra) by Henri Dutilleux, *Chamber Concerto* by Györgi Ligeti.

Piano entry in the 2nd movement (adagio) of the *First Piano Concerto in D minor* by Johannes Brahms.

Bach, Johann Sebastian

Concerto for harpsichord and strings No.5, v. 1730

F minor, BWV 1056

The emergence of the solo harpsichord

Chronologically first, Bach's harpsichord concertos, transposed from violin concertos, still link the soloist to the orchestra.

Built on the Italian model, the *Fifth Concerto* consists of three movements (fast-slow-fast). The initial *allegro* and the final *presto* are characterized by a vigorous rhythm and a complex thematic arrangement, where the solo instrument often forms one body with the orchestra. The central *largo* produces a gripping contrast: the right hand of the harpsichord trips nimbly through a melodic line which is the transcription of the old violin part, while the left hand merges with the strings in a pizzicato. This concerto is less a dialogue between soloist and orchestra than a polyphonic piece associated with the simultaneous play of the harpsichord and the strings treated as a whole.

Historical references

The eight concertos for harpsichord and strings BWV 1052–1059 were written between 1728 and 1735, for the Collegium Musicum ensemble, which Bach conducted in Leipzig.

Bach, Johann Sebastian

Italian concerto for solo harpsichord, 1735

BWV 971

Music as 'trompe l'oeil'

The culmination of all of Bach's concertos, the Italian Concerto *mimics the orchestral opposition between* soli *and* tutti.

Written 'according to Italian tastes', this work respects the division into three movements and the lively character of the Vivaldi-style concerto. The tone of the two extreme movements is particularly striking and the superimposition of the musical figures gives the impression of the *tutti*. But it is the central *andante* which best simulates the opposition between a solo instrument and an orchestra: the left hand of the harpsichord imitates the *pizzicatos* of a string ensemble and the melody is allocated to the right hand.

Historical references

Published in 1735, the Italian Concerto belongs to the second part of Bach's *Klavierübung* (Klavier Exercise). It is completed by a *Partita* which attempts to produce a French-style overture on the harpsichord.

Mozart, Wolfgang Amadeus

Concerto for piano and orchestra No.20, 1785

D minor K.465

A concerto commanded by drama

Added to several works also displaying a tragic nature, Concerto No.20 *established, for a long time, the idea of Mozart as a romantic composer.*

This concerto (three movements: 1, *allegro*; 2, *romance*; 3, *rondo allegro assai*) is the first that Mozart wrote for piano in a minor key. Beethoven thought extremely highly of it and the influence it had on his style is indisputable. Written one month before his *Concerto in C major No.21* K.467, it makes up, with this piece, a diptych of sorts; the serene grandeur of K.467 follows the dramatic colouration of K.466. Both pieces have conferred on the genre of Concerto the dignity of a musical form capable of holding its own against any other form.

Historical references

Mozart wrote his first concertos for harpsichord and orchestra (K.37, 39, 40 and 41) in London between April 1765 and April 1766. These were transcriptions of works by C. P. E. Bach, J. Schobert, etc. He was 10 at the time. His first 'real' piano concerto, *No.5 in D major* K.175 was composed in Salzburg in 1773. Four years later, still in Salzburg, Mozart abandoned the 'gallant style' with his *Concerto in E flat major No.9* K.271. The *Concerto in D major No.26* K.537,

called 'Coronation', disparaged by some and considered by others to be 'progressive' on a formal level, dates from 1788. In the year of his death, Mozart composed a last concerto for piano and orchestra, *No.27 in B flat major* K.595, another very beautiful and profoundly melancholy work.

---

28 Concertos

If we include *Concerto No.7* for three pianos and orchestra K.242, *Concerto No.10* for two pianos and orchestra K.365 and the *Rondo* for piano and orchestra K.382, Mozart composed a total of 28 concertos for piano and orchestra.

The series of great Viennese Concertos (14–25) also includes other essential works, such as the *Concerto in C minor No.24* K.491, the second and last piano concerto written in a minor key. Charles Rosen, comparing it to Concerto No.20, said that 'it is less operatic and closer to chamber music' and 'it makes up in refinement what it loses in grandeur'. Both moving and graceful, the *andante* of the *Concerto in E flat major No.22* K.482 (another famous passage) was encored at the first recital (Mozart was playing the piano). The *Concerto in A major No.23* K.488 seduces with its 'lyricism tinged with melancholy' (C. Rosen).

Of the *Concerto in G major No.17* K.453, one recalls primarily the finale in the form of variations; very original in many respects, *No.19 in F major* K.459 is also famous for its finale: a brilliant *allegro assai* which Mozart wrote making use of counterpoint in a humorous way.

Beethoven, Ludwig van

Concerto for piano and orchestra No.5 'Emperor', 1811

E flat major, opus 73

A symphony with obligatory piano (G. Gould)

Beethoven's last piano concerto, Emperor, owes nothing regarding its instrumental and orchestral style, to Haydn or Mozart.

Emperor, like all Beethoven's other piano concertos, respects the traditional division into three movements. Contrary to the custom which demands that a movement end in a solo cadenza, the *allegro* (the first movement) is preceded by the cadenza which acts as an introduction, with the brilliancy of an improvisation. In the form of a sonata, this *allegro* develops in more than 600 measures an immense dialogue between piano and orchestra. The second movement, an *adagio, un poco mosso* in lied form carries on without solution of continuity to the last movement, an astonishing *rondo* whose 'vigorous rhythmic lines' (André Boucourechliev) make one forget

entirely the grace and gentleness of the classical *rondo*.

Like *Symphony No.3*, which it resembles in its 'heroic' theme, *Emperor* is written in E flat major, one of Beethoven's favourite keys because of its ability to express the idea of greatness and give the impression of power. In the amplitude of this concerto, in its quasi-symphonic construction and in the frequent interpenetration of the piano and orchestra, specifically in the second movement, it breaks away from the traditional limitations of the concerto. In the same sense, it also foreshadows the third and last of Beethoven's styles (1815–26), in which his artistry, 'a great dramatic force, conceived of in terms of action, becomes nonetheless more and more meditative' (Charles Rosen).

Historical references

In the year Beethoven composed his *Concerto No.5*, Austria and France were at war. Vienna, beleaguered by Napoleon's army, was bombarded. Archduke Rodolphe, dedicatee of the work, had fled the Austrian capital with the imperial court. Beethoven felt lonely without his student and patron. Staunchly moral, he soon renounced working on this concerto which had originally been given the patriotic heading of 'a song of triumph in combat' (as written in the margin of his sketches). He did not complete the score until autumn, after the French troops had left and a peace treaty had been signed (14 October 1809).

Emperor was first played for the public in Leipzig on 28 November 1811. Johann Schneider played the piano. It was very enthusiastically received and Leipzig's music critic gave a very favourable review of a work which was so 'original' that only its 'slightly exaggerated' length diminished its value.

Schumann, Robert

Concerto for piano and orchestra, 1845

A minor, opus 54

An out-of-the-ordinary concerto

While the piano was the favourite instrument of Schumann, a man not entirely at ease in the symphonic domain, his concerto shows that he knew how to use the orchestra without submitting it to the hegemony of the soloist.

Although he never managed to create a symphonic work perfectly adapted to the density of his musical ideas, Schumann's piano concerto succeeded in renovating the form to make it perfectly suited to the expression of his moods and of his 'broken world, woven with whirlwind aspects' (R. Barthes). Far from a return to the balance of the Mozartian concerto or an attempt (as Beethoven often engaged in) to establish a conflicting piano-orchestra rapport, Schumann was content to give the soloist the opportunity to shine; he created, as he himself said, something between concerto, symphony and grand concerto. The piano is not set against the orchestral mass, rather it integrates with it; the piano has a dialogue with each group of instruments and the orchestration, with allusion to chamber music, is without any imposition of will by the soloist.

In the first *allegro affetuoso*, after a brilliant but very brief orchestral introduction, the piano introduces the first theme, a magnificent melodic design which predominates throughout the movement, enriching itself with the two secondary motifs which have undergone many transformations. Shortly before the end of the *allegro* the soloist emits a cadenza whose style precludes any demonstration of virtuosity. The orchestra and the piano then modify the rhythm of the first theme in order to develop it spiritedly, bringing the ensemble to the conclusion. The second movement is an *intermezzo*. Based on an intimate dialogue between piano and orchestra, it includes a beautiful cello solo in its middle section. The ensemble creates a very specific atmosphere, very like that of chamber music. With the main theme of the finale similar to the grand melodic design of the first movement, the concerto clearly brings to light the cyclic principle to which the entire work is formally bound.

Historical references

In 1841 Schumann wrote a *Fantasia in A minor for piano and orchestra (allegro affetuoso)*, considered by him at the time to be a complete musical piece. But he added to it, in 1845, an *intermezzo* and a finale, thus resulting in the composition of his *Concerto for piano and orchestra in A minor*. The work is contemporary with the first outlines of his second symphony.

The concerto was first played at the Gewandhaus in Leipzig on 11 January 1846, with Clara Schumann as soloist.

Liszt, Franz

Concerto for piano and orchestra No.2, 1857

A major

The orchestra equalled by the piano

A long way from the classical form, Liszt's Second Concerto *allowed the composer to show off his virtuosity, his technical qualities and his talent as an orchestrator.*

The adoption, for the *Second Concerto*, of the six connected movements and the complex interweaving of a principal theme with secondary themes does not come from the sole concern of distancing himself from the classical form. They were also necessary for the attainment of a succession of contrasts and for the mastery of them. The work is characterized by its harmonic innovation and by a principle of variation of motifs which brings it closer to the *Sonata in B minor* by the same composer; no more orthodox in its treatment of a classical form.

But even more surprising is the use made of the piano: often a simple orchestral instrument, the piano, is capable of competing with the full orchestra, so much so that the latter sometimes seems to be

nothing more than an extended echo of the soloist. By solidifying some of the principles implemented in the *First Concerto in E flat major* (four movements, three of which were connected, and the use of cyclic themes), the *Second Concerto* 'frees itself from some earlier traditions and moves closer to the symphonic poem' (Alfred Leroy). These two concertos by Liszt are not isolated creations, as they owe much to Weber's three concertos.

In one of history's many paradoxes, Liszt's concertos, which turned Mozart's and Beethoven's classical notion upside down, actually approximate, in the osmosis that they create between the soloist and the orchestra, the concertos by J. S. Bach.

Historical references

Begun in 1839–40, Liszt's two piano concertos were interrupted by his career as an instrumentalist. But if his liaison with Marie d'Agoult brought him to this career, the Princess Sayn-Wittgenstein, whom he met in 1847, convinced him to dedicate himself exclusively to composition. He was able to finish his two concertos in 1849 at Weimar, where Liszt had been named chapel master in 1842. The first was performed in 1855 with the composer on piano at a concert conducted by Berlioz. The second was first played for the public in 1857 with Liszt conducting the orchestra and one of his students on piano. The two works were subsequently revised; the first in 1856 and the second in 1861.

Two other works by Liszt for piano and concerto: *Totentanz*, contemporary with the two concertos, which inspired Moussorgsky; *Malediction*, an early work for piano and orchestra which was only published in 1915.

Brahms, Johannes

Concerto for piano and orchestra No.1, 1861

D minor, opus 15

A work created in 'a stroke of genius'

Brahms's first major orchestral work, the Concerto in D minor *was more popular than his symphonies due to less compact instrumental content.*

Encouraged by Schumann to compose a symphony, the young Brahms, dissatisfied with the results he was getting, gave his score the form of a Sonata for two pianos and in reworking it transformed it into the work we know as *Concerto No.1 in D minor*.

This concert piece of grandiose style was, at the time of its creation, assimilated with a symphony with obligatory piano. The composer imposes a symphonic treatment on the orchestra part and the piano part, but far from being a virtuoso piece intended to compete openly with the tutti, it does not really contrast with it at all. Moreover, the disproportion of the length of the first movement (*maestoso*) which almost equals that of the other two (*adagio* and *rondo-allegro non troppo*), introduces a structural imbalance which leaves one feeling that the work is less successful than the *Concerto No.2 in B flat*

'... the concerto is subjected to rather fanciful attempts at interpretation. One wants to see in its sombre first movement the terrible impression left by Schumann's suicide attempt' (Karl Geiringer, *Brahms*, 1982).

major opus 83 (a late work written between 1878 and 1881).

An early work admittedly, the Concerto No.1 affirms its value by 'incomparable strokes of genius' according to Glenn Gould who also notes the extraordinary fluctuation of key right from the beginning, which does not give way to the established key of the piece (D minor) until the 11th bar.

In this piece Brahms devotes himself to a very elaborate thematic work. We also recognize in it the distinctive timbre which characterizes his music, his very personal way of sounding the orchestra (Clara Schumann said of this piece that it is a composition where 'almost everything sounds wonderful') and a dynamism perfectly in tune with the dramatic emotional content of the work.

Historical references

Composed between 1854 and 1858, the *Concerto No.1 in D minor* was played for the first time to a private audience in Hanover on 30 March 1858. Joseph Joachim conducted the orchestra and Brahms was on piano. On 22 January 1859 the public at the Royal Theatre in the same city gave it a cool reception. But it was the concert at Leipzig's Gewandhaus on 17 January in 1859 which can be described as nothing short of a 'total fiasco'. The public and the critics found the work to be 'dry' and 'difficult to understand'. Two months later (30 March 1859) Brahms played in his home town of Hamburg where it was very well received.

Grieg, Edvard

Concerto for piano and orchestra, 1868

A minor, opus 16

Pure lyricism

Highly representative of Grieg's melodic style, the Concerto in A minor *remains one of his most popular works.*

Constructed according to the usual structure (1. *allegro molto moderato*, 2. *adagio*, 3. *allegro moderato molto et marcato*), the concerto clearly displays the influence of Schumann although Grieg managed to differentiate it from the German romantic tradition by inserting specifically Scandinavian folklore themes, melodic and rhythmic elements. This is not a very detailed work, but it is tuneful and pianistically brilliant.

Historical references

Composed in 1868 in Solloeroed, the *Concerto for piano* was first performed the same year in Rome during a visit Grieg was making to the Italian capital to present his work to his friend Liszt.

Tchaikovsky, Piotr Ilyich

Concerto for piano and orchestra No.1, 1875

B flat minor, opus 23

A regard for virtuosity

Despite a definite melodic complacency this concerto is not devoid of formal originality nor of originality in style.

In an apparently traditional form, the work is made up of three movements; but considered separately none of these respects the usual concerto structure. The 1st movement, an *allegro*, is preceded by an introduction; the central *andante* is interrupted by a *prestissimo*; and the third movement 'substitutes a savage Cossack dance for the final rondo' (Michel Hofmann). As for the work's virtuosity, it is not gratuitous, but rather a component of the musical style.

Historical references

Nicolaï Rubinstein, pianist and conductor of the Russian Orchestra to whom Tchaikovsky had originally dedicated his concerto, felt the work to be unplayable and without merit. It was performed without him in Boston on 28 October 1875.

Rachmaninov, Serge

Concerto for piano and orchestra No.2, 1901

C minor, opus 18

A sense of the past

Displaying an old-fashioned romanticism, Rachmaninov's famous Second Concerto *is a musical work by a master pianist.*

Exhibiting a more traditional structure than that of the models he claims to imitate (Chopin, Liszt, Tchaikovsky), Rachmaninov's *Concerto No.2* consists of three movements (*moderato, adagio sostenuto, allegro scherzando*). The style is primarily melodic, even sentimental, and its somewhat trite lyricism often grandiloquent.

Nonetheless, many performers have found within it an opportunity for displaying their virtuosity.

Historical references

After the failure in 1897 of his first symphony, Rachmaninov sank into a deep depression. Only psychotherapy was able to give him back the desire to write music. Once this was restored he quickly finished a part of this concerto which he played in Moscow at the end of 1900. The success gave him the determination to finish the work which he presented in its entirety in October 1901.

Prokofiev, Serge

Concerto for piano and orchestra No.3, 1921

C major, opus 26

A superficial modernism

Alternately post-romantic and neo-classical, lyrical and percussive, Prokofiev's Third Concerto *demands virtuoso performers.*

Prokofiev's *Third Concerto* was written both for the composer and the performer that he was. Its spectacular aspect comes from the fact that the musician's piano playing was meant to be quasi-hammering. The work abounds in contrasts, for it also contains lyric themes, some of which had been noticed in Russia previously. This somewhat eclectic concerto, neo-classical in places but full of colour, consists of three traditional movements.

Historical references

The writing of this concerto coincided with Prokofiev's first major voyage. Having left Russia after the Revolution he divided his time, from 1918, between France and the United States. Begun in 1916, the *Third Concerto* was first performed in Chicago on 16 December 1921.

Ravel, Maurice

Concerto in D for the left hand, 1931

Ravelian tones in a tragic atmosphere

Although Ravel's two piano concertos were written simultaneously, the one for the left hand *seems more modern than the* Concerto in G.

The *Concerto in D* only contains one movement, articulated in two sections (*lento/allegro*). The orchestra introduction, almost tragic, originates in the low register. It first brings out the rather lugubrious first theme introduced by the double bassoon; then the second introduced expansively by the brass instruments (these are the two principal themes of the work). It then swells to explode in a symphonic *crescendo* to which a spirited piano cadenza responds. A seductive piano solo precedes a passage of dialogue between the soloist and the orchestra before the second part begins. This part immediately establishes a rhythmic beat in the form of a march on which is superimposed, at first simulating a jazz improvisation, a network of melodic lines in which we recognize, modified in various ways, the two themes of the first part. The whole is of a great formal rigour and we are given the impression that both hands of the pianist had been used.

Historical references

Ravel was commissioned by the Austrian pianist Paul Wittgenstein (who had been injured in war and had had his right arm amputated), the *Concerto in D for the left hand*, composed in 1930–31, was first performed by Wittgenstein in Vienna on 27 November 1931.

When he wrote the *Concerto in G major* Ravel considered making him the soloist in the first performance. The work was eventually played by Marguerite Long (1874–1966) in Paris at the Salle Pleyel on 14 January 1932. The Lamoureux Orchestra was conducted by the composer.

The Concerto in G

Lacking the impetuosity and the controlled dramatic effects of the *Concerto in D*, the *Concerto in G* comes from a more traditional style which has been called neo-classical. The work is divided into three movements; *allegramente, adagio assai, presto*. It was originally intended to be a Basque rhapsody (its first movement evokes in many places the folklore of this region), then conceived in the spirit of a *divertimento* by Mozart. Ravel did not hide the fact that he had turned to Mozart for the construction of the *adagio assai* built on the model of the *larghetto* of the Clarinet quintet K.581. The last movement, dynamic, brilliant and precipitous, is not lacking in concessions to virtuosity. Here one finds jazz like 'a reflection of a domesticated exoticism' (H. H. Stuckenschmidt).

The two piano concertos are the last of the instrumental compositions by *Bolero*'s composer who, in the summer of 1933, felt the first symptoms of a serious brain ailment (Picq's disease), which resulted in a total incapacity for musical creation.

Bartók, Béla

Concerto for piano and orchestra No.2, 1933

Sz 95

The transformed concerto

*While Bartók's three piano concertos
are not among his major works, the
first, and certainly the second, are
rich in new tones.*

In his *First Concerto*, Bartók treated the solo piano as the equal of the percussion instruments. The primary role accorded to the rhythmic element had practically banished all melody.

With his *Second Concerto*, Bartók decided to reuse some of what he had learnt from the first (the innovation of piano formulas, the distinguishing of instrumental groups and the organization by rhythmic motifs), all in integrating, as he himself said, 'a more attractive thematic material'.

The work begins with a triumphant (and slightly teasing) trumpet call. In terms of its form, the *Second Concerto* consists of three movements: two *allegros* framing a central *adagio* which is itself split in three, as it gets interrupted in the middle by a *presto*. According to a favourite construction of

Bartók's, the work is thus perfectly symmetrical and this symmetry determines not only the organization of the movements, but also the distribution of themes. The unity thus established by the use of identical themes in the corresponding movements, Bartók strove to thwart it by the instrumentation. The strings are left out of the first movement, the wind instruments excluded from the slow parts of the second, and the full orchestra is not used until the last movement and in the central *presto*, a passage which is more interesting in terms of the orchestration.

Historical references

Disappointed by the reception given to the performance of his *First Concerto* for piano and orchestra in 1932, Bartók, on writing his second in 1930, decided that it would be less severe than the first. But, interrupted on several occasions by tours as a pianist in Switzerland, Spain, Portugal and Austria, he was not able to complete his work until 1931. The work was performed in January 1933 in Frankfurt with the composer on piano and Hans Rosbaud conducting.

> Bartók's piano concertos, like those by Stravinsky or Schönberg, may not be indispensable to the evolution of musical history, but the *Second Concerto* remains one of the rare works of its time to have postponed the demise of a form, albeit one that had reached the end of its usefulness.

Vivaldi, Antonio

'The Four Seasons', four concertos for violin and strings, 1725

Opus 8, Nos.1 to 4

Musical mimicries

*A very detailed portrayal of events
linked to the passing of the seasons,
The Four Seasons is one of the
most beautiful examples of synthesis
between pure and programme music.*

The Four Seasons is a musical transposition of a narrative in the form of four sonnets. This transposition is meant to be so exact that a system of letters, found in the margin of the score and text, makes it possible to pick out the corresponding passages. Furthermore, the musically transposed events appear simultaneously, interwoven among themselves. In this way the second movement of *Spring* superimposes three different levels of musical description: the complaint of a shepherd, conveyed by the solo violin; the barking of a dog and the rustling of leaves expressed by the string orchestra.

But the work would have remained as just one imitative score among others if Vivaldi had not had the courage to bring together his climactic evocations with the strict form of the concerto. He brought about a 'transition never yet achieved' (M. Marnat) between the tradition of imitative music — that of the Venetian operas in particular, which were full of descriptive episodes — and the establishment of a specifically musical form. From here on the rest of the scenes respect the form of three movements fast-slow-fast, and the second movements still correspond to a lull. For example, the last movement of *Summer* is a storm and the second of *Autumn* simulates the drowsiness of tipsy peasants.

This exceptional play of sounds was rediscovered only recently, thanks to Nikolaus Harnoncourt's analytical interpretation, showing once again that the musicological analysis turns out to be indissociable from good interpretations.

Historical references

The Four Seasons make up part of a collection of twelve concertos grouped under the title *Il Cimento dell' Armonica e dell' Invenzione* opus 8 (The confrontation between harmony and invention). They were published with the explanatory sonnets in 1725; but their composition goes back to an earlier time we cannot date precisely. The work was very well received and its circulation outside Italy developed rapidly.

Beethoven, Ludwig van

Concerto for violin and orchestra, 1809

D major, opus 61

In praise of classical phrasing

Beethoven's only violin concerto is the first of its kind to exhibit such vast proportions, as much by length as by its symphonic conception.

Written for a large instrumental complement (1 flute, 2 oboes, 2 clarinets, 2 bassoons, 2 horns, 2 trumpets, kettledrums and strings), Beethoven's *Violin Concerto* respects the traditional division into three movements; *Allegro ma non troppo, larghetto, rondo* (*allegro*).

The first movement, spacious and impressive, opens with a rhythmic motif of four notes repeated and confined to the solo kettledrums which, picked up by and spread throughout the orchestra, acquire a thematic dimension. This method of repeated notes is much liked by Beethoven, as he has already used it in his *Fourth Concerto for piano* and reused it, to get an entirely different effect, with the fundamental motif of his *Fifth Symphony*. But it is also one of the most spectacular examples of the 'clarity of definition' (Charles Rosen). Again according to Charles Rosen, the ease with which the arrangement of the classical phrase is detected is due to the fact that the motifs of which it is made are isolated from each other and well emphasized. The solution adopted by the violin concerto (a motif which breaks away from the solo kettledrums) is thus particularly clear.

The second movement of the piece, a *larghetto*, which is a series of variations entrusted to the soloist and to the reduced orchestra, links up without interruption to the final *rondo* in which the atmosphere is already that of the *Pastoral Symphony* and of its folk dance. The work finishes, not without humour, in an ascending virtuoso passage by the soloist abruptly interrupted by two chords of the full orchestra.

Historical references

Dedicated to his childhood friend Stephan van Breunig, the *Violin Concerto* was composed in 1806. It was first performed on 23 December of the same year by the director and first violin of the An der Wien theatre, Franz Clement, who had commissioned the work. But it was not published until March 1809. The *Concerto* dates from a happy and particularly productive period in the life of the musician who, during these years (1805–7) wrote his *4th Piano Concerto*, his *4th Symphony*, the sonata *Appassionata*, the three string quartets *Razumovski* and sketched out his *5th* and *6th Symphonies*.

Opus 61a

In 1807, for financial reasons, Beethoven transcribed his *Violin Concerto for the piano*. The result is debatable but the cadenzas were written by Beethoven and the one in the first movement is significant in that it is accompanied by a kettledrum solo.

Mendelssohn-Bartholdy, Felix

Concerto for violin and orchestra, 1845

E minor, opus 64

To the glory of the violin

It was the formal balance, the measured virtuosity and the melodic charm that ensured Mendelssohn's Concerto in E minor *its complete success.*

The work is divided into three movements which follow one another without interruption. From the second measure of the first movement (*allegro molto appassionato*) the violin tackles with authority a lyrical cantilena picked up by the orchestra before the soloist goes on to a more impetuous secondary theme. The development of the principal theme and the secondary motif move towards an integral cadenza of the movement which finishes with a brilliant variation of the secondary motif.

The *andante* is connected to the *allegro* by the bassoon. This may be the most beautiful passage of the piece; in it we recognize the Mendelssohn of the *Romances sans paroles* for piano, passionate but with restraint and handling his effects without romantic pathos. This *andante*, prolonged by a melody in the form of an *arioso* which the soloist executes on the foundation of *pizzicato* by the strings, gives way to an evocation of the initial cantilena. This precedes the introduction of an *allegretto non troppo* (beginning of the third movement), moving carefully towards a scherzo written in a style which recalls the 'ethereal music' of *A Midsummer Night's Dream*. The development of the last movement (*allegro molto vivace*) is accompanied by the reappearance of the initial cantilena, which is made the object of the soloist's variations during the coda by the melodic line.

In this work, in which the violin is almost always in the forefront, there are 'no acrobatics as in Paganini, but rather a perfect integration into the symphonic discourse, outside of all conventional formulas' (Remi Jacobs).

Historical references

The composition of *Concerto in E minor*, undertaken beginning in 1838, was completed in the autumn of 1844. The work was first performed on 15 March 1845 at the Gewandhaus in Leipzig. Ferdinand David, to whom the work is dedicated, was the soloist. This great virtuoso was all the more aware, as technical adviser, of the difficulties (arpeggios, trills, double strings, etc) of the violin part that Mendelssohn had introduced.

Brahms, Johannes

Concerto for violin and orchestra, 1879

D major, opus 77

A concerto for and 'against' the violin

'A kind of symphony with principal violin' (Claude Rostand), Brahms's Concerto for violin *joins those by Beethoven and Mendelssohn, in a Germany trilogy of sorts.*

In its formal structure, Brahms' *Concerto* is reminiscent of Beethoven's: the same imbalance between the first movement which is much longer than the other two, the same key (D major), the same way in which the soloists during the *allegro non troppo* take up and develop the themes introduced by the orchestra. Nonetheless, it is specifically Brahmsian and somewhat less reserved than usual due, without a doubt, to the use of the violin.

The *Concerto* is divided into three parts: *allegro non troppo, adagio, allegro giocoso ma non troppo vivace.* A glorification of the Beethovian legacy, the 1st movement with its three violin solos which correspond to the three traditionally arranged parts (introduction, development, reintroduction) links together two major themes and finishes on an *animato* passage which is one of Brahms's most beautiful.

The principal theme of the second movement, launched into unaccompanied by the oboe, is then taken up by the violin. The violin develops it freely with arabesques before introducing the median part (built on a theme in F sharp major) in which we see the Brahmsian emotion so typical both in what it holds back and in what it delivers. The *adagio* finishes with the return of its initial theme.

Animated in a gipsy style, the third movement (in *rondo* form) rests upon two melodic figures. It consists of a coda which, despite the acceleration of pace, gives the *Concerto* a conclusion which allows it to reach its end smoothly.

Historical references

Just as Mendelssohn sought advice from the violinist Ferdinand David in writing the solo part of his concerto, Brahms, when he wrote his in 1878, sought the advice of his friend Joseph Joachim. The minor alterations made by Joachim reduced the difficulties of the violin part which some critics felt were written not for, but 'against the violin'. With the technical progress made by the instrument, the difficult passages are easily surmounted today. Nonetheless, the work still demands from the soloist a flawless technical skill.

Brahms' *Concerto* was played for the first time at the Gewandhaus in Leipzig on 1 January 1879, with the composer conducting and Joseph Joachim as soloist. This was Brahms' first major success in the Saxon capital.

Tchaikovsky, Piotr Ilyich

Concerto for violin and orchestra, 1881

D major, opus 35

In the interests of the soloist

Without echoing any of the personal conflicts of its composer, the themes in Tchaikovsky's Violin Concerto *evoke a picturesque vision of Russia.*

Constructed according to the traditional structure, the *Concerto in D major* contains three movements. The first (*allegro moderato*) alone takes up half of the composition. It begins with a simple introduction by the strings which presents a first theme taken up again by the violin during a brief cadenza. This initial theme is abruptly substituted by a second motif which ends with a new cadenza 'where the technical difficulties accumulate: double strings, glissandi, sudden jumps, trills and vertiginous passages.The soloist is well-served, the music less so' (Michel Hofmann). A lilting reintroduction of the second theme follows this perilous passage. The coda, played *con brio*, reminds one of the finale of a ballet.

A complete change of atmosphere occurs from the beginning of the second movement; an *andante* in minor entitled 'canzonetta'. It contains a pretty melody meant

to emphasize the violin without privileging the virtuosity of the soloist who integrates the cantilena, 'of a slightly Italianized profile' (Michel Hofmann), into a lyrical musical discourse without excessive effusiveness. From the canzonetta, the piece moves to a vigorous finale (*allegro vivacissimo*) in which the principal theme is a Cossack dance developed over 92 bars.

Historical references

In March 1878 during a stay in Clarens (Switzerland), Tchaikovsky took up an idea he had had in 1875 of writing for violin and orchestra. He had not managed to do so, except for a fairly mediocre exploitation of the idea, first in 1875 (*Serenade Melancholique* opus 26) and then in 1877 (*Valse-scherzo*, opus 34). His resolve was hardened by the enthusiasm he had felt on reading the score of Edouard Lalo's *Spanish Symphony for violin and orchestra*.

The work was composed in just over 15 days. Its first dedicatee, the violinist Leopold Auer, found it impossible to play (he did, nonetheless, make it triumph around the world several years later). Another great violinist, Adolph Brodsky, to whom the concerto was next dedicated, managed to convince the conductor Hans Richter to ensure him the performance in Vienna in December 1881; this received few favourable reactions: 'savage' music, composition of a 'disconcerting strangeness', etc.

> **Leopold Auer** (1845–1930), illustrious Hungarian violinist, was also a great teacher; he trained, among others, Jascha Heifetz and Nathan Milstein.

Berg, Alban

Violin Concerto 'To the memory of an angel', 1935

'A world of quotations' *(Dominique Jameux)*

The last of Berg's works, but not his actual requiem, the Concerto *for Violin is primarily an attempt at reconciliation between serialism and tonality.*

The last work by the composer, who renewed the genre of opera in the 20th century with *Wozzeck* and *Lulu*, is an instrumental work. But it is not actually a work of pure music for it draws up a portrait of a young adolescent too soon departed, the 'angel' to whom the concerto is dedicated. The first movement, composed of an *andante* and an *allegro*, evokes the life of the young girl, and the second — an *allegro* followed by a *largo* — her death. This somewhat sentimental 'programme' did not prevent Berg from writing a rigorous work which strictly follows the serial doctrine invented by Schönberg. The *Concerto* is entirely based

on a dodecaphonic series. But this series is unusual in that it contains some tonal elements. This allowed Berg to integrate smoothly a popular melody, Bach's chorale 'Es ist genug' (extract from the cantata BWV 50) and the last chord of *Song of the Earth* by Gustav Mahler.

Discredited for a long time by serial orthodoxy, *The Concerto to the Memory of an Angel* is of interest today for its synthesis of popular and erudite styles and of tonality and serialism. Of interest also is the way in which the passages develop back and forth between these heterogeneous elements. For, 'the rich and turbulent images which emerge along the border of these two systems' (Jean-Paul Olive) are among the most enigmatic in the history of music.

Historical references

In 1935 Berg was working on his second opera, *Lulu*, when he received a commission for a concerto from American violinist Louis Krasner. At first hesitant, he finally accepted as his financial situation was precarious and the Nazi wave which was breaking out across Europe did not give him any hope for the success of *Lulu* in the near future. The death at the age of 15, on 22 April 1935, of Manon Gropius (daughter of Alma Mahler and Walter Gropius the founder of Bauhaus) affected him strongly enough to impel him to write the concerto based on a portrait of the deceased girl. These circumstances explain, in part, why Berg's most 'romantic' work — written in only a few months — was the first to have been played extensively; especially given that some critics had expected it to be the composer's 'requiem'.

Another contribution by Berg to the genre of concerto: the *Chamber Concerto* for violin, piano and 13 wind instruments (1925).

The School of Vienna
Alban Berg is, with Anton Webern, one of the two great disciples of Arnold Schönberg, the inventor (1922) and theoretician of serialism. The three of them were part of the 'Second School of Vienna'.

Vivaldi, Antonio

Concerto for flute and strings 'La Notte', 1730

Opus 10, No.2

The ideal concerto

The Six Concertos for flute *opus 10 by Vivaldi are the first written for the instrument.* The Second Concerto *does not respect the traditional division into three movements.*

The distribution of movements in this work is closer to that adopted by the concerti grossi by Corelli or Handel than to the 'fast-slow-fast' model Vivaldi almost always respected.

La Notte is made up of six movements which are played freely one after the other and change key each time. The first, a *largo*, in which the flute and strings play in unison, precedes a *presto* subtitled *Fantasmi* (phantoms) whose eerie atmosphere is achieved by the use of unusual modes (minor scales ascending without alternations). Next comes a second *largo* and then a second, very rhythmic, *presto*. The fifth movement, again a *largo*, also has a subtitle: *Il Sonno* (the Sleep). The lethargic mood suggested by this title is translated by a slowed rhythm

Another of Vivaldi's concertos was also entitled 'La Notte', but the solo instrument was a bassoon.

(the solo instrument and the muted strings are treated as extended notes) and a veiled timbre (the flute is doubled by the first violins). The work closes with a very virtuosic *allegro*. The two subtitles of this nocturnal piece (Phantoms, Sleep) help to explain its particular structure of six episodes: *La Notte* is more a vision of a concerto disturbed by a dream than of an Italian concerto proper.

But this concerto — as well as the five others of opus 10 — is even more remarkable in the way it widens the scope for the solo instrument. 'In this collection Vivaldi establishes what are to become classical traits of the flute: rapid scales, arpeggios and trills' (Carl de Nys).

Historical references

Published around 1730, the *Six Concertos for flute opus 10*, the first three of which have descriptive titles (*The Tempest*, *The Night*, *The Goldfinch*), were written for the orchestra of young girls that Vivaldi had directed in Venice from 1716 at the Ospedale della Pietà, a hospice for foundlings, where the most gifted students received musical instruction of a very high level. The experimental nature of a good number of Vivaldi's concertos and 'the draconian technical demands imposed on the soloists of each instrument showed that these works were written for first-rate virtuosos' (N. Harnoncourt). This 'singular boarding school orchestra' which Vivaldi made use of was, at the time, highly reputable.

Mozart, Wolfgang Amadeus
Concerto for clarinet and orchestra, 1791
A major K.622

An intimate melodic flow

Understated in its expression of pathos, the Concerto for clarinet *has none of the dramatization usually found in the concerto form and is more evocative of the climate of chamber music.*

With its themes expressed by the overlapping of multiple musical phrases with rhythm, the first movement (an *allegro*) gives the impression of perfect continuity; of a song based on the development 'of a series of melodies that flow one into the other without a break' (Charles Rosen). From treble to bass and inversely, Mozart exploits like no one else of his time the tone-colour possibilities of a clarinet (which had a lower sound than the present-day model in B flat). But the sonorities produced by the unaccompanied instrument, proof of a perfectly mastered, complex arrangement, exist only in terms of the whole discourse with which they become integrated by establishing a dialogue with the orchestra less contrasting than the one imposed by the piano. This then facilitates the predominance of strings in a *tutti* which does not contain trumpets or oboes or percussion instruments.

A model of Mozartian *cantabile* lacking virtuosic effects, dense without ever creating a feeling of gravity, and of significant melodic amplitude; the *adagio* in D major (second movement) represents the emotional peak of the work. This is a piece both melancholy and serene in which the theme evokes the *adagio* of the *Piano Concerto in A major* K.488, *L'Ave verum* K.618 and above all the *larghetto* of *Quintet in A for clarinet and strings* K.581. It clearly illustrates Mozart's exceptional ability to move people with the most simple means.

The finale, a *rondo* with a fairly fast refrain framed by two verses, finishes the work in an atmosphere of joyless diversion.

Historical references

Composed in October 1791 between the *Magic Flute* (May 1791 to September 1791) and the *Requiem* (October 1791, unfinished), the *Concerto for clarinet and orchestra in A major* was the last instrumental work that Mozart was able to finish. With the completion of the concerto, he honoured a commission made at least two years earlier by his friend, clarinettist Anton Stadler (1753–1812). The initial plan for the work is attested to by the outline of a *Concerto in G for basset-horn* K.584b which probably dated from the end of 1789 and constituted a pre-original version of the first movement of the *Concerto for clarinet*.

Bach, Johann Sebastian

Concerto for two violins and strings, 1720

D minor, BWV 1043

The Italian model surpassed

Conforming to the form developed by Vivaldi, this Concerto *by Bach testifies to an even more complex style.*

Bach's violin concertos give evidence of thematic developments and room given to the soloist as rarely before. In this respect they can be seen as the violin equivalent of the *Brandenburg Concertos*.

In the *Concerto for two violins*, the two extreme movements, rhythmically very fast and rich in contrasts, frame a very melodic central *largo*. Throughout the work the dialogue is not held between the two soloists, but rather between the orchestra and the bow instruments 'on an absolutely equal level' (Alberto Basso).

Historical references

The three concertos for one or two violins were all written in 1720 when Bach was the musical director for the Prince Leopold d'Anhalt in Cöthen.

Mozart, Wolfgang Amadeus

Concerto for flute, harp and orchestra, 1778

C major K.299

A musical compromise

Even though it concedes to the gallant French style, the Concerto for flute and harp *nonetheless offers an unusual combination of soloists.*

This concerto is actually a *symphonia concertante* for two instruments. The harp was considered to be too much of 'a poor relation of the piano' (Jean and Brigitte Massin) to claim the role of soloist. However, the work, with its three move- ments, is more of a success because of the balance achieved between the soloists and the orchestra, the French and German styles, and between convention and invention.

Historical references

The *Concerto for flute and harp* was written by Mozart in 1778 during his second trip to Paris. There he gave courses on composition to a young harpist, the daughter of the Duke of Guisnes, himself a flautist; and was responsible for bringing out the best in the two amateur virtuosos.

Brahms, Johannes

Concerto for violin, cello and orchestra, 1887

A minor, opus 102

The *concerto grosso* reinvented

The Double Concerto *allows the soloists to make the most of their respective tones within a symphonic blending which often makes them sound like 'a single instrument with eight strings'.*

While reminiscent, in its formal structure, of the old concerti grossi for two violins and cello and of some works by Bach (*Concerto for two violins and strings*), Mozart (*Sinfonia Concertante*), and Beethoven (*Triple Concerto*), Brahms's *Concerto for violin, cello and orchestra* differs in its symphonic scope and its instrumentation. The latter establishes a relationship of equal proportions between the solo instruments and the orchestra, which is doubled by a subtle balance of cello and violin.

The work respects the division into three movements. The first, a freely constructed *allegro* in A minor, contains three principal themes enriched by eight secondary motifs. This is a passage which shows Brahms to be extraordinarily inventive on the level of polythematism. The introduction (four bars of orchestra) brings out the vigorous, emphatic and insistent first theme. This is

followed by a very beautiful cello solo, the first of many interventions by the soloists (sometimes one or the other, sometimes the two together), distributed alternately with the orchestral parts up until the coda.

The *allegro* is followed by the elegiac climate of the second movement, an *andante* in D minor, built as a tripartite lied, 'a grand and mysterious ballad of sorts entirely typical of the Nordic inspiration of Brahms' (Claude Rostand). The middle section of this movement contains a magnificent melodic line.

The third movement, *vivace non troppo*, is a finale in A minor formulated like a *rondo* with a tripartite structure, yet different from that of the traditional *rondo*. Using popular, lively themes, the Brahmsian rhythm has a certain heaviness, notably in the folk dance, fourth theme of the central motif.

Historical references

Brahms finished writing the *Double Concerto* in the summer of 1887 during a visit to Thun in Switzerland. The concerto was first performed on 18 October 1887 in Cologne. The composition, quite favourably received, was Brahms's last symphonic work. From then on he dedicated himself exclusively to the creation of piano works, lieder and chamber music.

Webern, Anton

Concerto for nine instruments, 1934

Opus 24

Didactic art

One of the most basic works of Occidental music, the Concerto opus 24 *had an enormous influence on serial music between 1950 and 1960.*

The title of the work, *Concerto for nine instruments*, tells us that it is a piece written for nine soloists 'concertant' among themselves. In this sense, the work is fairly close to some of the concerti grossi and follows the classical structure of three movements 'fast-slow-fast'. The instruments also obey the number three — three groups of three instruments: the woodwinds (flute, oboe, clarinet), the brasses (horn, trumpet, trombone) and the strings (violin, viola and piano).

The *Concerto opus 24* follows the dodecaphonic system invented by Schönberg

---

The magic square

Webern saw the sequences of his *Concerto opus 24*, because of the extensive connections set up by the twelve notes, to be a transposition of the Latin magic square in which the five words can be read in all directions, and form pairs of words which read as the inverse of each other.

```
S A T O R
A R E P O
T E N E T
O P E R A
R O T A S
```

---

and is composed from a series of 12 notes. But this series is unique, as it is derived — according to diverse principles of transposition — from a musical figure of three notes presented in four different ways. The whole work, barely more than six minutes long, is thus a series of variations on a motif of three notes.

What strikes the listener first is that the music passes continuously from one instrument to another. In order that this variation of the three-note figure remains detectable, Webern entrusts each of these arrangements to a different instrument. This appropriateness of timbre to the musical writing is most obvious at the beginning of the work where the figures are exposed most clearly. Webern strives to blur the location of these three notes by making them heard simultaneously in the form of chords (entrusted to the unaccompanied piano or to many instruments) and by subjecting them to rhythmic irregularities and to gaps in the instrumentation. According to Pierre Boulez, the value of the *Concerto opus 24* lies in the way the music respects this figure of three notes or, at other times distances itself from it in order to approach completely different ones.

Historical references

Begun in 1931, the *Concerto opus 24* was not finished until September 1934 because Webern had had to constantly interrupt the composition because of his tours in Spain and the rise of the Nazis. After the *String Trio opus 20* and the *Symphony opus 21*, the *Concerto for nine instruments* constitutes the end of the composer's 'didactic' period.

Ligeti, Györgi

Chamber Concerto for 13 instrumentalists, 1970

An illuminating confusion

Although it superimposes so many elements that the detail of the music is often obscured (according to one of Ligeti's favourite processes), this Concerto *as a whole displays a very clear development.*

The title chosen by Ligeti is explicit. This is a chamber concerto because it is written for an orchestral complement limited to 13 instrumentalists (four woodwinds, two brasses, four keyboards played by two instrumentalists and a string quintet). This chamber work is a concerto because the '13 instrumentalists all have parts of equal importance to play', and because the music consists of 'continuously new groupings of soloists standing out from the ensemble' (G. Ligeti). However, the work does not include the three traditional movements, but rather has four, a structure which is more reminiscent of the symphonic division.

> Ligeti's *Chamber Concerto* takes its title from a work by Alban Berg entitled *Chamber Concerto for piano, violin and 13 wind instruments* (1927).

> Another contribution by Györgi Ligeti in the form of a concerto: *Double Concerto* for flute, oboe and orchestra (1972).

In terms of its actual composition, the *Chamber Concerto* proposes a whole approach. The elements (timbre, melodic line, interval) are rarely perceptible individually and only make sense in the sonorous mingling created by their superimposition. The interest of the work is in the transformations and sequences of its diverse mixes or textures. In order to achieve this blend of instruments, rhythms and intervals, Ligeti uses many processes such as the superimposition of very close melodic lines, the very rapid rhythmic beat, etc. Furthermore, as different textures are worked on, the musical confusion brought about can involve more or less directly according to the movements, the timbre, harmony, rhythm or melodic line.

However, the value of Ligeti's concerto is not just attractive ensemble tone. Besides being very original, the way in which different musical figures stand out from the ensemble, sometimes only just, sometimes very blatantly, often with humour, and then retreat back with the same continuity into the group by progressively losing their contours, makes this piece unique.

In brief, this is a piece of music with a very complex style but one where the recognition is almost instantaneous.

Historical references

Written in 1969–70 for Friedrich Cerha's Viennese ensemble 'Die Riehe', Ligeti's *Chamber Concerto* is a synthesis of his second string quartet and his *Ten Pieces for wind quartet*. In its entirety the work was first performed in Berlin on 1 October 1970.

Dances

The word *dance* describes the activity of a body in movement in accordance with certain rhythmic principles and the music which accompanies these movements. This practice takes different forms according to social and historical evolutions: thus we find peasant dances as well as court dances. Furthermore, specific dance music gradually gets taken over by individual composers which makes the form more complex and causes it to lose its primary function of accompaniment which gives way to concert pieces that are only inspired by dance rhythm.

The *basse-danse* was the first major dance of the Renaissance: the music which acted as the accompaniment was adapted to the steps invented by the dancers. Next came the *gaillard*, a popular dance, the *pavane* which was a Court dance, and to name just a few others; the *courante*, the *minuet*, the *bourrée* which was used by many composers, including Lully and Bach.

The *waltz* appeared during the 18th century and derived from German peasant dances and Austrian *Ländler*. In the 19th century, in Vienna, this dance of three movements triumphed with Johann Strauss (the Elder and Younger) in pieces such as *The Champagne Waltz* and *The Blue Danube*. However many composers had used the form earlier: Schubert (piano dances), Weber (*Invitation to Waltz*), and of course, Chopin with 19 waltzes for piano. The waltz is perhaps the only dance to have successfully incorporated both popular and erudite music. For, as Michel Chion noted, it 'has the particularity of being a dance capable of adaptation to complex and baroque styles, all the while conserving its fundamental dance characteristics'. This is why such diverse composers have been able to integrate it into very different works: symphonic pieces, ballets and operas. It also explains how the waltz can be both a piece of music without pretension and a very sophisticated piece, or can even lend itself to a consequential musical effort, as in the cases of Liszt, Ravel and Schönberg.

Already widespread by the 18th century, but most celebrated in the romantic era, the *polonaise* and the *mazurka* are triple time dances of Polish origin. The first is a Court dance and the second, choreographically very complex, a folk dance. Telemann and Bach, Chopin and Liszt, among many others, wrote polonaises but it was really only Chopin who wrote a piece based on the *mazurka*, giving it an original harmonic colour which was reflected in Wagner.

The *polka*, a Czech dance in double time which was also very famous, never went beyond the status of music for amusement.

From the 19th century, and at the beginning of the 20th, it was principally the other side of the Atlantic that produced new dances. The United States of America, as a place of ethnic convergence, favoured the advent of new dance forms: ragtime, the foxtrot, the Charleston, the boogie-woogie... And Latin America saw the emergence of the tango, the samba, etc.

Some 20th-century composers seized upon these dances to integrate them into their works. Stravinsky was the composer most aware of these new rhythms, as can be seen in his *Ragtime* for eleven instruments (1918) and his *Tango* for piano (1940, orchestrated in 1953).

Chopin, Frédéric

Grande Valse brillante No.1 for piano, 1834

E flat major, opus 18

'Gravity in Frivolity' (Baudelaire)

The Grande Valse brillante *penetrates Chopin's dandy side; the lightness of the manners of an apparently phlegmatic young man 'smitten, above all, with eminence' (Baudelaire).*

Graceful, surging from one section to another, the *Grande Valse in E flat major* reveals a more rigorous piano style than it seems to have. To offset the disadvantages of rhythms which could get monotonous, Chopin increases the sound intensity on the third beat of each bar, so that the melody in each section is treated in a condensed and elliptical way. This concern for avoiding rhythmic monotony, which existed during the creation of the 19 waltzes, is most obvious in the *Valse Brillante in A flat minor* opus 34 No.1, a piece full of contrasts, rich in subtle and frequent transitions from one key to another. The *Waltz in F major* opus 34 No.3 consists of a series of appoggiaturas which can be compared, a bit simplistically, to the coming and going of a cat on the

keyboard. Among these evocations of imaginary ballrooms (remember that Chopin wanted us to refrain from dancing his waltzes as they were not written for dance), it is also worth mentioning the *Waltz in A flat major* opus 42.

Most famous of these so-called allusive waltzes is the very beautiful *Waltz 'du Regret'* in *A minor* opus 34 No.2 (to be played *lento*, that is, more slowly than an *adagio*), which comes from a truly refined melancholy aesthetic. It was, supposedly, Chopin's favourite waltz. Other famous splenetic 'trifles': No.2 (in F major), No.3 (in D flat major), from opus 70 and, of course, the *Waltz in A flat major* opus 69 No.1 called 'de l'Adieu'.

Historical references

Chopin composed his 19 waltzes between 1829 and 1848. The *Grande Valse brillante* No.1 in E flat major opus 18, dedicated to a Miss Horsford was written in 1834 and published in Paris the same year.

---

14 Waltzes

In their near total, the recordings of Chopin's waltzes include only 14 pieces; the works numbered 15 to 19 (posthumous) were generally excluded.

The three pieces of opus 64 belong to the series of *salon waltzes* (a title objected to by the composer). The first (in D flat major) was nicknamed 'Waltz of the Little Dog' because it is supposed to be like the animal chasing its own tail: its *tempo molto vivace* often acts as a pretext for interpretations by virtuosos, transforming it wrongly into a 'minute-waltz'. A meticulous circular phrase (*piu mosso*) animates the central part of *opus 64 No.2 in C sharp major* (theme of the 'drop of water').

Chopin, Frédéric

Polonaise, 'Héroïque', for piano, 1843

A flat major, opus 53

Metamorphosis of a national dance

Chopin literally recreated the traditional polonaise, accentuating its modal and rhythmic ambiguities through the harmonic subtleties of the piano.

The first of nine musical episodes of *Héroïque* is an introduction (bars 1–16) which increases its intensity to arrive at the introduction of the principal theme, ardent, solemn, almost declamatory. This famous theme, in two repeats of sixteen bars each, also serves as the conclusion of the piece. Between the introductory passage and the coda comes the sixth episode, a well-emphasized and eloquent melody which develops its vigorous chords over forty bars, before finishing with a spellbinding *fortissimo* more epic than lyric. Some have viewed this work as a heroic poem inspired in Chopin, the exile, by nostalgia and a feeling of indignation; others see it as a polonaise of regret, an expression of heartache. Whatever the personal echoes (Chopin did not like his music to be scrutinized for its autobiographical aspects), this composition is valuable, primarily for its remarkable formal qualities, notably the conclusion and the balance between harmonic subtleties and rhythmic force.

Historical references

Chopin is the composer of 16 polonaises for piano written between 1817 — when he was eight — and 1846; the first seven, written in his native country, were early works; in the domain of polonaises he did not really discover his style until 1835 (four years after moving to Paris).

The *Polonaise in A flat major 'Héroïque'*, composed in 1836, was published in Paris in 1843.

The other polonaises

The *Polonaise in A major* opus 40 No.1, called 'militaire' is harmonically very poor. Its fairly rudimentary rhythmic effects exaggeratedly underline its martial mood. Written by the composer at the age of 20, the *Grand Valse brillante* in E flat major, opus 22 prefaced by an *andante spianato* makes too much of virtuosity. It is the last of Chopin's seven early polonaises which, without a doubt, brought this type of dance to its apogee with *opus 44 in F sharp minor*, a magnificent piece in the centre of which is a mazurka. Of an extremely free stylistic conception, the *Polonaise-fantaisie in A flat major*, opus 61, a very striking work, does not resemble the polonaise except in its intermittent rhythmic allusions.

Another dance of Polish origin, the *mazurka*, served as a musical basis for Chopin. As C. Bourniquel said, his 57 mazurkas (1824–48) 'often resort to themes which ignore the classical scale and the distribution between minor tones and major tones'; as such they are the 'places privileged by Chopinian modernity'.

Liszt, Franz

Mephisto-Waltz No.1 for piano, 1863

Myth as a pretext for musical pursuits

Of the four mephisto-waltzes written by Liszt, the first is the most illustrative and yet not just simple programme music.

Faust and Mephisto enter an inn where peasants are dancing. To help Faust win over the innkeeper's daughter, Mephisto seizes a violin and leads the audience in a 'wild' waltz. Responding to the call of a nightingale, Faust disappears in the night with the young girl and leaves Mephisto to his diabolical ball.

The first *Mephisto-waltz* follows this succession of events fairly closely, linking a series of 'devilish' dances with occasional amorous interludes. The dances receive virtuoso piano treatment in which the timbre work rivals the effect of cascading trills and arpeggios, notes repeated in the high range of the keyboard and rhythmic acceleration.

The *amoroso* passages are organized around a chromatic theme, composed of a simple ascent repeated several times — not without a foreshadowing of Wagner.

Historical references

With the composition of his *Faust-symphony* based on Goethe barely finished, Liszt wrote, between 1858 and 1860, an orchestral diptych based on Lenau's *Faust* and including: 1. *Nocturnal Procession*, 2. *Mephisto-waltz*. The transcription for piano that he wrote shortly after the second part of this diptych and which he published in 1863 made up the first *Mephisto-waltz*. The second, also transcribed from the orchestra, dates from 1881 and the third, written directly for piano, was composed in 1883. The fourth, whose manuscript is dated March 1885 (16 months before Liszt's death) is unfinished.

4th mephisto-waltz

It is customary to add to this Faustian cycle the *Bagatelle without key*, initially entitled *4th Mephisto-waltz* (without key), and a *Mephisto-polka* dating from 1883.

Of the 1200 pieces by Liszt now itemized, only 24 make references to dance, among which are: *Valse-Impromptu*, and *Mazurka brillante* (1850), Two *Polonaises* (1851), three *Czardas* (1882–4) and three *Valses oubliées* (1883), all piano pieces.

Composed 28 years later, the other three *Mephisto-waltzes* are quite different from the first. Their frequently bare style is much more linear and the virtuosity is relegated to secondary importance to leave room for the harmonic innovations which foreshadow Scriabin. While the second still follows closely the programme of the first, the last two are much more abstract, content to organize freely the *staccato* motifs and the more melodic phrases by making references, respectively, to the dance and love episodes. Even more surprisingly, the last two *Mephisto-waltzes* have even dispensed with the triple-time rhythm of the waltz.

Strauss (the Younger), Johann

The Blue Danube, waltz for orchestra, 1867

Opus 34

A celebrated musical stream

The famous Blue Danube *has remained, rightly or wrongly, the symbol of a flaunting of love for luxury, merriment and all the pleasures of society.*

Mechanical, tense, solid and powerful but too abrupt in the succession of themes which almost never last longer than 16 bars, Strauss the Elder's conception of the Viennese waltz lacks cohesion.

The melodious works of Johann Strauss the Younger created a more subtle structure: the introduction — a veritable miniature overture — saw his symphonic style accentuated, the melody enlarged and made more flexible and the themes more harmoniously based on each other.

The enlargement of the melody is clearly perceptible if one listens to the *Blue Danube*, but the fact that this waltz (in D major) was originally composed for a men's choir and orchestra creates a conflict between the

Other great successes by Johann Strauss II: *Tales from the Vienna Woods* (1868); *Wine, Women and Song* (1869); *Vienna Blood* (1873); *Emperor Waltz* (1889).

use of the human voice and the musical treatment of the rhythm. Lacking the 'winged gliding' (H. E. Jacob) which gave value to so many other pieces of the genre, it still retains a great variety of tones. The 44 bars of its introduction are followed by the waltz itself, divided into five sections (many of these begin with an entry) and a very long coda (148 bars).

Historical references

By emphasizing the swirling, brilliant and majestic characteristics of the waltz, Johann Strauss (1804–49) and his son Johann Strauss (1825–99) contributed to a dance music style which, from 1825, was extraordinarily fashionable in Vienna and soon spread throughout Europe.

It was Johann Herbeck, director of the male chorale association of Vienna, who gave the commission to Strauss the Younger for a waltz for a men's choir and orchestra which the composer, having written his work without any precise descriptive intentions, entitled 'The Beautiful Blue Danube'. A member of the choir, Josef Weye, was chosen by Herbeck to write the words to Strauss's music. The mediocrity of Weye's text was one of the reasons for the very reserved response to *The Blue Danube* at its public première in Vienna on 15 February 1867. Six months later the orchestral version of the work triumphed when it was played in Paris for the World Exposition.

Sibelius, Jean

Valse Triste for full orchestra, 1904

Opus 44

Auditory hallucinations in triple time

Written in Sibelius' 'romantico-national' period, the Valse Triste *is celebrated for its expressive pathos.*

In the half-light of a derelict room a dying woman in the throes of delirium listens to the ethereal music of a waltz (the muted melody, *pianissimo*, of silence in the key of G minor) coming from an imaginary ballroom. A stranger, who she believes to be her dead husband, asks her to dance (the theme previously introduced develops along a rhythm which gently accelerates, slows down, then accelerates again). The couple whirl round suddenly, *appassionato*; then the theme, having been abruptly reintroduced in a minor key, the waltz ends slowly, the violin invoking the last sigh of the dying woman.

Taken from the music of a scene from the drama *Kuolema* (Death), the *Valse triste* remains, with *Finlandia* (opus 26, No.7), Sibelius's most famous work.

Ravel, Maurice

Valses nobles et sentimentales for piano, 1911

The rigour of a calculated artifice *(Roland-Manuel)*

Although there is a reference to Schubert in the title, these waltzes are nevertheless very progressive pieces of piano writing.

Highly representative of clear, forceful writing, marked by a condensing and a hardening of the system of chords that they obey, these eight *waltzes* are rich in percussive tones (first waltz), light (third waltz) and sometimes slightly sombre (epi-logue). This is an 'advanced' work in which Ravel — especially in the last four compositions — by 'playing with discords, juxtaposing contrasting material' (Michèle Reverdy) innovatively presents the results of harmonic experiment.

Historical references

The *Valses nobles et sentimentales*, composed in 1910, were performed in Paris 'amidst protests and boos' (Ravel) on May 1911 in the Salle Gaveau.

Ravel, Maurice

La Valse for full orchestra, 1920

A fantastic and fateful whirl

Originally conceived of as an 'apotheosis of the Viennese waltz', Ravel's Valse *is not a light piece and its implacable rhythm produces an indisputably tragic effect.*

Written as a tribute to the memory of Johann Strauss the Younger, *La Valse* is actually a 'series of waltzes' linked to each other without any gap. The unifying principle of the work comes from the fact that it is more or less framed by an immense crescendo and that it is 'entirely derived from a central rhythm' (H. H. S-tuckenschmidt). But the significance and the originality of this 'choreographic poem' comes from the choice of subject — the Viennese waltz — and from the way it is handled. Unlike the traditional symphonic poems which illustrate extra-musical anecdotes, this *Waltz* uses the music itself, in this case the famous Viennese triple-time rhythm, as its subject. Ravel's Waltz

involved, principally, the restructuring of preorganized and well-known musical material. As Jules Van Ackere justly noted 'it is not so much the subject which creates the tone, as the potential for development of the material; in other words, the technical perspective'. In this sense Ravel's process is very similar to Gustav Mahler's, who composed his symphonies based on the military marches of Ländler.

La Valse also benefits from Ravel's large-scale orchestration, especially as the instrumental complement used is very significant. Included are consecutively linked effects 'as varied as flute tremolos, violin harmonics, bow or harp *glissandi*' (Jean Dupart). Returning to a process used in the *Concerto for the Left Hand*, the beginning of the work seems to emerge from the midst of noise. Then, gradually organizing itself, it heads rapidly towards its inexorable conclusion.

Historical references

As the composer's correspondence indicates, the idea of writing a work as a tribute to the Viennese waltz goes back to 1906. But the project was postponed for a long time due, particularly, to the profound disarray Ravel had been plunged into by the years of war. The work was therefore not returned to until 1919 on the request of Diaghilev who planned to present the choreographed version for the 1920–1 season. Finished in the Spring of 1920, *La Valse* was performed in concert on 12 December the same year and conducted by Camille Chevillard. Diaghilev refused the work. He considered it unplayable.

Ida Rubinstein (1885–1960), dedicatee of *Boléro*, started out as a dancer in Serge Diaghilev's Ballets Russes (1909). She created her own company in 1921. Ravel, as well as Debussy, Stravinsky, Honegger and Milhaud, composed for her.

Her company produced *La Valse* as ballet in 1929.

Ravel, Maurice

Boléro, for orchestra, 1929

Obsessive rhythm

Although it does not figure among Ravel's major works, Boléro *is nonetheless a unique exercise in instrumentation and rather fascinating.*

'A specifically orchestral adaptation of the principle of the *chaconne*' (André Hodeir) or of the *passacaglia*, this work repeats seventeen times a unique theme of 16 bars without developing it.

This theme is introduced initially by the unaccompanied flute on a foundation of drum beats and *pizzicati*. At each recurrence, always played in a 'very moderate and consistently uniform movement' (Ravel), which underlines the unchanging rhythm of the drum, a different instrument is emphasized: clarinet, then bassoon (high register) followed by a clarinet in E flat, the oboe d'amore, etc. The only diversification: a subtle orchestral crescendo.

The sound intensity increases virtually imperceptibly alongside the progressive superimposition of many instruments (for example we hear in the ninth repeat of the theme the oboe, the oboe d'amore, the clarinet and the cor anglais accompanied by the rest of the orchestra), but it remains in the obsessive key of C major, without a change in the rhythm, until, shortly before the conclusion, a sudden modulation in E major intervenes. The piece, an 'amazing carousel of tones' (M. Mantelli), finishes with a *tutti* at an impressive volume.

Historical references

Composed in 1928 to fulfil a commission from the dancer and patron Ida Rubinstein, *Boléro* was performed for the first time at the Paris Opera on 22 November 1928 (choreography by Bronislava Nijinska, sets and costumes by Alexandre Benois). Walter Straram conducted and Ida Rubinstein had the role of dancer. It was a great success. The first concert performance also took place in Paris on 11 January 1930, where the Orchestre des Concerts Lamoureux was conducted by Ravel.

Ravel appears to have accepted the somewhat simplistic choreographic plot reluctantly.

He had imagined a different scenario: an open air set with a factory exit and workers dancing among themselves; over this he pictured the story of a bullfighter killed by a jealous lover.

The plot
The action takes place in a Spanish inn. A gipsy, standing on a large table, starts to take a dance-step, hesitates and then gains confidence and gets carried away by the rhythm in double time (the standard rhythm of a bolero is in triple time), which gradually becomes less obsessive. The attention of four men is drawn towards her. They approach the table and surround it. The rhythm manages to intoxicate each of them progressively.

Theme of Boléro
(beginning):

Études

Études are didactic pieces generally intended for solo instruments, particularly the piano. Quite short, and usually put together in a collection, études make a point of exploring a technical problem of instrumental execution or of style.

Although the title étude was not given to a musical piece until the 19th century, the principle of didactic compilations had emerged much earlier. In this regard it is worth mentioning, in England: *Lessons*, by Purcell (1659–95) and by Handel (1685–1759), in Italy: *Sonates* by Domenico Scarlatti (1685–1757) published as 'Essercizi' (exercises). Certain pedagogical pieces by Telemann (1681–1767) excepted, the German didactic collection par excellence is the *Well-Tempered Klavier* by J. S. Bach (1685–1750), even though it is much more associated with the learning of particularities of a musical language than with their execution, questions of touch or instrumental technique. Finally, some works by French harpsichordists, such as F. Couperin (1668–1733) and J. P. Rameau (1683–1764) can be allied to this didactic genre as they demand a new method of playing.

In the 19th century the emergence of great piano virtuosos (Liszt, Hummel) as well as violin virtuosos (Paganini) favoured the development of compilations of études and the exploration of specific problems associated with these instruments: 'scales, arpeggios, trills, thirds, octaves, parallel chords, etc., for the piano, double strings and rapid passages for the violin' (Michel Chion). However, the virtuoso stylistic innovations are primarily punctilious and are often made to the detriment of the ensemble structure which remains simple. The 19th century saw the proliferation of compilations of piano études (J. B. Cramer *Études in 42 exercises*, (1804–10), Clementi, *Gradus ad Parnassum* (1817–26), Czerny, Moscheles, Hummel, etc.), but it was not until Chopin, Schumann and Liszt came on the scene that the étude went beyond its teaching role and became a fully-fledged concert piece. Among the series of études written by these three men it is necessary to mention: Chopin's *24 Études*, opus 10 and 25 (1833, 1837), Schumann's *Études Symphoniques* for piano opus 13 (1837) and Liszt's *12 Études d'execution transcendante* (1851).

Although the étude survived until the beginning of the 20th century with, notably, Scriabin's *24 Études* (opus 8, 42 and 65, composed, respectively, in 1895, 1904 and 1912), the last important collection published under the title of *étude* was Debussy's, whose *12 Études* for the piano (1916) prolonged and renovated the genre.

Displaying a certain similarity to Debussy's études, the *Quatre Études du rhythme* (1949) by Olivier Messiaen count among the last études written for the piano. More recently, the title étude has more and more been applied to electroacoustic works (Pierre Schaeffer, Pierre Henry, Karlheinz Stockhausen...). Finally, the series of *sequenzas* for an unaccompanied instrument, composed by Luciano Berio in 1958 may be considered, for now, to be the last, highly successful, manifestation of this genre.

Chopin, Frédéric

Études for piano, 1833 and 1837

Opus 10 and opus 25

When the playing 'directs the writing' (M. Chion)

Intended for the resolution, by the player, of a specific problem of instrumental technique, the Études *have contributed greatly to the musical evolution of the modern piano.*

Among the best known of the *Études* is the *third étude in E major* (first book of *12 Études*, opus 10), inappropriately nicknamed 'Tristesse' (sadness). The hackneyed tune with which the piece starts and finishes, of an apparently simple execution, presents a melodic line which the pianist must play *legato* by extending his/her fingers to a tremendous degree. Limited to the exclusive use of the black keys, the *Étude No.5 in G flat major* is a training exercise requiring rapid, brilliant and polished playing. Like the *Étude No.8 in F major*, it requires working the thumb. *No.6 in E flat minor*, 'a very beautiful polyphonic *andante* and very like a nocturne' (Camille Bourniquel), teaches

how to play *cantabile*. It contrasts strongly with *Étude No.12 in C minor*, 'La Revolutionnaire', a celebrated work in which the dynamic and brilliant qualities of scherzos are mixed with the unleashing of the most lyrical polonaises. With its obstinate augmentation of sound intensity in single time and its abrupt crescendos, this piece demands exceptional force and speed in the left hand.

In his second book (*12 Études*, opus 25) Chopin tackles other problems: arpeggio chords for both hands combined in the principal melody (*Étude No.1 in A flat major*), polyrhythm involving rapid playing by the right hand (*Étude No.2 in F minor*), chromatic thirds (*Étude No.6 in G sharp minor*, sometimes called 'La Sibérienne'), octaves played staccato (*Étude No.9 in G flat major*), etc. He completed this second collection with two pieces in which the pure musicality visibly outweighed its didactic content: *Étude No.11 in A minor*, which treats piano like a potential orchestra, and *Étude No.12 in C minor*, vehement, tragic and rich in broken chords for two hands.

Historical references

The first collection of *Études*, composed from 1828 to 1831, is dedicated to Franz Liszt; the second, which dates from 1831 to 1836, is dedicated to Countess Marie d'Agoult whose daughter, Cosima, became Wagner's wife.

Besides the series of opus 10 and 25, Chopin composed, for Moscheles and Fétis' *Méthode des méthodes*, three other *Études* published in 1840 without an opus number.

Debussy, Claude

12 Études for piano, 1916

The threshold of contemporary piano
(A. Boucourechliev)

Dedicated to the memory of Chopin, Debussy's Études *pave the way to a definition of music as the arrangement of sounds as well as notes.*

This last collection for the piano by Debussy contains two books, each of six études. The first focuses on problems of fingering, the second on tone. The first étude, 'for the five fingers' based on Czerny, plays around with a pedestrian piano motif (the first five notes of the scale in C major). The following four ('for thirds', 'for quarters', 'for sixths', 'for octaves') are each written according to the interval they are named after and which serves as their thematic material. As André Boucourechliev noted, Debussy rejects all classical thematic methods and the titles which he gives his *Études* are themes only in a more general sense. As a result 'these abstract thematic ideas free the musician from any restraint on the levels of motif, phrase and especially development'. In this way, the motifs which are based on intervals allow these four études to explore new harmonic principles. With the étude 'for eight fingers' which concludes the first book, Debussy makes the modification of timbre dependent on the very rapid speed of its development.

The six études of the second book are focused more on tones: (7: 'for chromatic degrees', 8: 'for grace notes', 9: 'for repeated notes', 10: 'for opposing tones', 11: 'for compound arpeggios', 12: 'for chords'). They resume and develop the harmonic and rhythmic innovations of the first book, and emphasize the differentiation of attack and intensity. With the tenth étude Debussy proposed 'a contrapuntal arrangement of registers, nuances, dynamics, tempos and speeds of development', (Jean Barraqué), in other words, a structuring of the components of sound.

Étude for chords

The beginning of the 12th and last *Étude* is associated with a particular musical parameter: the chord (superimposition of simultaneously emitted notes). The discordant harmony emerging from the succession of chords put into play here is reinforced by the vigour of the attacks; also, the piano appears to be treated in an almost percussive way.

Historical references

Composed between August and September 1915, the *12 Études*, published in 1916, were performed in the same year.

Messiaen, Olivier

4 Études de rythme pour piano, 1949 and 1950

A new conception of musical time

The Études de rythme *are the most experimental of Messiaen's piano works, and the second étude,* Mode de valeurs et d'intensités *led to the generalization of serialism.*

Put together into a single collection, and meant to be played in that order (1: *Île de Feu I*; 2: *Mode de valeurs et d'intensités*; 3: *Neumes rythmiques*; 4: *Île de feu II*), the *Quatre Études de rythme* are actually in two distinct groups.

The first includes the first and last études, whose poetic title, *Iles de feu* (*Fire Islands*) I and II, are explained by the fact that they are dedicated to Papua (New Guinea). The first is a very short 'series of variations on a "martelé" theme in the low register, supported by a tom-tom *ostinato*' (Harry Halbreich). The second, also a series of variations, but even more jubilant, is supported by a rhythmic theme played like the ringing of bells or chimes.

The second group is made up of the two

central études, and their title refers explicitly to the problems of stylistic technique. *Mode de valeurs et d'intensités* is probably the most calculated piece Messiaen wrote. It consists in permuting a certain number of notes (in this case 36), spread out along three superimposed registers (high, medium, low). Each of these 36 notes is characterized by a duration (one of a possible 24), an attack (one of the 12 proposed) and an intensity (one of 7); and each time a note reappears it is always associated with the same characteristics (which are only allocated once for the entire piece). It consists thus of a permutation of sounds, each one distinct, but constantly changing place. The produced effect is very static and makes it impossible to pick out any beat, or *a fortiori*, any regular rhythm; more than the others, this étude introduces a new notion of musical time. The interest of *Neumes rythmiques* lies, among other things, in the work carried out on the piano resonances.

Historical references

The two central études were composed in 1949 and the two *Iles de feu* in 1950. Messiaen presented the work in Tunis in 1950, and the French première on 7 June 1951 in Toulouse was performed by Yvonne Loriod.

While these four études — especially the second — had an enormous influence on the younger generation, they were at the same time very important to the pedagogical aims of the composer, and to the ideas which they gave him the opportunity to develop. This importance is testified to by the fact that Messiaen was able to attract to his Conservatory classes nearly all the composers considered major today.

The success of *Mode de valeurs et d'intensités* was due to its being the first attempt at the systematic pre-establishing of musical parameters (heights, intensities, durations, attacks). Many composers (Stockhausen, Boulez...) made use of this method to engage in all the possible transformations of sound space, within the framework of the generalization of Schönberg's series. And yet, Messiaen's piece does not actually transform any of the elements of sound.

Fantasias

Fantasias are essentially instrumental music works which evolved in the 16th century by adopting the structure of the *ricercare* (the Italian for 'research'), a contrapuntal form already used in Italy (*fantasias* by G. Gabrieli, O. Vecchi, etc.). It was also associated with the *ricercare* in England (W. Byrd's *Fancies for viol ensemble*), in France (*viol fantasias* by C. Guillet and E. du Caurroy) and in Spain (*tientos* by A. de Cabezón).

For the French polyphonists of the 17th century (L. Couperin, N. Lebègue) fantasias were similar to harpsichord preludes in that they were written in an improvisational style. In Germany, S. Scheidt's fantasias were inspired by the *ricercare* and the English *fancy*, while J. J. Froberger's were related to the instrumental *canzona*.

After the death of G. Frescobaldi (1643), the Italian masters of the 18th century abandoned the fantasia permanently in favour of the sonata and the *sinfonia*. J. S. Bach, on the other hand, took an interest in this imprecise form, giving the name fantasia to his organ and harpsichord compositions which were organized like preludes or toccatas (*Fantasia in C minor* BWV 562; *Chromatic Fantasia and Fugue* in D minor BWV 903). With Wilhelm Friedmann and Carl Philipp Emanuel Bach, fantasias expressed the 'preromantic' desire to stir the passions (the *Empfindsamkeit* movement) by giving the impression of being impromptu.

The classical style transformed the fantasia dramatically; it became 'a sonata of sorts with less rigid construction' (André Hodeir): Mozart's *Fantasia in C minor* for piano K.475; the slow movement of Haydn's *Quartet* opus 76 No.6; and Beethoven's *Sonatas quasi una fantasia* opus 27.

From Schubert (*Wanderer-Fantasia* for piano opus 15) to Brahms (*Piano Fantasias* opus 116) and including Mendelssohn, Chopin, Schumann (*Fantasia for piano* opus 17) and Liszt, all the romantic composers who wanted to break away from the framework of classical rules, adopted the fantasia form. Most often they gave it the form of an irregular sonata with a free variation. Towards the end of the 19th century the name 'fantasia' was also given to the assortment of opera or opera-comique motifs for piano or small orchestra, constituting a pot-pourri without much musical value (*Fantaisie sur Carmen*).

In the 20th century several musicians episodically revived the form, such as Fauré (*Fantasia for piano and orchestra*), Darius Milhaud (*Pastoral Fantasia for piano and orchestra*), André Jolivet (*Fantaisie-caprice for flute and piano*), Vaughan Williams (*Fantasia on Greensleeves, Fantasia for string orchestra on a theme by Thomas Tallis*) and Schönberg (*Fantasia for violin and piano*).

Bach, Johann Sebastian

Chromatic Fantasia and Fugue, for keyboard 1720 or 1730

D minor, BWV 903

A contradictory arrangement

In this diptych, virtuosity of style and a rigorous construction are linked by a common chromaticism.

The *Fantasia* (called chromatic due to its many passages in semitones) is divided into three sections. The lively and sparkling character of the first (bars 1–48) is very like a *toccata*. The second (bars 49–61) is a recitative of exceptional dramatic force which ends with a magnificent descending chromatic line (the last five bars). The third (bars 62–79) brings together in a clever mix, the constituent elements of the first two. The second piece of this work is a fugue for three voices. It, too, is chromatic and very rich in modulations, and perfectly completes the work by easing down the tension of the work.

Historical references

No manuscript of Bach's *Fantasia and Fugue* exists today. It was published for the first time in 1802.

Mozart, Wolfgang Amadeus

Fantasia for piano, 1785

C minor, K.475

Dramatic tension mastered

As the introduction to the Sonata in C minor, *the* Fantasia *forms with it one of the peaks of Mozart's unaccompanied piano works.*

The *Fantasia* K.475, in the guise of an improvisation, in reality displays a subtle structural balance. It contains four successive movements (*adagio, allegro, andantino* and *finale*) divided into six clearly distinct sections. From one section to another the piece goes progressively from a stability of key (C minor) — deliberately weakened — at the beginning of the piece to a sophisticated play of uninterrupted modulations (third section), returning gradually to the key of C minor (end of fifth section), which asserts itself unreservedly in the sixth and last section.

Historical references

The *Fantasia* K.475 was composed in May 1785, seven months after the *Sonata* K.457 which it was intended to introduce. The two pieces are dedicated to the pianist Theresa von Trattner, one of Mozart's first Viennese pupils.

Schubert, Franz

'Wanderer-Fantasia' for piano, 1823

C major, opus 15 D.760

Unity as the governing principle

Besides the virtuosity which it demands, the Wanderer-Fantasia *distinguishes itself by its bold unitary concept: all the themes used are in strict relation to each other.*

Obeying the principle of the classico-romantic fantasia, this brilliant work by Schubert only barely follows the traditional sonata form. Although it respects the division into four movements (*allegro, adagio, presto, allegro*), it joins them without interruption, by providing subtle transitions. The reduction of thematic material is not the only thing which gives the *Fantasia* its unity; there is a rhythmic formula which circulates throughout the work.

The first movement — *allegro con fuoco ma non troppo* — begins with a series of *fortissimo* chords which sets out the rhythmic formula of the work and makes it easily recog-

nizable. In order to respect the thematic economy this *allegro* 'disregards the dualist principle of constructing a principal sonata movement on the basis of two opposing themes' (Frieder Reininghaus). Thus, the sonata-form is very quickly exploded. Also full of numerous modulations, this movement allows for the smooth transition without any gap to the adagio which follows by growing gradually quieter.

This *adagio* is a series of variations on *Der Wanderer* lied, but the rhythmic motif of its theme is derived from the initial formula of the *Fantasia*.

After a *presto* which follows the same technique of unification, comes the final *allegro*, a bravura in which the last bars achieve an entirely Beethovian breadth.

Historical references

Hastily written in November 1922 at the request of a virtuoso pianist, the *Fantasia* opus 15 had to bring out the virtuosity of the pianist. This explains its brilliant style and its complexity — Schubert himself was not able to play it properly.

The work was published under the title of *Fantasia for piano* in 1823; the allusion to the lied *Der Wanderer* — written by Schubert in 1816 — was not acknowledged until the end of the 19th century. Schubert had to restrain himself from projecting too readily the tragic mood of the lied ('The sun seems so cold, the flowers are wilting, I am weary of life . . . I feel I am a stranger everywhere I go'). on to the *Fantasia*.

Schubert composed the *Wanderer-Fantasia* at the same time as the *Symphony in B minor* ('Unfinished') and the *Mass* in A flat.

Because it had served as an example for his Sonata in B minor (1853), also a unitary conception, Franz Liszt created a piano and orchestra version of Schubert's *Fantasia* in 1851, entitled *Great Fantasia*.

In 1828 Schubert composed a piano *Fantasia* in F minor for four hands, opus 103, D.940.

Schumann, Robert

Piano Fantasia, 1839

C major, opus 17

The monument to the death of the classical style
(Charles Rosen)

Schumann exploded the notion of the classical sonata form with his Fantasia in C minor, *opus 17, a revolutionary work described as the 'charter of musical romanticism'.*

The first of this composition's three movements is the most developed; Schumann had specified that it was to be 'played from beginning to end in a fantastic and impassioned manner', with a steady touch, to best convey the intense emotional turbulence. From the beginning 'the rhythmic framework definitive of the classical style is rejected in favour of a more open sonority from which the theme gradually takes shape' (C. Rosen) within a general tonal instability. This instability continues until the appearance of C major, imposed by the verbatim citation of a lied by Beethoven (the sixth of his cycle *An die ferne Geliebte* (To the Distant Beloved)) in the very last bars of the piece. The effect of the initial section, made up of two distinct themes (the second, introduced in D minor then developed in F major, is similar to the first) combined with an independent central section in C minor, gives an impression of dislocation which makes it difficult to perceive the formal tone

colours despite their being clearly laid out.

A constant and obsessive use of dotted rhythm signals the second, moderate and energetic movement: a triumphant and heroic march in E flat major which contrasts with the preceding movement in its splendour and its recourse to virtuosity.

Contrasting strongly with this central section, the third movement (slow, with gentle nuances) is reminiscent of a lied, with echoes alternately of Beethoven and of Schubert (*Impromptu* in B flat opus 90 No.3 is explicitly cited on two occasions). This is an admirable piece of pure romantic contemplation which abounds in innovative modulations and in which 'the stasis completely turns its back on the dialectic of the sonata' (Harry Halbreich).

Historical references

Started in 1836 when Schumann set himself the task of selling one hundred copies of his piece to contribute to the erection of a monument to the glory of Beethoven, the *Fantasia in C major* was originally entitled *Great Sonata*. When the composer found the work was taking on a more and more subjective character associated with his frustrated love for Clara Wieck, he abandoned the original project. Revised in 1838 and published the following year, the *Fantasia* is dedicated to Franz Liszt.

Fugues

From the Latin *fuga* (flight), the *fugue* is the most rigorous of all musical forms connected with polyphony. The behaviour of the different voices makes use of all the resources of contrapuntal skill. Firstly, a fugue results 'exclusively from the combination of melodic lines, all of equal importance, without any note being able to form part of a chord without having first been justified melodically' (Jacques Chailley). Obeying strict principles of imitation, each of the voices — which have successive entries — is thus derived from a base theme which dominates, called the subject (in Latin *dux*: leader).

Fugues always begin with the subject played by the first voice then, entering in turn, the second voice gives the answer (in Latin *comes*: accompanist). The first voice — that which proposed the subject — is modified by this answer; we now hear in it a counter-subject whose function is to accompany the answer. In short, a fugue combines with its subject its own transformations which are created by taking bits from all of the resources of contrapuntal imitation. More technically, while the answer (or consequent) does not exactly reproduce the subject (or antecedent), it creates what we call irregular imitation; and these irregularities can be produced by the *augmentation*, or *reduction* of the rhythmic values of all the notes of the subject (which can thus be played twice as slowly or twice as quickly); by *inverse movement*, or *inversion* (the consequent is derived from the antecedent as if a mirror had been placed under it); by *backward movement* (here the consequent is the antecedent read backwards); or finally by a combination of these various processes. The number of voices — whose entries are successive — must remain constant throughout a given fugue. As a result of these principles no other musical form contains such a clear equivalence of voices or such a controlled stylistic unity.

Even though some of these principles were to be found in the motets of polyphonic songs of the 13th and 14th centuries, the term *fuga* was not used until the 15th century, to designate either simple *canons* (polyphonic pieces defined by the similarity of voices replicating themselves after a certain time interval) or vocal compositions, such as those by Ockeghem, constructed 'on sequences of imitative expositions built on many different subjects' (A. Mellnäs).

Nonetheless, the fugue does not derive as much from these forms as from the *ricercare* (research), an instrumental form which emerged in 16th-century Italy and issues from the polyphonic motet, but which can be better distinguished in terms of the notion of contrapuntal development based on a freely devised theme. Becoming widespread throughout the 17th century in Spain, France and England and with the organists in the North of Germany, the *ricercare* was gradually modified. A new type of unity was also conferred on this form, characterized principally by a greater thematic concentration (multiple themes tended to give way to a single subject) and the successive entry of the voices. Composers who contributed to this evolution towards the stricter sense of the fugue include Frescobaldi, Sweelinck, Froberger, Pachelbel and Buxtehude.

But the fugue culminated, undeniably, in the 18th century with J. S. Bach (1685–1750), in the diversity and the complexity of solutions he brought to the form and in the level of development to which he took it. On one hand, this resulted from the reliability of the tonal system, for the fugue is best able to integrate tonality into its structure by exploiting the different possible relationships between keys. (For tonality demands that, if the subject modulates from the tonic key to the dominant, the response must go from the dominant to the tonic. This rule means that the intervals which separate the first and last notes of a subject and its response cannot be, in this case, identical, as they are alternately a fifth and a fourth — C–G, then G–C for example; due to this fact, the tonal fugue response generally brings to its subject a light melodic modification, called a *mutation*.)

The importance of the fugue for Bach goes far beyond the works in which he explicitly referred to it, for the fugue style, based on imitation, is virtually basic to his writing. Furthermore, Bach's mastery in this domain is so great that the definitions given of fugue are usually inseparable from his production.

According to this model, the fugue — or rather the 'academic fugue' as it is usually called — must respect an arrangement in four parts: exposition, development, recapitulation and coda (this last part optional). Consisting of the successive introduction of the subject and its answers, the exposition allows for the gradual expansion of the composition to all the voices of the fugue. The development is made up of a series of sections of actual development, which are interspersed with *divertimenti*, also called *episodes*. As a general rule, the development sections have their own particular tone, while the *divertimenti* act as modulations (transitions). The last part of the development is called the *stretta*; it is an exposition in which the vocal entries are so close together that the subject and its answers constantly overlap; an example of predilection for contrapuntal virtuosity, the *stretta* corresponds to the point of greatest tension in a fugue. The recapitulation, which presents the subject in the principal key for the last time, advances either towards the conclusion or towards a coda.

Beginning of the Fugue No.10 *showing the successive entry of three voices (↓), an extract from Johann Sebastian Bach's* The Art of Fugue.

After Bach the fugue, was confined to Church music. It is mostly in the form of *fugatos* (fugal fragments) that the fugue is found in many classical and romantic works. While we find in Mozart very accomplished integrations of fugues, it was Beethoven, primarily, who revived the fugue within the framework of the classical style. Among the romantics, Liszt and Brahms, as well as Franck, used the form and increased the possibilities of modulation.

In the 20th century, the first movement of Belá Bartók's *Music for strings, percussion and celesta* (1936) is one of the rare instances of a fugue constructed outside the traditional tonal range (oscillating between very distant keys). And Anton Webern, in the third movement of his *Quartet* opus 28 (1938), even created a fugue which obeyed the organizational principles of serial music.

Bach, Johann Sebastian

The Musical Offering, 1747

BWV 1079

A combinatory art

The Musical Offering *is an almost conceptually abstract work which aims, through calculation, to produce a piece of music referring only to itself.*

A rigorous work, characteristic of later Bach in its very dense polyphony, the *Musical Offering* renounces all melodic and timbre allurements (the instrumentation, with only two exceptions, is not fixed), to devote itself exclusively to the fascinating laws of strictest counterpoint.

Nine of the thirteen pieces in this collection are actually canons, and this form — unlike the fugue with which it shares some features: the imitation of voices among themselves and the successive entries — is characterized by the lack of any departure from the chosen rules. More precisely, the structure of a canon 'is entirely determined from the start by the choice of melodic motif (subject), by the formula of imitation and

by the position of entry of the voices' (Roland de Candé). In other words, a canon is a kind of perpetual motion, entirely derivable from its first few bars. In order to get the maximum varied musical effects from the *Offering*, Bach had to diversify as much as possible the imitation formulas among all the voices.

This exceptional work also includes a canonic fugue, two *ricercares*, and a trio sonata. The *ricercares* are actually fugues; the first, in three voices, is fairly close to an improvisational style; the second, in six voices, is one of the vastest fugues that Bach ever wrote and the only one to have so many voices. The trio sonata is of a freer style and Bach specified its instrumentation: a flute, a violin and a basso continuo, keeping its royal dedicatee in mind, who was a flautist.

Historical references

The composition of *the Musical Offering* originated from a meeting in Potsdam on the 7 May 1747, between the composer and the King of Prussia, Frederick II. On that day, at the request of the King and based on a theme proposed by him, Bach improvised a fugue in three voices but refused to do the same for a fugue in six voices, on the pretext that none of the themes lent themselves well to it. But on 7 July Frederick II received from Bach, who had returned to Leipzig, the first of a series of pieces all composed on the basis of the royal theme, which included a fugue in six voices. The order of the pieces was not specified and the canons, indicated for a single voice, still had to be completed. One of these, which left room for several possible solutions, had written in its margin 'Seek and ye shall find'.

In 1935, Anton Webern transcribed for chamber orchestra the *ricercare* in six voices of the *Musical Offering*. 'My instrumentation', he wrote, 'attempts to expose the motivic relationships'; in fact, the distribution of timbre did not respect the distinction between the contrapuntal voices and produced an effect of conflict between pitch melody and timbre melody. This transcription is, in any case, one of the most effective examples of the appropriation of one composer's work by another.

Bach, Johann Sebastian

The Art of Fugue, 1750 or 1751

BWV 1080

From the imagined to the realized: a musical sum

An impressive didactic composition based on musical mathematical skill, The Art of Fugue *magnificently typifies all the possibilities of fugal style.*

This work is a collection of contrapuntal variations elaborated from a principal subject in D minor which is very simple but designed to undergo a significant number of changes of form.

If we follow Wolfgang Schneider's numerical ordering (Bach Werke Verzeichnis, BWV), the composition begins with a first group of simple fugues (2,4,1,3) in four voices, the third and fourth fugues exposing the subject (or theme in a countermovement (with the intervals inverted). A second group has three counter-fugues (5,6,7) whose complex ordering brings out a prodigious variety of rhythmic combinations. The fugues 8,9,10 and 11 constitute a third group in which the initial base subject is combined with new ones. A rest of sorts intervenes in the curious guise of four canons in two voices (14,15,16,17) in which the melodic lines stem from variations on the principal theme whose rhythm is almost always greatly transformed and sometimes inverted (canons 15 and 16). Three pairs of fugues, labelled 'mirrored' because the second (*inversus*) reflects exactly, in a complete inversion, the intervals of the first (*rectus*) represent a fifth group for two harpsichords: counterpoints 12a and 12b, 13a and 13b, 18a and 18b.

A great unfinished fugue (19) developing three subjects which differ from the principal subject of the cycle, and where the third (bar 193) goes by the name B.A.C.H. (B flat, A,C,B in German notation) is generally considered to be an integral part of *The Art of Fugue*. According to Gustav Leonhardt, it was not a necessary part of *The Art of Fugue*, which was a beautiful and finished whole work.

Historical references

The Art of Fugue, composed between 1745 and 1750 was first published in 1750 or 1751 (the second edition is dated 1752). Its first performance, orchestrated by W. Graeser, was in Leipzig on 26 July 1927.

> There is some disagreement about the number of pieces that make up The Art of Fugue and their order of presentation. Jacques Chailley, who sees the work as an unfinished collection of 24 fugues (19 complete, two incomplete and three missing), proposed a new classification of 12 pairs of fugues forming six groups, each divided into three families (The Art of Fugue by Johann Sebastian Bach, Leduc edition, 1971).

> Bach did not specify what instrument his piece was intended for. Some people thought that it was more a piece to be read; others, such as G. Leonhardt, hoped to prove it was specifically intended for the harpsichord. Alberto Basso felt the work had two sides: its polyphonic realization could be experimentally tried out on the keyboards, but its complex texture also demanded study 'on the speculative level without become obsessed with the corresponding sound'.

Overtures

Taken in its wider sense, the term *overture* means an orchestral composition which serves as the introduction to a lyric work (opera, opera-comique, oratorio) or to certain suites. The little fanfare used as the prologue to Monteverdi's *Orfeo* (1607) is the oldest known prefiguration of the 'Italian Overture' — or *Sinfonia* — which was inaugurated by P. Cesti (*Il Pomo d'Oro*, 1667) and was given its definitive tripartite form (allegro, largo, vivace) by A. Scarlatti.

Another form of opera overture, the 'French Overture', of which Lully was the instigator, developed in France and then in the rest of Europe, except for Italy. J. S. Bach masterfully used this type of overture in his four *Orchestral Suites* (BWV 1066–69). But the flourishing of this form also owed a lot to Muffat, Telemann, Hasse and Handel. A modification to its structure was introduced by Rameau: the tripartite form was abandoned and the overture became limited to one slow movement followed by a fast and shorter one.

Up until this point the overture had been separated from the work for which it was meant to serve as a preface. But with Gluck (*Alceste*, *Iphigénie en Aulide*) it became tied directly to the main work in order to justify its raison d'être (Mozart's *Don Giovanni*). From then on it was modelled on the initial movement (*allegro*) of the classical symphony.

Beethoven's *Leonora III* ushered in a new type of overture which was a virtually independent orchestral composition meant to summarize the action of the drama to follow (C. M. von Weber's *Freischütz* or Wagner's *Phantom Vessel*). This new genre gave rise to the 'Concert Overture': Mendelssohn's Overture to *A Midsummer Night's Dream*, Berlioz's *Carnaval romain*, Brahms's *Tragic Overture*, etc.

The 19th century also saw the emergence of the 'pot-pourri overture', reduced to a simple arrangement of musical phrases drawn from a lyric work (Rossini's *The Thieving Magpie*) and the Wagnerian 'Symphonic Prelude' (*Tristan und Isolde*) intended to create an instant atmosphere appropriate to the piece.

In modern opera, the overture is reduced to a brief orchestral introduction (Debussy's *Pelléas et Mélisande*) or to a miniscule prelude (Berg's *Wozzeck*), in cases where it has not disappeared altogether (as in R. Strauss's *Salomé* or *Elektra*), to allow for an immediate entry into the action.

Mozart, Wolfgang Amadeus

Overture to Don Giovanni, 1787

D minor, K.527

Overture to an opera of conflict

Far from just being the narrative introduction to the opera, the Overture to Don Giovanni *exposes the dramatic principle which rules the entire work: the mixing of genres.*

The great syncopated chords which begin the overture to *Don Giovanni* create a tragic atmosphere right away. This mood perpetuates throughout the slow introduction, most of the elements of which get taken up again just before Don Juan's final descent into Hell. Notable, in this regard, is the famous sequence of ascending and descending scales. 'But this has barely had the chance to penetrate and impress when the mood turns around: in an instant it becomes a brilliant and decisive irruption' (Pierre-

Jean Jouve): the sombre introduction gives way to a spirited and breathless *allegro*. In a few bars, the entire principle of the work is set out; Don Giovanni is neither an *Opera seria* nor an *Opera buffa*, but both at the same time. 'The fusion is so perfect that we no longer notice the mixing of genres; at the end of the 18th century, however, people were greatly aware of it and often reacted with condemnation'. For 'mixing genres was seen to be a violation of convention' (Charles Rosen). Furthermore, and it was this that led to the indisputable success of the piece, the dramatic conception is indissociable from the musical form on which it rests: the sonata. The overlapping of different levels is such that the conflict of genres is undeniably reflected in one of the themes of the libretto: the conflicts among different social classes.

Historical references

The first performance of Don Giovanni took place in Prague on 29 October 1787. The night before, Mozart still had not written the overture. This reveals Mozart's working method. As Jean and Brigitte Massin said: 'while the overture to *Don Giovanni* may not have been put down on paper until that night in October, it was certainly, at that time and probably long before then, entirely composed in his head'. This is certainly not meant to suggest that Mozart wrote with little effort, but rather to show that his art came from within — a fact that allowed him quickly to bring his musical ideas to life.

An arrangement of ascending and descending scales (played by the first violins) which are increased by a semitone at the beginning of each bar, and sometimes at the high end of the ascending scale. (D, E flat, F, F sharp, G). This principle of linking from one scale to another produced a very powerful chromatic tension. This connection of scales is a key element of the drama: at the end of the opera, it is associated with the character of the Commander who leads Don Juan to Hell.

1st violin

1st violin

70

Rossini, Gioacchino

Overture to The Barber of Seville, 1816

A celebrated 'melodic cynicism' *(Berlioz)*

Based on a facile orchestral style, the Overture to the Barber of Seville *flaunts a preference for ostentation.*

Two themes are exposed in this fairly short piece: the principal, introduced and developed by the orchestra, is successively taken up by the oboe, the horn and the clarinet. The piece finishes on a crescendo which precedes a spectacular finale with massive use of brass instruments.

Historical references

The original score of the *Overture to the Barber of Seville*, if it ever existed, was lost. Rossini substituted a composition that had already been used as the overture to *Aureliano in Palmira* (1813) and *Elisabetha, regina d'Inghilterra* (1815).

It is said that Rossini composed the *Barber of Seville* in less than 15 days. The work, presented for the first time at Rome's Teatro Argentina on 20 February 1816 (the composer conducted), was the victim of a cabal before it achieved a huge success not long after.

Weber, Carl Maria von

Overture to Freischütz (The Freeshooter), 1821

A musical representation of the fantastic *(Debussy)*

This work is based on the idea of summarizing the plot of a lyrical drama by borrowing some of its themes.

From the beginning the fantastical atmosphere of a forest is evoked by the strings playing *lento* in unison, and then by the horns. Violin tremolos, rhythmic beat by the double bassoons, kettledrum beats and a cello recitative then come in to convey the appearance of Samuel the black hunter, a character with demoniacal powers who has stolen the infallible bullets from the hero

Max's gun which will allow him to win a shooting contest. This contest is of great importance as Max's marriage to the young Agatha hinges on its outcome. Agatha is symbolized by a jolly melody played on the clarinet with a string accompaniment. The orchestra evokes the dark presence of evil forces once again before suddenly launching into a brilliant finale.

Historical references

Composed in the summer of 1817, the *Freischütz* was first performed on 18 June 1821 at the new Berlin Opera which it inaugurated. Weber was at the podium.

71

Wagner, Richard

Overture to Tannhäuser, 1845

The Almighty versus 'the universal Venus'

The overture to Tannhäuser *marks an important evolution of Wagnerian orchestral language in the search for its own distinct sound.*

Like the plot it synthesizes, the 'concert vision' of the overture, dated 1845 and different from the 1861 and 1875 overtures, is based on two antinomic themes engendered by 'man's conflict between religious ascetic love and voluptuous sexual love' (Dominique Bossuer). These contrary themes are evoked through the opposition of two major musical themes.

The first, that of the pilgrims, begins in E major. Introduced *lento* by wind instruments (horn, bassoon, clarinet), it develops from an ascending melodic line which has created a distant music which gradually grows closer; then at the moment that the strings enter, it increases greatly in volume to rise *crescendo* to an impressive *fortissimo* (trombone, tuba) and returns *diminuendo* to its melodic starting place.

The second theme, contrasting strongly with the first one, centres on Venusberg (a legendary mountain in medieval Germany) and Venus's palace where the chevalier-poet Tannhäuser forgets his sad mortal condition amidst all the pleasures. The intermingled motifs evoking the magic of the setting and modulated by the orchestra are followed by the invocation by the hero to the goddess; a wild hymn which Baudelaire described as the expression of a 'frantic, all-encompassing and chaotic love, elevated to the level of a "counter-religion"'. After a return to the Venusberg motifs, Tannhäuser's invocation to Venus is heard once again.

The insistent Venusberg motifs continue until they have to give way to the religious theme of the pilgrims, a symbol of Christian Saving Grace working over two deaths: that of Tannhäuser's young virgin lover Elizabeth and the death of the hero himself caused by the sight of this chosen victim of God.

Historical references

Wagner composed *Tannhäuser* (music and libretto) between June 1842 and April 1845. The work was performed on 19 October 1845 in the theatre of the Saxony royal court in Dresden, where it was received with reservation. For its première at the Opera de Paris the composer modified the ending of his opera by adding a bacchanale to support the ballet which demanded a certain degree of tradition. This magnificent composition disconcerted a public who, for the majority, belonged to a celebrated cabal in the annals of opera.

Verdi, Giuseppe

Overture to La Forza del destino (The Force of Destiny), 1869

Centering on a fixed theme

A brilliant symphonic passage organized around a preponderant theme (destiny), the overture to this opera determines the atmosphere of the drama which follows.

There is a paradox in isolating Verdi's overtures from the dramatic works they are inseparable from. Their strictly musical quality does not justify our exempting them from their theatrical function and treating them as entirely separate concert pieces. Nonetheless, two of them — the exception which proves the rule — have achieved this status. These are the overtures to *The Sicilian Vespers* (1855) and to *The Force of Destiny*.

The arrangement of the overture to *The Force of Destiny* following quite closely the principle proposed by Weber in his overtures, is supported by the preponderant themes of the opera. 'The theme of destiny, exposed straight-away, serves also as the

principal link throughout the piece which is orchestrated in an exemplary fashion' (Jacques Bourgeois). The work closes on a particularly dynamic *allegro*.

Historical references

The Force of Destiny is the result of a commission given to Verdi by the Imperial Russian Theatre in St Petersberg. Verdi originally suggested adapting Victor Hugo's *Ruy Blas* but this idea was met with a refusal by the Czar who did not think much of this critic of the monarchy. Verdi finally chose the Spanish drama *Don Alvaro o la fuerza del Sino*, written 25 years earlier by the Duke of Rivas Don Angel de Saavedra. Verdi entrusted Piave with the task of creating a libretto for this piece which was, to say the least, strange as it consisted in a series of coincidences each more unbelievable than the one before, but always explained in the same way: 'the force of destiny'. (However, this fairly lame dramatic plot seems to have pleased the composer because it allowed him to mix together very different styles; it is sometimes tragic, sometimes burlesque.)

The opera was performed in St Petersberg on 10 November 1862 in a first version which included, instead of the overture we know today, a short instrumental prelude. It was at the performance of *The Force of Destiny* at La Scala in Milan that Verdi gave it its definitive form.

> Several of Verdi's operas begin, not with an overture, but with a prelude. The two most interesting examples, orchestrally speaking, are those of *Macbeth* (1847) and *La Traviata* (1853).

Beethoven, Ludwig van

Leonora III, 1806

C major, opus 72b

An abandoned overture

Leonora III *is the overture that Beethoven intended for the second version of his opera* Fidelio, *originally entitled* Leonora. *But this piece is musically so rich that it stands on its own.*

'When a piece of music achieves absolute intelligibility without the drama, it detaches itself and lives on independently; like the overture to *Leonora III*'. This statement by Charles Rosen summarizes well the particular case of this symphonic piece which, despite its successive modifications, has remained so fully developed that it anticipates too much the unfolding of the opera itself and does not prepare us at all for the 'happy' atmosphere of the first scenes.

Considered on its own, *Leonora III* strikes us with its compositional strength and the dynamism of its thematic developments; its heroic style is the result of a synthesis of French and Viennese influences. The progression of the overture corresponds roughly to the succession of the major events of the opera. A slow introduction evokes the suffering of the lead character, Florestan,

who is being held prisoner for political reasons. Then an *allegro* centres mainly on the theme of Leonora, the heroine of the opera and Florestan's wife who devises a strategy to become reunited with Florestan: disguised as a man, and going by the name of Fidelio, she succeeds in entering the prison where her husband is being held. A trumpet call offstage interrupts the piece and symbolizes Florestan's release. The overture is thus able to finish with its 'hymn to joy' which prepares the way for a section dominated by a flute solo which, swelling gradually, leads us to a stunning final *stretta*.

Historical references

The opera *Fidelio* was the work which gave Beethoven the most difficulty, attested to by the fact that there were no less than three versions. The first, written between 1803 and 1805, included the actual overture known as Leonora II. (*The overture Leonora I* had been written in 1805 but Beethoven, dissatisfied with it, abandoned it for *Leonora II*). The performances resulted in failure, and the overture *Leonora II*, which was very unconventional and innovative, was judged to be banal! Beethoven modified his opera in 1806, and preceded it with a new overture, *Leonora III*, which was more concise and which had an entirely different conclusion. This version was performed on 19 March 1806. In 1804, when he gave his opera its definitive form, Beethoven gave up transforming the material of his overtures and replaced them with a solemn prelude.

> While *Leonora III* is today most often performed in its concert version, it is also still customary to play it during the second act of *Fidelio*, just before the final chorus.

Mendelssohn, Felix

Overture to A Midsummer Night's Dream, 1827

Opus 21

Shakespeare assimilated

The Overture to A Midsummer Night's Dream *shows off equally well the young Mendelssohn's skills as an orchestrator and his rhythmic and melodic brilliance.*

At the beginning of the overture, the six chords played by the wind instruments and 'the delicate and ethereal harmonies of the first strings' (Raymond Leppard) create a general atmosphere of celebration of nature and of sensual pleasure (summer heat on a starry night, the fluttering of wings, rustling of leaves). Throughout the musical discourse these evocations leave very little room for the descriptive elements which refer to Shakespeare's fairy-comedy piece whose name it carries. In fact, the Shakespearian dramatic plot is only very subtly suggested here; the horns of Theseus's court, Nick Bottom's braying, the man wearing

a donkey's head, the dance by Bottom's artisan-comedian companions. The tripartite melodic structure established on the basis of the initial chords fits the classical pattern of the sonata *allegro*: exposition, development, recapitulation and coda. From beginning to end the work, written at a time when Mendelssohn was much more influenced by Mozart and Weber than by J. S. Bach's contrapuntal style, 'manifests in its whole the suggestion of where it is heading'.

Historical references

Composed in Berlin during the summer of 1826, (7 July to 26 August), the overture to *A Midsummer Night's Dream* was first performed on 20 February 1827 in Stettin.

In 1843, sixteen years later, when Frederick William IV, King of Prussia, requested a set-music piece to accompany a performance of Shakespeare's fairy-comedy in Potsdam, Mendelssohn returned to the phantasmagorical theme of *Dream*. Keeping the overture, he followed it with 13 pieces (the third and 13th required two sopranos and a female choir) which constituted the whole of the work entitled *A Midsummer Night's Dream* (opus 61). All these pieces were treated in the light-hearted and playful spirit of the overture but the one which has the famous '*Wedding March*' (piece No.9) which is cited again in the composition's finale (piece No.13).

Of the seven overtures composed by Mendelssohn, only the overtures to *Dream*, *The Hebrides* (Fingal's Cave opus 24), *Fair Melusina* (opus 32) and *Ruy Blas* (opus 95) have been rescued from oblivion, though the last two are rarely played.

Berlioz, Hector

Le Carnaval Romain, overture, 1844

Opus 9

A return to the previously stated

Both an independent symphonic work and the second overture to the opera Benvenuto Cellini, Le Carnaval Romain *exhibits all the brilliant qualities of Berliozian Orchestra.*

This piece, constructed as a rondo, first presents, in a tiny introduction (strings and *tutti allegro con fuoco*), a very lively theme copied from the tune *venez, venez, peuple de Rome* ... which is sung by the choir at a carnival scene at the end of the first act of *Benvenuto Cellini* (the 1838 version in two acts). Immediately after, the cor anglais — alto oboe in F — introduces a cantilena, this time taken from the love duet between Cellini the carver-adventurer and the young Teresa also in the first act of the lyric drama (1838 and 1852 versions in three acts). This cantilena (one of the most beautiful of Berlioz's melodies), which is

Besides *Benvenuto Cellini* (1838) and *Le Carnaval Romain* (1844), Berlioz's overture works include: *Waverley* (1828), *Les Francs-Juges* (1828), *Rob Roy* (1833, disclaimed by the composer), *King Lear* (1834), *Le Corsaire* (1855) and *Beatrice et Bénédict* (1862). These works clearly reflect the stylistic evolution of the author of the *Symphonie Fantastique*.

developed in canon by the violas, flutes and a string ensemble, constitutes the essence o an *andante* which ends with the return o the saltarello rhythm from the introduction The *allegro vivace* which follows and finishes the overture on a thundering *fortissimo* is a spectacular series of recapitulations (varied or in canon) of the initial *allegro con fuoco* theme. Here again, from time to time and very skillfully integrated into these recapitulations, we find the cantilena, which emerges from the turbulent sounds portraying the festivities of a carnival.

Historical references

Berlioz wrote the so-called 'characteristic' overture to *Le Carnaval Romain* in January 1844 in order to salvage a fragment of his opera *Benvenuto Cellini* which, in its two-act version, had been taken off the stage after only two performances given in Paris in 1838. (The definitive version in three acts was performed with great success in Weimar on 20 March 1852 with Liszt conducting). At the first performance of *Le Carnaval Romain*, on the other hand, the audience brought the house down with demands for an encore. This performance also took place in Paris and was conducted by the composer. The work, one of the most popular of the romantic classical repertoire, is also the most famous of Berlioz's overtures, along with the overture to *Benvenuto Cellini*, another 'turbulent, powerful musical work whose irresistible spirit is adorned with lavish instrumentation' (Claude Ballif).

Symphonic Poems

The *symphonic poem* is a composition for orchestra which generally consists of one movement and is explicitly determined by an extra-musical descriptive or poetic idea. It stems from programme-music and its genre was principally developed in the second half of the 20th century. Primarily concerned with illustrating the narrative thread which is its inspiration, the symphonic poem cannot be defined by any specific musical form. However, in order to establish a stronger dramatic cohesion, a symphonic poem can follow pre-existing formal structures (sonatas, themes and variations), or can be organized around very obvious leading motifs (leitmotivs) or ones endowed with a symbolic value. Furthermore the symphonic poem is indissociable from the full orchestra development whose possibilities it fully exploits.

Even though the symphonic poem did not appear until the middle of the 19th century with Liszt, we can partially recognize this genre in some symphonies by Haydn (*Le Matin, Le Midi, Le Soir,* around 1761) and Beethoven (*Pastoral Symphony,* 1808), as well as in Mendelssohn's overture *The Hebrides* (1830). But the principal precursor to the symphonic poem was Berlioz (1803–69) who, with his programme symphonies (*Symphonie Fantastique,* 1830; *Harold en Italie,* 1834; *Roméo et Juliette,* 1839) made use of orchestration for dramatic ends.

Franz Liszt (1811–86) was the first composer to have suggested the title of symphonic poem, and to have explicitly set out its principles. His works contain 13 symphonic poems (the first 12 written between 1849 and 1858, the 13th in 1882), whose means of illustrating an extra-musical subject generally goes beyond that of simple description, and approaches psychology with a very general symbolism. Of these 13 works of unequal value, the best known is *The Preludes.*

After Liszt, the composer who made the most of the symphonic poem and certainly brought it to its peak was Richard Strauss (1864–1949). But the genre appealed to many other musicians, in fact there were very few, from the second half of the 19th century and the beginning of the 20th, who did not attempt it. In France there were Camille Saint-Saëns (*La danse macabre,* 1874), César Franck (*Le Chasseur maudit,* 1882), Paul Dukas (*The Sorcerer's Apprentice,* 1897) and above all Debussy, many of whose works can be included in the genre (such as *La Mer,* 1905). The Russian School is also well-represented with Moussorgsky (*Night on the Bare Mountain,* 1867), Borodin (*In the Central-Asian Steppes,* 1880), Rimski-Korsakov (*Scheherezade,* 1888), Tchaikovsky (*Manfred,* 1885) and more recently, Scriabin (*Poem of ecstasy,* 1907; *Prometheus,* 1910). Finally, the symphonic poem resulted in several examples of national music, with Smetana's Czech cycle (*Ma Vlast,* 1874–9, including the famous *Moldau*) and a Nordic series by Sibelius (*Finlandia,* 1900; *Tapiola,* 1926).

Few of the 20th-century composers expanded this genre which was almost indistinguishable from Romanticism. The two works by Schönberg which could be considered to belong to it belong to the very earliest of his productions (*Transfigured Night,* 1899; *Pelléas et Mélisande,* 1903).

Moussorgsky, Modest

Night on the Bare Mountain, 1867

Original version

Cries and scattered calls *(Moussorgsky)*

Left out of Rimsky-Korsakov's version, the audacious score of this poem has recently been restored to it.

Moussorgsky wrote this piece to depict a witches' sabbath. Although, following Liszt's example in his own symphonic poems, it only consists of one movement, it is nonetheless made up of four sections: the reunion of the witches, Satan's cortège, black mass, Sabbath. But the 'Satanic' programme mainly allowed Moussorgsky to come up with a very innovative treatment of the orchestra, by separating the different instrumental groups (strings, winds and percussion).

Historical references

The work, written in its original version in 1867, was severely criticized by Balakirev and was revised twice by Moussorgsky.

In 1886, Rimsky-Korsakov drew from the three versions a symphonic poem in his own style. The original score was not published until 1968.

Rimsky-Korsakov, Nikolaï

Scheherazade, 1888

Opus 35

A kaleidoscope of mythical images

The complex arrangement of motifs and a sparkling orchestration are the major assets of this first musical tale from the Orient.

The four episodes of *The Thousand and One Nights,* served as the starting point for the composition of *Scheherazade* and allowed Rimsky-Korsakov to create a purely musical and instrumental piece suggestive of the Orient. The piece is not only illustra- tive, but consists also in circulating and interweaving a certain number of motifs throughout the piece. Played by the solo violin, the theme representing the character of Scheherazade reinforces the cohesion of the whole.

Historical references

Completed in July 1888, the work was per- formed in St Petersberg on 28 October of the same year and conducted by the com- poser.

Strauss, Richard

Don Juan, 1889

Opus 20

The orchestra blooming with 'rhythmic colours' (Debussy)

Unlike other symphonic works by Strauss, Don Juan *does not tell a story, but rather evokes the youthful and passionate figure of a 'Faustian' (A. Tubeuf) philosopher.*

The interweaving of the Faustian metaphysics and the musical writing brings *Don Juan* into a dramatic setting reminiscent of a miniature opera. Based on the alternation of themes alluding to the hero (episodes in the form of refrains) and of themes evoking female characters (episodes in the form of verses), the work has the structure of a rondo.

It abounds in 'the expressive moments of moments' (Glenn Gould) which we discover, from the beginning, with the violent and rapid beat of the first refrain (*allegro molto con brio*) which ascends abruptly and is very rich in rhythmic modulations and variations. Shortly before the end of the first part, after the melodic motif developed *molto appassionata* by the violas

and the cellos, the cantilena played in G major by the oboe and the brief repeat of the ascending refrain, the main theme (in C major) of *Don Juan*'s romantic exaltation which, *molto espressivo e marcato*, evokes his character for the third time, appears; introduced by horns. Maximum dramatic tension is achieved with the almost immediate repeat of this theme by the horns. Then a bacchanale of sorts follows a veritable torrent of sound where Strauss demonstrates an extraordinary mastery of instrumentation. The spectacular horn theme returns one last time and then, on a thundering descendent string motif, there is a suggestion that we are nearing the end. A replaying of verses which fleetingly recalls the female figures, precedes a broken-up *pianissimo* chord (intervention of the trumpets) which symbolizes the approach of death (descending string tremolos) while the music, *sempre più lento*, turns imperceptibly to silence.

Historical references

The third of Richard Strauss's symphonic poems (the first two were *Aus Italien*, 1886 and *Macbeth* 1886–7), *Don Juan*, composed in 1887–8 'established its author as the initiator of an orchestral art form which attained in the years to follow, with Mahler, Berg and Ravel, an impressive posterity' (Dominique Jameux). The work, freely inspired by a dramatic poem by Nikolaus Lenau (1802–50) with the same title, was played for the first time in Weimar on 11 November 1889, conducted by the composer.

> The symphonic poem is also represented in Richard Strauss's works by *Tod und Verklärung* (*Death and Transfiguration*), 1889; *Till Eulenspiegel*, 1895; *Also sprach Zarathustra*, 1896; *Don Quixote*, 1897; and *Heldenleben* (A Hero's Life), 1898, which makes reference to all the previous ones.

Dukas, Paul

The Sorcerer's Apprentice, symphonic scherzo, 1897

A story of water

The Sorcerer's Apprentice *captivates by its instrumental colour and its humour.*

The work (principal key of F minor) is structured according to the classical sonata-form. It opens with a brief introduction (*lento*) in which four themes are outlined: 'The magic spells', 'the magic broom', 'the apprentice' and 'the master'; the motifs of the broom and the apprentice are developed in the lively movement of the

actual sonata-form. The piece ends with a short coda (*lento*): the master sorcerer, having returned, restores order to his house where the apprentice has created a flood in his absence by putting a spell on a broom which he is incapable of stopping.

Historical references

Inspired by a ballad by Goethe, Dukas wrote and first performed *The Sorcerer's Apprentice* in 1897. It was an immediate and great success.

Scriabin, Alexander

Poem of ecstasy, 1907

Opus 54

Story of the superman

In the Poem of Ecstasy, *Scriabin musically exalts a kind of Nietzschean superman.*

Based on a philosophical poem of four stanzas written by the composer, the work issues both from the symphony and the symphonic poem. Its form adopts the *allegro* structure of the sonata but is considerably expanded. Intended for a gigantic orchestra, the *Poem of Ecstasy* is a grandiose appli-

cation of sound tensions capable of conveying the spiritual exaltations of the author; its harmonic complexity is clearly linked to a post-Wagnerian chromatic texture.

Historical references

Scriabin worked from 1905 to 1907 on the *Poem of Ecstasy* which was first performed on 10 December 1908 in New York, and had its Russian première on 19 January 1909 in St Petersberg.

Schönberg, Arnold

Verklärte Nacht (Transfigured Night), for string sextet, 1899

Opus 4

An illicit union

Although Transfigured Night *reconciles Wagner and Brahms, it still transgresses genres, as it is both a symphonic poem and a piece of chamber music.*

The plot used by Schönberg for the composition of *Transfigured Night*, his first major work, came from a poem by Richard Dehmel. The text evokes a walk taken by two lovers on a moonlit night. The man agrees to acknowledge the child that the woman admits to having conceived with someone else. 'Our love', he says, will 'transfigure' it.

The score roughly follows the text and is made up of five connected sections. The odd-numbered sections depict the forward movement of the lovers in the night and the other two, which overlap, correspond to the words of the woman and the man. However, the different themes are interwoven to such an extent that the structure of the work is able to show us the concern, inherited from Liszt, for the whole work within a single free movement.

Furthermore, this piece 'exalted on the melodic, polyphonic and harmonic levels'

(H. H. Stuckenschmidt), and which 'illustrates neither action nor drama, but is content to depict and express human emotions' (A. Schönberg), can, doubtlessly for these reasons, be appreciated as pure music. All the more as the instrumental choice — a string quartet — is conventionally associated with pure music.

But *Transfigured Night* is above all the first work to reconcile Wagner and Brahms. Wagner in the treatment and the tone of the instruments, and Brahms in the use of certain variation techniques. This reconciliation was a necessary preliminary to the decisive innovations of the later Schönberg. The work already includes some passages with an indeterminate tonality which are, in the composers own words, 'an allusion to the future'.

Historical references

Composed very quickly in September 1899, *Transfigured Night* was performed in Vienna in 1903. It caused a scandal due to its harmonic and explicit audacities. However, the piece soon became one of Schönberg's most played pieces. He later produced two versions for string orchestra in 1917 and 1943; the latter was more precise, for the benefit of its interpreters.

Debussy, Claude

La Mer (The Sea), three symphonic sketches, 1905

An innovative sound

La Mer *does not reflect the sounds of an expanse of water; its title only serves as the platform, by analogy with the movement of waves, for a radically new development.*

La Mer strikes one first with the incessant attention paid to sound (the timbre work and the intensities are unprecedented) and to the variability of the rhythms (all regular metrics are rejected).

But these two preponderant elements are further enriched by a compositional method of superimposing autonomous wholes. This technique 'creates besides the effects of "depth"', the *provisional obliteration* of certain parts of the space, thus creating, in an alternation of absence and presence, a '*discontinuity*' (Eveline Andréani). Irregularities, heterogeneous superimpositions and discontinuities are some of the most innovative formal characteristics of the piece, but there are many more as well. With *La Mer*, 'even the notions of exposition and development co-exist in an uninterrupted flow which allows the work to

move forward under its own impetus' (Jean Barraqué).

The first movement, *De l'aube à midi sur la mer*, is characterized by an ascending and continuous progression of musical discourse which begins quietly and finishes with a particularly brilliant conclusion. This movement is composed of two virtually equal sections, the first of which closes with one of the most complex rhythmic passages of the piece; a superimposition of seven different metres. The produced effect is 'flamboyant' and the contrast even stronger in the following section which is introduced by a theme played by the cellos.

The second movement, *Jeux de Vagues*, appears to be a prismatic dissection of sound space. The constant dispersion of timbre, the continually renewed development of form makes this one of the piece's most prophetic passages.

The last section of the work, *Dialogue du vent et de la mer*, is more dramatic: its arrangement around two contradictory 'forces' brought Debussy to discover new means of linking.

Historical references

Started in September 1903, *La Mer* was completed in March 1905. The first performance took place on 15 October of the same year under the more than mediocre direction of Camille Chevillard. The work was not really heard until January 1908, when Debussy conducted it himself. But some people were disconcerted: it did not sound like the sea ...

Although it does not go by the title and consists of three movements instead of the one which is generally required, *La Mer* can be considered a *symphonic poem* in that the idea which it is based on is extra-musical.

Honegger, Arthur

Pacific 231, 1924

A rhythmic force on Bach-style foundations

A work which appears based on imagery, but whose subtitle, symphonic movement, seems intended to reduce the effect of its descriptive elements, Pacific 231 aims to recreate a tradition.

A symphonic poem as well as a symphonic movement, *Pacific 231* (whose name is taken from a steam locomotive used for high speed passenger trains) constitutes the first section of a triptych which also included *Rugby* (1928) and *Symphonic Movement No.3* (1932–3).

Honegger, in reference to Pacific 231 had originally said (*Dissonances* magazine, April 1924) that he had not sought to 'imitate the noises of a locomotive but rather to convey a visual impression'. Whatever the case, the 'chosen *subject*' (Honegger) which supplied the work with a dramatic time-frame and the descriptive intention associated with the subject — based only on the rhythmic machine-music similitude — effectively conveys the idea of a symphonic poem dedicated to the glory of a moving mechanical force.

But, without a doubt wearied by the trivializing interpretations by critics who were interested solely in the programme music aspect of *Pacific 231*, the composer was later induced to give a corrective explanation of the genesis of his work which actually only further obscured the matter, as he explained the piece only in terms of pure music: 'In truth, I pursued, in *Pacific*, a very abstract and entirely idealistic notion by giving the impression of a mathematical acceleration of rhythm, while the movement itself was actually getting slower. Musically, I composed a kind of varied great chorale, punctuated with counterpoints in the first part which make it reminiscent of Johann Sebastian Bach'.

Thus *Pacific 231* has become a symphonic poem, a symphonic movement and now a 'varied great chorale'. Orchestrated on the basis of a tightly-woven polyphonic structure, it is built like a figured chorale (key of C sharp), having as its principal subject a *cantus firmus* of 41 semibreves. A subtle work of gradually shortening rhythmic values, from the semibreve to the semiquaver via the crotchets, quavers, etc, it produces the spectacular effect of acceleration right from the beginning; while the deceleration effect results from the opposite process: the return from the semiquavers to the semibreve via the quavers, crotchets...

At the time of steam traction engines, the various types of locomotives were classified according to a designation system based on the number and relative position of the motor and booster axles; the *Pacific* (a six-axled engine with 12 wheels) had the following pattern seen laterally from left to right: two booster axles for four small wheels, three motor axles for six big wheels, one booster axle for two medium sized wheels.

Historical references

Honegger composed *Pacific 231* between January and December 1923. The work, dedicated to Ernest Ansermet, was performed in Paris under the direction of Serge Koussevitzky.

Equal Temperament

Equal temperament results from an arrangement of the 'natural' scale which is composed of tones produced by the natural resonance of a sound-producing body (harmonic tones generated by a fundamental tone) and contains *unequal* tones and diatonic semitones *greater* than *half a tone*. While such a scale can be played on the violin, *no instrument with fixed tones* (principally the keyboards) can keep in time with it. In order to overcome this 'inconvenience', equal temperament is introduced arbitrarily to divide the scale into *12 equal semitones*. This division leads to creating a C sharp and an E flat, which are slightly different acoustically) from *the same note*. With this acoustical/musical compromise *all* the diatonic scales thus become of *equal value*, and can be played on any keyboard instrument. Due to this principle Johann Sebastian Bach was able to write the two books of his *Well-Tempered Klavier* (1722, 1744) (see p. 86) as well as the *24 preludes and fugues* which correspond respectively to the *24 diatonic scales* set out in the order presented here (from high to low).

Note
ut is the early notation for **do**
gamma de means scale of

Preludes

Originally a simple sequence of sounds improvised on the flute or organ to test the instrument or to set the pitch for singers (the *intonazione* that was practised in Italy in the 15th century), the *prelude* made its first public appearance as a musical genre with the organ tablature pieces by Adam Ileborgh (1448).

From the 16th century it was used as an instrumental piece (generally taken from the writings for lute) to 'open' either a particular piece with which it integrated, or any piece written in the same key as its own — on condition that it kept to the same type of instrument — but from which it remains separated, serving ultimately as the introduction to another piece.

Having very probably originated in lutanist music, the unmeasured 'French' prelude became established in the 17th century as an extremely free piece which presented, on the basis of minimal notation, an improvisational tone (harpsichord pieces by L. Couperin, N. Lebègue, L. Marchand). It is not stylistically unlike the fantasia and the toccata which often substitutes for it as an introductory piece (*Toccata and Fugue in D minor* BWV 565 by J. S. Bach).

The genre of prelude and fugue, which has a rigorous construction, developed with J. Pachelbel and D. Buxtehude before achieving a degree of perfection with J. S. Bach, for whom several preludes to the *Well-Tempered Klavier*, constructed on three themes, foreshadow the form of the classical sonata.

Almost entirely abandoned by the 18th-century composers who were promoting the gallant style (Telemann, J. C. Bach, etc), the duo of prelude and fugue reappeared in the 19th century as a kind of tribute to J. S. Bach: Mendelssohn's *Preludes and fugues for organ* opus 37, *Fantasia and fugue for organ B.A.C.H.* by Liszt, and *Prelude, aria and finale* for piano by Cesar Franck, etc.

But the 19th century was primarily the century which witnessed the birth of the piano prelude, a self-contained short piece (*Preludes* by Chopin, and Debussy). In this tradition of independent piano pieces we find, in the 20th century, Fauré's nine *Preludes* opus 103, Rachmaninov's 24 *Preludes* opus 3, opus 23 and opus 32; Satie's four *Preludes lasques pour un chien* and Messiaen's eight *Preludes*.

As for the symphonic prelude (created in the 20th century), it is found in the form of a free composition, most often for full orchestra (Debussy's *Prelude à l'après-midi d'un faune*). It is also sometimes associated with the symphonic poem (Liszt's *Preludes*) or replaces the overture of an opera (Wagner's *Prelude and death of Isolde*).

Bach, Johann Sebastian

The Well-Tempered Klavier, 1722 and 1744

BWV 846–869 and 870–893

For an egalitarian musical system

In composing the Well-Tempered Klavier, *Bach wrote in all keys with so much musical inspiration that the work contributed greatly to the establishment of the tonal system.*

The collection of the *Well-Tempered Klavier* groups together two independent books, each consisting of 24 preludes and fugues. Each diptych is attributed one of the 12 possible keys, alternately presented in major and minor. For each book, the sequence of keys is presented thus: C major, C minor, C sharp major, C sharp minor, D major, etc., up to B minor (see page 84). The title of the work indicates that the use of all the keys is conditional on the adoption of *equal temperament*.

Unlike the preceding musical systems which claimed to be 'natural', but actually favoured certain keys, the *equal temperament* system rests on 'an arbitrary regimentation of tone levels' (Alberto Basso). More precisely, this arbitrariness consists in arti-

---

In 1722, the year Bach finished the first book of the *Well-Tempered Klavier*, Rameau published his *Treatise on Harmony*. Without any knowledge of the other's work, the two composers simultaneously elaborated; Rameau the theoretic justification of the tonal system, and Bach, the practical proof.

---

ficially subdividing the octave into 12 *equal* semitones. It thus becomes possible, by approximation, to give each key the same importance (see p. 84). With the *Well-Tempered Klavier*, Bach took definite possession of this new more egalitarian system and effected the musical proof of its validity.

The formal structure, in a prelude and a fugue, inherited from Buxtehude, was to take on a very different form. For while the two sections of each of these diptychs appear to be unrelated (the form of the prelude is free and 'recreative' while that of the fugue is more regular and didactic), they are linked by a common key which gives them the same 'atmosphere'. And this principle of coherence is at the origin of the eventual attribution of a specific character to each key.

Historical references

Although we cannot date precisely the composition of these 48 preludes and fugues which Bach worked on for a long time, we do know that the first book — the only one to have the title the *Well-Tempered Klavier* — was completed in 1744. The work was not published in Bach's lifetime (1801), but its success was considerable even before then, thanks to the numerous copies that had been made.

The *Well-Tempered Klavier*, unlike many of Bach's other works, never fell into oblivion; the romantics in particular — despite or because of their very pianistic sensibilities — considered it to be their 'daily bread' (Robert Schumann).

Chopin, Frédéric

Piano preludes, 1839

Opus 28

Musical snapshots

Composed with the intention of forming a whole based on the alternation of moments of tension and relaxation, the 24 Preludes *each reveal 'the same exquisite and elegant writing' (Schumann).*

Long considered a descriptive musical piece conceived to convey a particular 'mood' (Alfred Cortot, for example, saw in the third *Prelude* the equivalent of 'the song of a stream', and the 11th evoked for him 'a young girl's desire' etc), the *Preludes* actually obey the logical development of a purely musical conception, which does not have to deprive them of the extra-musical connotations usually given to the romantic style: sombre charm (Nos. 7, 11, 17, 23), passion (Nos. 8, 16, 22), héroïco-fantastic feelings (Nos. 12, 14, 18, 24), anguish (Nos. 4, 9, 15, 20). They were tonally ordered in such a way that each piece written in major

(*Prelude* No.1) was followed by its corresponding minor (No.2), but as each piece was in itself so rich in modulations, this rule did not represent anything more than a kind of formal tribute to the *Well-Tempered Klavier*.

Almost all of Chopin's pianistic vision is found in microcosm in this collection; certain *Preludes* could belong to the *Nocturnes* (Nos. 4, 13, 15, 20), others to the *Études* (Nos. 8, 12, 14, 16), No.22 has the character of a polonaise, others are stylistically like a romance without words (No.17), a mazurka (No.7), a recitative (No.18) or a funeral march (No.20). Two of them, The *Prelude No.2 in A minor* and *No.24 in D minor* also give us the opportunity to appreciate the Chopin who is more passionate and epic than intimate. They are at the origin of the cycle whose harmonic innovations they presage (they were judged to be bizarre, discordant and unplayable).

Historical references

It seems as though Chopin had intended, from as early as 1831, to write the series of *24 Preludes* which had been commissioned by the editor Camille Pleyel. If we can judge from the composer's own correspondence and by the written testimony of George Sand (*Story of my life*), the *Preludes* were completed during a visit to Mallorca in extremely difficult conditions: brutal temperatures, a bad state of health, the hostility of the population and the discomfort of the Chartreuse de Valdemosa. The *Preludes* were published in Paris in September 1839.

In the margins of the *24 Preludes* of opus 28, Chopin composed two other preludes: one of these was the *Prelude in C sharp minor opus 45* (1841), celebrated for its audacious treatment of modulation (30 passages of one key in another, carried out over a duration of only a few minutes).

Debussy, Claude

Preludes for piano, books 1 and 2, 1910 and 1913

From one sound region to another

Debussy's first major piano collection, the Preludes, *synthesizes the achievements of the previous pieces and is characterized by a structurally-fluid sound discontinuity.*

Pieces of fairly limited dimensions, many of which should not be played — according to the composer — 'except between four eyes' (in other words not before having listened to them attentively), Debussy's *24 Preludes* were conceived in conformity with their generic title, to be followed, in a concert performance, by works of more ample proportions. This preliminary function explains without a doubt why the specific titles — poetic or descriptive — of the *Preludes* are written only at the end of each piece. As if Debussy had wanted to indicate, in that way, the ability of his music to eventually symbolize, according to the principles of tonal equivalence, a particular subject (*Danseuses de Delphes, La Fille aux cheveux de lin, La Cathedrale engloutie ...*) and to warn against the temptations of natu-

ralism ('this is not a photo of a beach, a postcard for 15 August', wrote Debussy about *Voiles*, second prelude of book 1). In this respect, the title given to the first prelude of the second book, *Brouillards*, is fairly revealing; for this very innovative piece is primarily concerned with subverting (Debussy, always keen on aquatic comparisons, would have said '*drowning*') the key of C major, accorded to the left hand by the 'sound confusion of the right hand' (Harry Halbreich): in short, these fogs are extremely musical.

Some of the pieces in this very diversified collection — because they integrate into their composition musical potentialities, propose harmonically untested combinations, or turn blatantly to athematism — are among Debussy's most innovative. Besides *Brouillards*, there are *Les sons et les parfums tournent dans l'air du soir, Ce qu'a vu le vent d'Ouest, La Terrasse des audiences du clair de lune, Canope,* and *Feux d'artifice.* Some of the preludes have a more 'exotic' inspiration (principally Spanish: *La Sérénade interrompue, La Puerta del Vino*), and the collection even contains some humorous passages, tinged with the first hints of a nascent jazz (*Minstrels, Général Lavine-eccentric*).

Historical references

Book I of the *Preludes* was composed hastily from December 1909 to February 1910. The writing of Book II, on the other hand, was spread out over three years (1910–12). The first series was published in 1910, the second in 1913.

The first performances of the *Preludes* were always partial — the composer did not envisage, as is done today — presenting them in the form of a cycle.

Wagner, Richard

Prelude and death of Isolde, 1857 and 1859

A desire for eternity and prelude to modernity

Joined by Wagner with a symphonic version of the Death of Isolde, *the* Prelude of Tristan *exposes a complex musical plot intensified by a frenetic amorous celebration.*

A short melodic motif, introduced *pianissimo* by the cellos, called 'de l'aveu' opens the *Prelude*. It is soon followed by the famous 'Tristan's chord' which is linked with the theme 'du désir', the ensemble repeats it while being interspersed with imposing rests. The cellos expose the very beautiful motif 'du regard', which establishes itself gradually as the principal theme of the piece; the symbol of the enigmatic language of passionate love. After a short evocation of the 'love-potion' and 'death-potion' themes, a long *crescendo* derived from the motif 'du regard' announces the theme 'de

la delivrance par la mort', the sixth and last motif of *Prelude*. This finishes solemnly with the return of the first three themes which are followed by an admirable elegy to Tristan and the fulfilment of a wish for annihilation, *La Mort d'amour d'Isolde*. An ascending musical figure, comparable to the incessant ebb and flow of the sea, marks the extraordinary melody which is played out in submerging sound waves, 'from where the irresistible *movement* of this passage, its continuous *crescendo* which is even more irrefragable than the *tempo*, remains constant' (Dominique Jameux).

On the level of pure music, *Tristan* inaugurates the 'later Wagner' and marks an important evolution, for it is a work of exacerbated chromatic tension, a veritable 'network of delayed harmonies and false conclusions in the shimmering changes of key' (Martin Gregor-Dellin) at the front of a development that was to result, at the beginning of the 20th century, with the Vienna School (Schönberg, Berg, Webern), in the disappearance of the traditional tonal system.

Tristan's Chord

If the musicologists, instead of focusing their attention on the single chord of the third bar, had gone on to study the different appearances of this same structure, they would certainly have detected the *elusive nature of its identity*. A nature which is 'explained by the *enharmonic double properties* of the chord which is evident from its first appearance ... It thus contains all of the *strongest* elements of the tonal system' (Évelyne Andréani).

Historical references

Wagner conceived the plan for *Tristan* in 1854. He began writing the text of the poem in August 1857 and finished it in September the same year. The composition of *Prelude* and Act 1 also dates from 1857, while the second and third acts were not finished until 1859. The work was played for the first time on 10 June 1865 in Munich, for King Louis II of Bavaria. Hans von Bulow conducted.

Chord harmony:
The notes F, B, D sharp, G sharp can also be read F, C flat, E flat, A flat.

Debussy, Claude

Prelude à l'après-midi d'un faune, 1894

A renewed musical art

Debussy's first major orchestral experiment, the Prelude à l'après-midi d'un faune, *due to its formal and tonal originality, is considered to mark the opening of the era of modern music.*

The work planned to illustrate Mallarmé's *l'Après-midi d'un faune* was originally intended to be in the form of a triptych entitled *Prélude, interludes et paraphrase pour l'après-midi d'un faune*. But having set out, in the single Prelude, 'the successive sets in which the desires and the dreams of the faun are played out in the heat of the afternoon' (Debussy), the composer decided to stick with this short piece of only ten minutes duration. This statutory function of the preliminary passage with a nonexistent development indicates, on Debussy's part, an a priori rejection of the traditional development. In reality, however, the principle of development adopted in the *Prelude* proceeds less from the rejection of any predetermined form than from 'an amalgam of known forms' (Jean Barraqué). These forms, recognizable despite their considerable modifications, are those of the sonata (exposition, development, recapitulation), the lied (construction by sections) and of variation. Analysed in this way, the work turns out to have five sections. The first (exposition) consists of four varied and commented upon presentations of the slightly Oriental wonderful theme which is played by the flute, at first alone and then accompanied by the orches-

tra. This exposition links up with the first *development*.

The third part (middle) in which the *Prelude* reaches its climax, goes to considerable effort to superimpose — a favourite technique of Debussy's — different rhythms. Then it dwindles into a dialogue between a violin solo and a horn, an oboe and a clarinet, causing a change in the musical discourse's emphasis with the entry of the second development: the initial theme, reappearing on the flute, but distended, gives the impression of a dream.

With the *recapitulation* (fifth part), Debussy indulges in new developments of the theme and colours these with the use of antique cymbals. A coda, based on a mix of muted horns and violins replays the theme one last time on the flute, but in a ghostly way: reduced to only four notes.

Historical references

Started in 1892, the *Prélude à l'après-midi d'un faune*, was not completed until September 1894 when Debussy had already begun working on his opera *Pelléas et Mélissande*. When the work was performed on 22 December 1894 it was a great success despite its boldness; it was even encored.

> Mallarmé, at first unsure about the idea of a musical illustration to his poem, was very impressed by the music to *Prelude*. He wrote to Debussy — in a compliment that has since become famous — saying his illustration 'is not discordant with my text, except in that it goes even further into nostalgia and into light, with sensitivity, with disquiet and with richness'.

String Quartets

The *string quartet* is an instrumental formation made up of two violins, a viola and a cello which generally play parts of approximately equal importance. It does not have a set form, but because it emerged in the classical era, it has for a long time taken the structure of the sonata with a division into four movements.

When it appeared around 1760, the string quartet created a new musical category. Its 'invention' was due to the synthesis, brought about simultaneously by composers like Boccherini and Haydn, of various instrumental forms of Baroque music, put together bit by bit, around 1720. And the influence of the tighter contrapuntal four-part writing of the Italian *sonata*, *concerto* and *sinfonia* was particularly decisive. Furthermore, the progressive emancipation of string instruments from the midst of the nascent baroque orchestra and the develop-ment of a 'chamber' style, represented primarily by the Austrian *divertimento* for small solo ensemble, also played a role in the creation of the string quartet.

The importance of Joseph Haydn to the definition and evolution of the string quartet is considerable and stems not just from the fact that he was the first composer, with Boccherini, to have written them, but mainly from his being the first musician to have brought this new formation to a very high level. Of the 68 quartets he created, we must draw particular attention to four series, of six works each: opus 20 (1722) subtitled *Sun Quartets*, opus 33 (1781) called the *Russian Quartets*, opus 64 (1791), and, last but certainly not least, opus 76 (1799).

Despite Mozart's 23 works for the quartet, his role in terms of its development was less decisive. Nonetheless, some of his works certainly rivalled musically the greatest of Haydn's quartets. This is particularly true of the group, written between 1782 and 1785, of his *Six Quartets* dedicated to Haydn.

Beethoven's 16 string quartets constitute one of the greatest collections in musical history. After a first group of *Six Quartets* opus 18 (1801), still fairly similar to those by Haydn and Mozart, Beethoven brought the quartet to entirely new dimensions with the three following works: the *Razumovsky Quartets* opus 59 (1806), and *Harp Quartet* No.10 opus 74, and the 11th, opus 95 (1810). And finally, his last five quartets, composed between 1823 and 1826, carried the classical forms to their absolute limit.

Schubert's last two quartets, which were exact contemporaries of Beethoven's five 'peaks', *Death and the Maiden* (14th D.810; 1824) and the 15th D.887 (1826), are the only ones to have taken substantially different paths at that time.

After Beethoven and Schubert, and up until the beginning of the 20th century, numerous composers tried out string quartets: Mendelssohn, Schumann, Brahms, Tchaikovsky, Dvorak, Janacek, Franck, Fauré, Debussy, Ravel.

In the 20th century, despite Darius Milhaud's 18 quartets, and the 15 by Dimitri Shostakovich, the composers who most renovated this form were Bartók, Charles Ives and the musicians of the Vienna School (Schönberg, Berg, Webern). More recently, from 1948 to the beginning of the 1980s, the quartet has been revived in the works of Pierre Boulez, Elliott Carter, Györgi Ligeti, André Boucourechliev, Henri Dutilleux, Brian Ferneyhaugh and others.

Simultaneously with the string quartet, other types of four instrument for-mations were developed, usually for a solo instrument and a string trio. Mozart was one of the first composers to have written such a piece with, among others, three quartets for flute and strings and two quartets with piano. In the 19th century the most often exploited formation included a piano and string trio; principally by Schumann, Brahms and Fauré.

Quintets, sextets, septets and octets

Alongside the string quartet and the quartet with piano, other chamber music formations were gradually established which grouped together more instruments (between five and eight).

While the string quintet (two violins, two violas, one cello and, more rarely, two violins, one viola and two cellos) appeared simultaneously, around 1760, with the quartet, the quality of works which it gave rise to has always been quantitatively inferior to that written for the four-instrument formations. But this limitation of number says nothing at all about the musical quality of quintets, for those by Boccherini — who inaugurated the formula — are as good as his quartets, and among the six composed by Mozart, four are considered to be high points in the whole of his chamber music production.

In the 19th century, Beethoven, Bruckner and Brahms also wrote string quintets, but Schubert's composition far surpassed theirs; it was one of his greatest works. Quintets with piano and strings are best illustrated by Schubert again, with the *Trout*, as well as Schumann, Brahms, Franck and Fauré. It is also worth mentioning the quintets for clarinet and strings by Mozart, Weber, Brahms and, more recently, the wind quintets by Arnold Schönberg, Karlheinz Stockhausen and Györgi Ligeti.

The repertoire of string sextets (two violins, two violas, two cellos) is even smaller than that of the quintets because, with the exception of Boccherini's quintets, musical history has only retained three; two by Brahms and one by Schönberg, *Verklärte Nacht*.

While there are very few examples of septets (Beethoven, Saint-Saëns, Janácek and Stravinsky), the octet, on the other hand, is very well represented. Beethoven, Schubert and Mendelssohn each wrote an octet, respectively for wind instruments, strings and winds and for strings alone. In the 20th century, the octet captured the attention of many composers, including Enesco, Stravinsky (for wind instruments), Milhaud (for strings), Hindemith, Shostakovich and even Iannis Xenakis.

Mozart, Wolfgang Amadeus

Quartet No.19 'Dissonanzen', 1785

C major, K.465

'Melodicity' rediscovered

With Dissonanzen, *the last of six quartets dedicated to Haydn, Mozart reconciled his melodic style with new principles of thematic elaboration borrowed from Haydn.*

The slow introduction which precedes the initial *allegro* and whose chromaticism explains the quartet's sub-title, is one of the

These six quartets are Mozart's most significant contribution to the genre. His aim was not to imitate but to integrate into his own thematic pursuits the new thematic language introduced by Haydn's opus 33 which was characterized by the total independence of the four instruments, and endow the quartet with a 'specific perfection' (J. and B. Massin). But this elaboration of thematism led to the renunciation of the appeal of melody for its own sake which Mozart had practised widely before then. The exploration of this new genre also resulted in his abandoning this primary melodicity in favour of a 'global melody ... where the interweaving and the thematic dynamism come together in the complete cohesion of a single instrument with four bows' (Jean-Victor Hocquard). With *Dissonanzen* in particular Mozart even succeeded in 'making the thematic language sing'.

most tense written by Mozart. This tension results from the way in which the key of C major is postponed, the C major chord appearing always as a reference mark, as the absent point of stability 'around which all the others revolve' (Charles Rosen). Furthermore, when the actual *allegro* begins, outright in C major, it gives the impression of an almost joyful release. But the next two movements (*andante cantabile*, minuet-trio), which have an almost tragic atmosphere, contain indications of the initial tension, which is ultimately resolved by the final *allegro* and its unexpected 'opera-buffa' coda.

Historical references

The publication of Haydn's *Six Quartets* opus 33 in 1782 encouraged Mozart to write this series. The first (No.14 K.387) was completed in 1782 and the sixth, *Dissonanzen*, was not finished until 1785.

In the Quartet K.465, Mozart experimented with a type of *discord* centering on a perfect C minor chord: C (cello), E flat (2nd violin), G (viola). The notes which make up the discords are A flat and F sharp on the viola (these notes are the closest to the concordant G) and A on the violin, which is justified only in the next bar where it belongs to a more harmonically-stable chord.

Haydn, Joseph

'The Lark' Quartet, 1791

D minor, opus 64 No.5

A conversational tone

Opus 64 No.5 is the most famous piece in a cycle of six string quartets, in which Haydn's creative skill brilliantly demonstrates its Apollonian nature.

The opening movement (*allegro moderato*) of this sonata-form quartet *alla breve*, based on a thematic cell which gives rise to a very spirited and light-hearted principal melodic motif played by the first violin with a *staccato* accompaniment from the other three instruments, progresses much like a conversation. This air of conversation which 'perhaps constitutes the most striking innovation of Haydn's writing for string quartets' (Charles Rosen) reinforces in this passage the clarity of musical discourse and gives it a definite appeal and a syntactic lucidity, which counters the opposite effect created by the confusion of the lyrical outbursts.

Dominated by variation, as with the other slow movements of opus 64, the *adagio* in A major (second movement) is in three parts. Its middle section, in minor, is based on thematic material derived from the first section. The whole, which puts into relief a beautiful melody enriched with an even more complex series of ornaments, seems to be typical of this formation which Haydn used extensively in his quartets and trios.

The third movement, an *allegretto* minuet (D major) with trio (D minor) presents a formal singularity which is not uncommon in Haydn's structures: its second section is much longer than its first (exposition) and includes unorthodox modulations. It also demands an execution in the style of a minuet.

With its progression interrupted by semiquavers, the finale in D major (*vivace*) comes across as an extremely vigorous and rapid perpetual motion. Here virtuosity plays an integral part in the style of the work, 'in spite of the continuous beat, the phrases are clearly articulated and never overlap; the strong off-beat accents of the middle section in the minor increase even more the diversity of the piece' (Charles Rosen).

Historical references

The collection of six string quartets of opus 64 to which *The Lark* belongs was composed by Haydn in 1790, shortly before his first trip to London (Jan 1791–June or beginning of July 1792). It was first published in Vienna in April 1791.

This quartet was sub-titled *The Lark* because of the impression of flight created by the high-pitched melody played by the first violin at the beginning of the piece.

Haydn, Joseph

'Emperor' Quartet, 1799

C major, opus 76 No.3

A famous patriotic emphasis

Opus 76 *is both a summary of Haydn's experimentation within the norms of classical style, and a prefiguration, in certain of its technical aspects, of the forms of later Beethoven.*

A motif of five descending notes (first bar) serves as the introduction to the first movement (*allegro*). This motif is carried out by the viola and cello and is responded to by the 'commentary' of the second violin established on the basis of a dotted rhythm which is essential to the development which characterizes a stunning 'Magyar' spirit. The epilogue, *più presto*, is preceded by a recapitulation with a long pause evoking the conclusive style of the *London Symphony* (No.104) finale.

In the second movement (*poco adagio, cantabile*), in G major, the melody of the Austrian imperial anthem remains constant from beginning to end; it develops on the basis of four purely harmonic variations, the last of which veils the theme in a restless chromaticism and makes it fluctuate between G major and E minor until the coda (five bars) re-establishes a tonal stability, probably representing the permanence of the political order.

Several themes derived from the base motif of the first movement impel the minuet (*allegro*) and the finale (*presto*). With this admirable finale dominated by the sombre key of C minor until it moves into C major in the last few bars, Haydn foreshadows the Beethovian pathos and places himself at the transitory border which separates the rigours of the classical music tradition from the pre-romantic emotional exaltation.

Historical references

The quartets opus 76 were composed in 1797 in Gumpendorf and Eisenstadt, and published simultaneously in Vienna and London in 1799. The *'Emperor' Quartet*, performed in Eisenstadt on 28 September 1797 at a gala concert given in honour of the visit to the city by Archduke Joseph, intensified the political impact of the imperial anthem (first sung in Vienna on 12 February 1797) which was considered to be the symbol of Austrian resistance to the approaching invasion by Napoleon's armies.

We must also include within this series two other great works with well-known sub-titles: *The Fifths*, opus 76 No.2 and *Sunrise*, opus 76 No.4.

As the author of the Imperial Austrian Anthem *God save Emperor François* in 1796, Haydn returned to this anthem as the theme and variations for his *Quartet in C major*, subtitled for this reason *Emperor*.

Beethoven, Ludwig van

'Razumovsky' Quartet No.9, 1808

C major, opus 59 No.3

For the times ahead *(Beethoven)*

Last of the three 'Razumovsky' Quartets *(almost of a symphonic style and revolutionary in their technical aspects), the* Quartet No.9 *stands out by virtue of its stunning final fugue.*

Called, in Austria, the 'heroic quartet' by analogy with the symphony of the same name, this ninth quartet contains four movements. But this traditional division is usually contested as each section does not possess the same 'relative weight' (Joseph Kerman). Undeniably, the entire evolution of this quartet tends to converge towards its monumental finale. This apparent disequilibrium disappears as soon as we bring the piece back into the cycle that it forms with the other two quartets of opus 59. For the monumentalism produced by the finale of this third *Razumovsky* is explained by its relation to the beginning of the equally grandiose first *Razumovsky* to which it is responding.

The three Razumovsky quartets were seen at the time of their creation to be, at best, too complicated and, at worst, provoked unprecedented violence in their critics. One violinist even said to Beethoven that it was not music, and was in return told 'it isn't for you, it is for the times ahead'.

The initial *allegro (vivace)* is preceded by a slow introduction marked *andante con moto*. But Beethoven was not content to stick with the harmonic digressions traditionally associated with slow introductions preceding a sonata-form allegro: instead he increases this effect of tonal indecision with a rhythmic and melodic instability, as well as with the use of rests. Just as soon as we are deprived of any reference point, the almost symphonic notes of the *allegro* itself burst forth. The second movement is an andante whose unique first sound — a cello *pizzicato* continually repeated thereafter — is almost capable of establishing the colour on its own.

In order to preserve the effects, Beethoven preceded the final fugue with a relatively more moderate minuet *grazioso* which is joined to the fugue without any gap. The modernity of this fugue, as André Boucourechliev noted, lies in its speed. It moves so rapidly that the listener perceives whole or 'sound tracks' rather than individual notes. But this grandiose fugue presents another tour de force when, just before the final cadenza, it is followed by a rest at the moment of its greatest tension, making the silence seem 'not an ending but an explosion' (André Bouchourechliev).

Historical references

The three quartets of opus 59 were composed in 1805–6, to honour a commission from the Count André Razumovsky. Published in January 1808, they were first performed the following month.

Beethoven, Ludwig van

Quartet No.13 with 'Grosse Fuge', 1826

B flat major, opus 130 and 133

Beyond the principle of disparity

Possibly the most enigmatic of Beethoven's works, the Quartet No.13 *is sometimes problematic, as its music is extremely differentiated and its final fugue is out of proportion.*

This quartet contains six movements, all very different from one another more in terms of duration than on a formal level; the shortest lasts just two minutes while the last one is sixteen minutes long, and one of them is an allemande, another a fugue. What is more, 'this principle of diversity and contrasts is found within each movement' (André Boucourechliev). It was because Beethoven had organized many links between the various sections that he was able to take the risk of such disparity.

The initial *allegro* is preceded by a slow introduction (*adagio*). But this *adagio*, far from its traditional introductory role is intended, through its numerous repeats, to contrast the character and the rapid tempo of the *allegro*. Thus, this quartet is a work of oppositions right from the beginning.

Because the *Grosse Fuge*, was published separately it was long considered a *quartet in its own right*. For this reason we often attribute Beethoven with the composition of 17 quartets instead of the actual 16 he wrote.

The three following movements confirm this impression: a very short *presto* (two minutes) and an allemande — *alla danza tedesca* — which is not much longer, frame an *andante* which is 'one of the most polished passages by Bach on the rhythmic level' (André Boucourechliev) and which is also not without humour.

Serving as the fifth movement, the Cavatine (*adagio molto expressivo*) is an extremely tense piece and, needless to say contrasting, which culminates in its middle section with 'anguished and oppressed accents of a melodic line lacerated with rests' (André Boucourechliev).

Only the gigantic, and itself conflictive, finale is capable of crowning, of resolving with excess, this quartet wrought with disparity. This task is fulfilled by the *Grosse Fuge*, which is itself divided into several opposing sections, and lasts more than quarter of an hour. Both a dramatic and a rigorous work, the effect of modernity which it produces is prodigious, and comes mainly from the radical unpredictability of its sound development.

Historical references

The *Quartet* was composed in its original version with *Grosse Fuge* in 1825 and performed in Vienna in 1826. Faced with utter incomprehension of the *Grosse Fuge* by the public, Beethoven resigned himself to composing a rondo as a new finale. The work was published in this form in 1827 and the *Grosse Fuge* as an independent work in 1830, as opus No.133.

Schubert, Franz

Quartet No.14, 'Death and the Maiden', 1826

D minor, posthumous opus, D.810

A dramatized moment

Composed at a time when Schubert had broken away from classical models, this quartet evokes, through a powerfully internalized musical language, the romantic notion of death.

A very incisive theme shines forth *fortissimo* from the first bar of the initial *allegro*. It renews itself continuously in a melodic design which gives its tormented mood to the developments of the second theme which are less dark and less violent but whose innovative modulations create an accent of pathos. In the last bars of this movement, after an animated *crescendo*, a relative calm is restored when the first violin exposes once more the extremely melancholy first theme.

The second movement (*andante con moto*) has, as its leading motif, the tragic air of the lied with the same name, but in the key (G

The quartet 'Death and the Maiden' takes its title from a lied in D minor, written in 1817, played in the form of variations in the second movement.

minor) of *Roi des Aulnes*, another funeral lied which the fourth movement re-echoes.

In order to create a relaxed atmosphere after these particularly gloomy sections without altering the dramatic weight of his composition, Schubert brings in a fairly brief scherzo (*allegro molto*) with vigorous rhythmic accents made even more intense by the alternation of major and minor. A trio at the centre of the scherzo creates 'a moment of joy' (Alfred Einstein) in an emotional turmoil which is brought to its peak by the last movement (*presto*).

The quartet finishes on a frenetically animated finale which combines the structure of the sonata with that of the rondo: in its rapid obsessive rhythm, the unbroken evocation of the principal theme and the constant base of the key of D minor, this last movement was obviously intended to give the impression of hurried completion.

Historical references

Only one of the fifteen quartets that Schubert officially composed was published in his lifetime. This was the *Quartet No.13 in A minor* (1824), another high point in his chamber music, along with *Quartet No.15 in G major* (1826). Rejected by B. Schott's Sons publishing house who edited Beethoven's last works, the *Quartet No.14 'Death and the Maiden'*, written in 1824, was performed for a private audience in Vienna at the home of a friend, Joseph Barth on 1 February, 1826.

Brahms, Johannes

String Quartet No.1, 1873

C minor, opus 51 No.1

'Progressive' musical language

In Opus 51 *the post-classical formal strictness is accompanied by rhythmic innovations, bold harmonics and an inclination towards an original thematic unification.*

The first movement of the *Quartet in C minor* is an *allegro* which is both energetic and sombre, constructed in a sonata-form of three themes. The initial theme, exposed by the first violin, already establishes an important thematic relationship between the different movements; we find it used in various ways at the beginning of the romance (second movement), and of the *allegretto* (third movement) and in the finale. This 'almost Straussian' (Claude Rostand) theme is followed by a second more melodic theme which is joined by a secondary motif to the third theme. Towards the end of the exposition the initial theme reappears to dominate the quasi-tonality of the development and to give a considerable unity to the movement.

The sombre atmosphere of the *allegro* is found in the second movement (*romanza, poco adagio*), a piece in A flat major with two themes which somewhat evoke the famous *Cavatina* of Beethoven's quartet opus 130.

The admirable third movement (*allegretto molto moderato e commodo*) is in F minor. Of a typically Beethovian tone, it presents itself as an intermezzo in the form of a scherzo very skillfully centred around a double melody. The central trio, un *poco più animato* in the major key, is responsible for breaking up the melancholy mood (with the use of *pizzicati*) before the repeat of the initial *allegretto* closes the movement.

The finale, an *allegro* in C minor, obeys both the structure of the sonata (without the central development) and the rondo form. A severe and invariably sombre fragment of 'musical prose' (Schönberg), it creates a great thematic richness (six different motifs) and represents the part of the quartet whose complex organization — with the repeat of the initial theme of the first movement — best substantiates the idea that the entire piece contains the 'cyclic method in embryo' (Claude Rostand).

Historical references

The 'maturation process' of the two quartets which make up opus 51 was exceptionally long. Started in 1853, shortly after the historic meeting between Robert and Clara Schumann, the diptych, from outline to outline and from draft to draft, did not find its definitive form until 1873. No.1 was played for the first time in public in Vienna on 11 December 1873. No.2 (in A minor) was presented on 18 October the same year.

Debussy, Claude

String Quartet, 1894

G minor

A work in search of a break

Debussy's unique quartet displays a lyricism which does not exist in his later works.

Despite its classical structure, Debussy's *Quartet* represents an already conclusive attempt to replace the development of traditional musical discourse with a formal freedom which is demonstrated by a refusal to make the recapitulation symmetrical with the exposition, as the rules of sonata-form dictate.

The second movement (a *scherzo* with trio) presents various transformations of the cyclic principal theme introduced at the beginning of the work. The third movement (*andantino*), in its languid harmonization, is fairly reminiscent of César Franck's style, while the finale reveals the beauty of well-worked sound in its own right.

Historical references

Completed in February 1893, the *String Quartet* was performed in Paris in December of the same year.

Ravel, Maurice

String Quartet, 1904

F major

Ravel the forerunner of Ravel

In certain of its harmonic innovations, the Quartet in F *foreshadows the 'reasoned' style of Ravel's most accomplished works.*

In sonata-form with two themes, the first of the four movements is a fast *allegro moderato* of an almost Mozartian polyphonic clarity. Its explosive melodic design gives way to the fairly lively rhythmic motif (exposed in *pizzicati*) of the second movement, the second theme of which has a lyrical and melodic quality uncommon for Ravel. The admirable third movement reintroduces the initial theme of the *allegro moderato* in variations. The last movement is a finale in quintuple time: lively and spirited, it finishes with the repeat, on a 'Russian' rhythm, of the very spirited theme with which the work started.

Historical references

The *Quartet in F*, composed at the end of 1902–beginning of 1903, is dedicated to Gabriel Fauré. Fauré criticized the finale but Ravel refused to change it.

Schönberg, Arnold

Quartet No.2, 1908

F sharp minor, opus 10

A singular farewell

Because it integrates a vocal part into its last two movements and gradually distances itself from tonality, just as far as to suspend it, this quartet is a historic first.

To move, within the same work, from tonality to its abandonment, and to attach to it a soprano voice, are the heterogenous factors that risk this second quartet losing all unity. In order to counter this risk, the work respects the classical division into four movements and the cyclic repeats of the different themes are carefully organized.

While the first 'moderate' movement with a post-romantic aspect is traditional in its allegiance to the classical structure of an *allegro* in sonata-form, the second movement, a 'very fast' scherzo characterized by a vaguely mocking rhythm and harmonic fluidity is considerably less traditional. For while its structure may be conventional (scherzo, trio, repeat of the scherzo), Schön-

berg undermines this by inserting, at the end of the trio, the ironic citation of a popular Viennese refrain 'O, du lieber Augustin'. Besides the straightforward role of foretelling the vocal part of the following movements, the instrumental integration of this song is ironic as well, for there is a hint of the imminent abandonment of tonality in the words 'Alas, my poor boy, all is lost'.

The last two movements ('slow' and 'very slow') are written for soprano and string quartet, and the texts they use are the poems by Stephen George, 'Litany' and 'Estrangement'.

The achievement of the third very dramatic movement — a theme followed by five variations and an instrumental coda — is perfect in terms of the confrontation created between the voices and the bows.

The last movement, 'Estrangement', from its instrumental introduction gives up all tonal functions and the verses — 'I feel the air of other planets' — take on a very different meaning because of this fact. Finally, when the chord of F sharp major, which concludes the work, reappears, one is able to appreciate the separation from tonality, but it sounds mainly, in this context, like a ghost from the past.

An ethical innovation.
Schönberg, who defines himself as a 'conservative forced to become radical', felt it was his duty — and not necessarily his choice — *to put an end to tonality*. He took this position when, in 1922, he invented *serialism*. During the war of 1914, a captain asked him if he was actually 'the Schönberg, the avant-garde musician'. He is reported to have replied 'Nobody else wanted to be, somebody had to be, so I volunteered'.

Historical references

Started in March 1907, the second quartet was finished in the autumn of 1908 and its performance, in December of the same year, created one of the greatest scandals in the history of music.

Certain rumours suggest that once Schönberg abandoned tonality his wife left him; she went back to him soon after. But it took Schönberg a lot longer to return to tonality.

Ives, Charles

String Quartet No.2 1913

The controversial quartet

Constructed on the scenario of four characters having a political debate, this quartet is an avant-garde work in terms of the techniques it experiments with and the independence of its voices.

'A string quartet for four men who converse, discuss, debate (politics), argue, shake each other's hands, fall silent and then climb the slope of a mountain to observe the view': this is the programme written by Charles Ives for his *Second Quartet*.

The first movement is reserved for the conversation, the second for the debate and the third for the appeasement achieved by climbing the mountain. The personification of the four instruments creates such an independence for the voices of the quartet that they appear sometimes to have no con-nection with one another. More specifically, this principle allows for the superimposition of melodies, harmonies, rhythms, dynamics and radically opposing methods of execution. In fact it allows for the co-exist-ence, in the same passage, of the most radical lack of theme with excerpts of well-known melodies.

In the first movement — Discussion: *andante moderato* — the citation of familiar tunes, such as 'Marching through Georgia' has the effect of indicating that the con-versation in question is about the Civil War.

The second movement — Altercation: *allegro con spirito* — is principally striking in its rhythmic independence of voices, and its pre-Bartókian accents. The most con-trasting sections follow one another in a very abrupt manner, as at the beginning of the movement when discordant rhythmic blocks unceasingly interrupt a melodious and almost sentimental cadenza. The het-erogeneity of the elements is brought to its highest level here, as Ives does not hesitate to cite, besides the familiar tunes, a frag-ment of Beethoven's *Hymn to Joy*. However, despite their disparity, all these elements come together in Ives' rigorous writing, and the arrangement he invented is more like a cinematographic montage than a pictorial one.

With his last movement — The Call of the Mountains: *adagio* — the quartet becomes contemplative and the effect of suspended time, achieved by the last bars, hints at grandiosity.

Principally self-taught, Charles Ives (1874–1954) is one of the strangest figures in 20th-century music. Although he ignored all the developments of European music, he discovered 'before the inventors and officially recognized users of the time: polytonality . . ., pure atonality (ten years before Schönberg), polyrhythmics . . ., metric modulation . . . and spatial music' (Claude Rostand).

Among these works, which are occasionally lacking in originality, it is worth mentioning five symphonies, the *Concord Sonata* for piano and isolated orchestra pieces.

Historical references

Started in 1907, this quartet was finished in 1913 but not performed until September 1946 by the Walden Quartet.

Bartók, Béla

String Quartet No.5, 1936

A tempered expression of harshness

Less grating and less tense than the preceding ones, the Quartet No.5 *establishes itself, within a harsh musical language, as a work of relative calm and melodic expressiveness.*

Not respecting the classical rule of four movements but divided rather, into five sections, this quartet was created according to the construction principles of an arch: the central movement (in this case a scherzo) serves as the keystone for the other parts built around it.

In the first part, an *allegro* in sonata-form played very energetically, three themes follow each other: the initial section which creates an extremely lively rhythmic tension, ends at the introduction to a dance style motif (second theme), itself joined to the lyrical and melodic third theme.

The second movement, *adagio molto*, replaces the violence of the beginning with a 'murmuring music which is similar to the *Musique de nuit* of the *Suite en plein air*, and other nocturnes by Bartók' (Michel Chion); it finishes with a very striking descending conclusion on the cello.

We return to the dance with the 'rein-vented' folk rhythms of the central scherzo *alla bulgarese*. Here Bartók assimilates so well the popular Bulgarian elements with the aim of transmuting them into integrated elements of his personal aesthetic that the impression of pure music predominates.

The fourth movement is an *andante*. More sombre than the almost romantic *adagio molto*, it shares many structural and thematic similarities with it. From the beginning, the *pizzicati* followed by *glissandi* testify to Bartók's fondness for abrupt tones wrenched out of silence.

In sonata-form like the first movement on which it is dependent, the finale, after 13 introductory bars, *allegro vivace*, returns to the original theme of the piece and quickly develops it in a fugue. It is in the most tense part of the quartet, and the most violent, where Bartók suddenly decides to indulge in the luxury of a gag: 'A simple little tune in A major accompanied by classical chords' (Pierre Citron). The composition finishes with a return to a vehement polytonal counterpoint.

Historical references

Bartók composed his *Quartet No.5* in Budapest during the summer of 1934. The work was published in Vienna in 1936 after having been played for the first time in Washington by the Kolisch Quartet on 8 April 1935.

STRING QUARTETS

Webern, Anton
String Quartet, 1938
Opus 28

Bach reinvented

A work of pure counterpoint releasing a new sound, the Quartet Opus 28 *follows from a motif of* B–A–C–H *(B flat, A, C, B in German notation).*

The *String Quartet opus 28* is no exception to the typically Webernian concern for a rarefaction of the musical material. In other words, the writing of this piece was based on the principle of 'serial economy' sought after by the composer. Thus, the 12 notes of the series used here consist of three groups of four, and the last two groups are derived solely from the first, made up of the motif B–A–C–H. While this division of the series into segments with many possible patterns is primarily a factor of musical organization, its principal and rather radical

> Webern had originally intended to put the middle section at the beginning of the piece. But he decided not to, in order to avoid having two pieces of similar tempo next to each other.

> The last composition published in Webern's lifetime, this quartet constitutes, with *Variations* for piano opus 27 and *Variations* for orchestra opus 30, his ultimate instrumental trilogy.

B   A   C   H

Base motif of the series B.A.C.H. (B flat, A, C, B).

consequence is to put an end to any thematism: too short for any theme to develop, the serial fragments from which this work is woven do not leave room for anything but motifs.

A major serial music piece, the *Quartet opus 28* is also a work of counterpoint, for its three movements contain only canons and a fugue, and thus stem from a system 'where the equivalence of different voices is, by definition, achieved' (Stéphane Goldet). For this reason no other quartet before this one attained such an equality among the four instruments. Furthermore, this union of the series and counterpoint created for Webern an element of dramatic tension.

Following the same principle of organization as their base series, each of the three movements of the quartet abound in symmetries and internal reflections. The first two ('moderate', 'at ease') even have a tripartite division A–B–A. The third ('very smooth') is more complex, for its structure is both that of a scherzo and of a fugue.

Although the completely systematized calculations of pitches is the dominating principle, this quartet also focuses on renewing the writing of rhythms and intensities. It even contains — just enough to create an effect — an undeniable study of sonority, as in the final fugue where trills are superimposed on *pizzicati*.

Historical references

Started at the beginning of 1937, the *Quartet Opus 28*, which is less than nine minutes long, was not completed until April 1938. Webern had received, during the composition, a commission for a string quartet from the American patron Elizabeth Sprague-Coolidge. The work was first performed in April 1939 in Krakow.

104

Boulez, Pierre

Livre pour Quatuor, 1949

A work of *passage (S. Goldet)*

The Livre pour Quatuor *is one of Boulez's first attempts at the systematic organization of all sound parameters.*

Unlike his earlier instrumental works, Pierre Boulez's *Livre pour Quatuor* is not based on any classical formal structure. Its six movements can even be played separately, or permuted, or grouped according to the whims of the interpreters. In its writing,

this piece represents the first attempts to apply the Schönbergian serial principles not only to pitch, but also to duration, intensity, and timbre. It focuses as well on the rhythmic values and treats them with a complexity never before achieved.

Historical references

Composed in 1948–9, and partially published in 1960, the *Livre pour Quatuor* is not played all that often. Boulez actually revised the score to make it easier to play.

Shostakovich, Dmitri

String Quartet No.8, 1960

C minor, opus 110

The role of citation

Shostakovich, in this quartet governed by humanitarian ideas, cites himself many times.

The *Quartet No.8* contains five movements, each of which develops several musical citations which the composer took from his own works. In the initial *largo* in the form of 'a fugal complaint', we can recognize one of the themes of the *First Symphony*. The second movement (*allegro molto*) recalls the toccata of his *Eighth*, as well as the poignant

motif in C minor of his *Trio* opus 67. With the *allegretto* (third movement), we discover the first theme of *Cello Concerto* opus 107. An aria from the opera *Lady Macbeth* is cited at the climax of the fourth movement (*largo*), while the finale, also *largo*, begins with a repeat of the theme of the *Cello Concerto*, played here like 'a cry of protest' (M. Hofmann).

Historical references

Composed in 1960, the work was performed in Leningrad on 2 October of the same year.

Carter, Elliott

String Quartet No.2, 1961

An 'anti-quartet' quartet *(D. Schiff)*

Carter's Quartet No.2 *is intended for instrumentalists who are both interpreters and 'actors' of an 'auditory plot', as it sets up a theatrical situation within pure music.*

A 'conversation' and 'debate' for four, in an atonal musical language almost always replacing the traditional repeat of themes with the development of a perpetually changing series of motifs, the *Quartet No.2* does not have the homogeneity usually found in pieces for four bows (a single sound mass apparently transmitted from the players to the listener). It was created according to a subtle dissociation of sounds, with each 'separated' sound corresponding to the autonomy of 'speech' engaged in by the performer-speaker who plays his/her part in terms of a relationship with the other performer-speakers which can represent a 'conversation' among 'disciples', 'friends' or 'adversaries'.

Divided into nine connected parts (introduction, *allegro fantastico*, viola cadenza, *presto scherzando*, cello cadenza, *andante espressivo*, first violin cadenza, *allegro* and conclusion), this 'quartet scenario' unravels its plot by developing the 'conversation'

within the six sections where a particular instrument will often assume the role of narrator (the *allegro fantastico* is carried by the first violin, the *andante* by the viola) and within the three solo cadenzas in which the player-speaker 'takes the floor' in a more isolated way. Carter himself emphasized the dead-pan tone of the *confrontation between the soloists and their adversaries*: after the *presto scherzando* when the cello is playing in its own romantic way, it is confronted by other instruments which demand a stricter tempo; finally, after the *andante espressivo* which revels the virtuosity of the first violins playing, it collides with the silence of the others who, even before it has a chance to finish its cadenza, launch into the '*allegro*'.

But at the heart of this complex piece, both fragmented and continuous, the personalized contribution of each instrument, while it is very important, is not the fundamental essence. Of prime importance is the ability of each part of the work to total the elements which it generates to produce a kaleidoscopic musical moment linked without obvious junctures to the following moment.

Historical references

Composed in 1959, the *Quartet No.2* was performed on 25 March 1960 in New York by the Juilliard Quartet. Published in 1961, it received the Pulitzer prize for music in 1960.

Ligeti, Györgi

String Quartet No.2, 1968

A quartet of references

Despite the radical originality of its sound textures, this work by Ligeti reflects all the traditional elements of the quartet.

Györgi Ligeti acknowledges having been principally inspired by classical models in writing his *Quartet*. But more than these sources, it is himself that he cites here. Furthermore, he makes reference to his first work in which the two main tendencies of his style are found: static music and fragmented music. And although the arrange-

ment in five movements is not conventional, one can detect within the structure 'an overture *allegro*, a slow movement, a scherzo, a *presto* and a finale' (Stéphane Goldet). The clarity of the writing and certainly the technique of development are undeniably founded on the classical spirit, and make particular reference to Haydn whose appeal, humour and subversion are reinvented by Ligeti.

Historical references

Composed in 1968, this quartet was first performed on 14 December 1969.

Dutilleux, Henri

Ainsi la Nuit for string quartet, 1976

A varied dream-like vision

Displaying a tempered modernism, Ainsi la Nuit is a work whose title perfectly describes its poetic dreamlike atmosphere.

A short introduction (eight bars) opens this *String Quartet* which is divided into seven connected parts. The first four ('Nocturne', 'Miroir d'espace', 'Litanies' and 'Litanies 2') are organically linked to each other by very brief interludes called 'parentheses'. At

the end of the fourth parenthesis, the last three sequences ('Constellation', 'Nocturne 2', 'Temps suspendu') follow without discontinuity. From sequence to sequence, the piece unravels sound lines of a kind of 'rhapsody in which the dynamics are founded on the dialectic between mobile and immobile elements' (Stéphane Goldet).

Historical references

Ainsi la Nuit was composed between 1971 and 1976. The Parenin Quartet performed it in Paris on 6 January 1977.

Fauré, Gabriel

Quartet for piano and strings No.1, 1884

C minor, opus 15

Academism foiled

Despite its conventionality, this quartet is surprising in the unexpectedness of its modulations and in the fusion of its very diverse themes.

Written for piano and string trio, in a concertant spirit, Fauré's first *Quartet* contains four traditional movements. Although the initial *allegro* is the first indication of the typically Fauréan vigour, the second move-

ment, a scherzo, unfolds 'in a serenade atmosphere' (J. M. Nectoux). The *adagio* is remarkable for its coda: a series of modulations played by the strings serves as the basis for a theme, played by the piano and finishing on arpeggios. With the final *allegro*, the *Quartet* returns to the same kind of atmosphere it had at the beginning.

Historical references

Composed between 1876 and 1879, this first *Quartet with piano* was performed in 1880. But Fauré rewrote the finale in 1883 and the definitive version was published in 1884.

Messiaen, Olivier

Quatuor pour la fin de temps, for violin, clarinet, cello and piano, 1941

New rhythmic irregularities

Referring to the end of the world the Apocalypse, this quartet exposes the totality of Messiaen's first rhythmic inventions.

The eight movements of the *Quatuor pour la fin du temps* differ greatly from one another, as one is a clarinet solo, two others are duets (cello and piano, violin and piano) and the fourth contains only keyboards. The most

exemplary moments of this piece are found in its first movement 'Liturgie de cristal' which is perfectly polyrhythmic; in the extraordinary and premonitory 'Abîme des oiseaux' for solo clarinet; and finally in the seventh movement 'Fouillis d'arcs-en-ciel', whose sonorous force is almost orchestral.

Historical references

The *Quatuor pour la fin du temps* was written in 1940 and performed by Messiaen in January 1941 during his captivity in Silesia.

Mozart, Wolfgang Amadeus

Quintet for clarinet and strings, 1789

A major, K.581

A new arrangement of timbres

Founded on a previously unpublished instrumental combination, the Quintet in A major *inaugurates a new genre exploited by Mozart with an exceptional sense of euphony.*

The first movement of the *Quintet*, an *allegro* in sonata-form, contains three themes. Each of these, initially exposed by the strings, is repeated by the clarinet which gives the piece the character of a concertante, tempered by the fact that the solo instrument, far from acting against the group, plays in accord with it throughout a musical discourse which is contemplative and solemn in the first of the three themes, radiant and frenetic in the second, and finally relaxed and calm in the third.

The exaltation displayed by the second theme of the *allegro* is found, although less internalized, in the second movement of the work, a magnificent *larghetto* in D major with such emotional force and complexity that it could be considered one of Mozart's most beautiful slow movements. The clarinet tune is spread widely throughout and supported by the softly playing strings, before it sets up a dialogue with the first violin which develops in a striking, euphonic perfection.

A minuet played by two trios follows the

larghetto. The initial trio (in A minor) which is interrupted only by the strings, marks the final return to the indefinable Mozartian dramatic atmosphere both intimate and remote. The second trio which restores the lead role to the clarinet, progresses on the rather harsh rhythm of a ländler, a country dance in triple time and an ancestor of the waltz.

The finale is an *allegro* of six variations on a lively and pleasant theme, although with less exuberance and more gravity in the third variation in A minor. A very striking *adagio* (fifth variation), in which the clarinet and strings play together, precedes a coda (*allegro*) full of energy.

Historical references

Mozart completed the *Quintet in A major* on 29 September 1789. The work was written for his friend and masonic brother, the clarinettist Anton Paul Stadler, who had probably guaranteed the performance of it on 22 December of the same year in Vienna's Burgtheater.

The friendship between *Don Juan*'s author and Stadler is responsible, not only for this chamber music piece, but also for Mozart's partiality for the clarinet at the time that he wrote his later works, evidenced in *Così fan tutte* (1789), *La Clemenza di Tito* (1791) and certainly in the *Concerto for clarinet and orchestra* K.622 (1791), also written for Stadler.

Schubert, Franz

Quintet with piano, 'Trout', 1819

A major, opus 114, D.667

The expansion of a lied

While it cites a fairly simple tune, this quintet is written for an uncommon formation: piano, violin, cello and double bass.

Schubert's *Quintet in A major* contains five movements. The first three (*allegro vivace*, *andante* and *scherzo-trio*) converge to announce the fourth, *andantino*, which is a series of variations on the famous theme of the lied called *The Trout*. This preparation for the fourth movement is made by allusion to the genre of lied (first movement), by use of the technique of variation, and the same key (D minor) in the scherzo's trio. The last movement, *allegro giusto*, seems, in its triumphant tone, to be commenting on the success of the citation.

Historical references

This quintet was commissioned in 1819 by a violinist who was impressed by the lied *The Trout*. Schubert gave the 'ungratifying' role of the fish not to the cello, but to a double bass.

Schubert, Franz

String quintet, 1828

C major, opus 163. D.956

Restless music

Written the year of his death, Schubert's Quintet with two cellos *represents the final revision of his style.*

While the four movements of this *quintet* appear to respect, in their structure, the classical Viennese tradition, this is only to better undermine it. Thus, in the first movement, *allegro ma non troppo*, it is not the two exposed themes that are developed, but a third which appears at the end of the expo-sition. The second movement, *adagio*, unique in its cello *pizzicati*, is interrupted by an almost phantasmal episode. And the extremely discordant scherzo contains a central trio, *andante sostenuto*, which echoes the *adagio*. And finally the *allegretto* succeeds, through the complex arrangement of its highly contrasting three themes, 'in defin-itively taking on all the restlessness it en-counters' (B. Massin).

Historical references

The work was composed in 1828, performed in 1850 and published in 1853.

Brahms, Johannes

Quintet for clarinet and strings, 1891

B minor, opus 115

The art of 'muffled sounds' *(K. Geiringer)*

This Quintet *is one of Brahms' most accomplished works, especially on the level of variation.*

This composition begins with an *allegro* in B minor in sonata-form with three themes, whose short initial motif acts throughout the piece as 'a sort of leitmotiv' (Claude Rostand).

The second movement, an *adagio* in B major, is constructed in three parts on a single principal theme magnificently developed in the middle section, *più lento*. Following a brief *andantino* in D minor, the finale (*con moto* in B minor) forms a series of five variations on a fairly simple melodic theme, and finishes with a motif derived from the leitmotiv of the *allegro*, before this leitmotiv is repeated in its original form to conclude the *Quintet* in a mood of melancholy.

Historical references

Opus 115, composed in the summer of 1891, was performed in Berlin in December the same year.

Brahms, Johannes

String sextet No.2 for two violins, two violas and two cellos, 1866

G major, opus 36

A polished Brahmsian polyphony

More carefully elaborated than the Sextet No.1 *(opus 18), opus 36 is full of thematic transformations.*

The first of the four movements of this *String sextet* is a sonata-form *allegro non troppo* evoking, in an elegaic manner, a woman whose name A.G.A.T.H.E is deciphered (A–G–A–(D)–B–E in German notation) after the exposition of the second theme.

The second movement (scherzo) in G minor, *allegro non troppo*, has the somewhat sombre and distant character of an intermezzo. Its central trio in G major, *presto giocoso*, takes on the rhythm of a lively country dance.

The third movement (in E minor and E major) is built on a lyric theme and five variations with great dramatic force, while the less spectacular *poco allegro* finale is somewhat like a dance.

Historical references

Brahms composed most of opus 36 in 1864.

Schubert, Franz

Octet for strings and winds, 1824

F major, D.803

The art of reproduction

Schubert's Octet *illustrates an important phenomenon: the proven obligation of an artist to copy a particular form handed down by a predecessor in order to boost his production.*

The *Octet in F major* is modelled after Beethoven's *Septet*. The parallelism between the two works is striking.

The *Septet* contains four string instruments (violin, viola, cello, double bass) and three wind instruments (clarinet, bassoon, horn); the *Octet* has the same instrumental complement, Schubert's only modification was to double the violin. Beethoven's work has six movements, as does Schubert's. Besides the number, the distribution and the succession of the tempos are homologous. Furthermore, the structure of the movements presents obvious analogies: the outer movements have an introduction, the fourth has a theme and variations, and the two works are also identical on the tonal level. Finally, even in the way it refers to itself, the *Octet* resembles the Beethovian model.

Beethoven's *Septet* (opus 20) was published in 1802. It very quickly became famous and established itself as the favoured work at musical sessions in Viennese homes. It is a relatively conventional piece which its author, irritated by such a success, declared not to be very Beethovian.

However, this composition cannot be seen as a simple exercise — regardless of its success — in mimicry. Although the wind instruments of the *Septet* 'are still reminiscent of the 18th century' (Dorel Handman), they receive from Schubert a treatment which foreshadows romanticism. Also, typically of Schubert, the 'copy' is different in its format, as it is almost twice as long as the 'original'.

The first movement (*adagio-allegro*) is distinguished by the complete use made of the range of tonal colours created by the richness of instrumental combinations. The following *adagio* entrusts the theme to the clarinet before developing the movement through dialogues between woodwind and strings. The *allegro vivace* is a rhythmically well-defined scherzo and the trio delegates the exposition of a march-like melody to the cello. The *andante* includes seven slightly mechanical variations of an operetta theme which Schubert wrote in 1815, *Die Freunde von Salamanka*. The only slightly weak movement of the piece is the fifth (*menuetto* and trio) which is responsible for putting into relief the finale (*andante molto allegro*). This is an ample construction in five parts which plays, as is common with Schubert, on atmospheric contrasts and abandons the playful spirit which existed at the beginning of the work.

Historical references

Composed in 1824 for a commission, the work was played for a private audience in 1825, and the first public performance did not take place until 1827. Published in 1853, without the fourth and fifth movements, the *Octet* only achieved its integral edition in 1875.

Rhapsodies

The *rhapsody* (from *rhapsode*, an itinerant singer of Ancient Greece who recited epic poems) is an essentially romantic instrumental or symphonic composition in a free style and form, fairly similar to the fantasia, but based on national or regional themes and rhythms. When it appeared at the beginning of the 19th century, the rhapsody reflected the Nationalist conscience of certain European peoples. It also led to the extension of musical language to the general population, as it integrated many folk elements.

Venceslas Tomasek, a Czech musician adept at improvisation, is considered to be the first to have composed pieces of this genre, but musical history tends to regard the *Hungarian Rhapsodies* by Franz Liszt as the first pieces. Throughout the 19th and up until the beginning of the 20th century, this free form was expanded in several works, such as Dvořák's *Slavonic Rhapsodies*, Lalo's *Norwegian Rhapsody*, Ravel's *Spanish Rhapsody*, Gershwin's *Rhapsody in Blue*, Rachmaninov's *Rhapsody on a theme by Paganini*, and Béla Bartók's two *Violin Rhapsodies*.

Liszt, Franz

Hungarian Rhapsodies for piano, 1853 and 1885

A magnified folk music

The famous Hungarian Rhapsodies *borrow their scale, their rhythms and their taste for ornamentation from the gipsy style.*

The extreme popularity of the most well-known of these *Rhapsodies* (No.2, No.6, No.12, No.15) has, for a long time, eclipsed Liszt's major works (*Sonata in B minor, Années de pèlerinage*, etc). In their place, and well-played, these pieces are pianistically skillful, seductive, sometimes a bit affected in their eloquence, and often less virtuosic than they appear to be.

Historical references

Composed between 1840 and 1853, the first fifteen *Hungarian Rhapsodies*, originally published in separate collections, were grouped together in 1853. The last four, written between 1882 and 1885, were published in 1885. Liszt orchestrated *Rhapsodies* No.2 and No.12.

Gershwin, George

Rhapsody in Blue for piano and orchestra, 1924

A succession of spectacular effects

Rhapsody in Blue *combines a concertante piano part inspired by jazz with other parts of symphonic character.*

Two of the four principal themes of *Rhapsody in Blue* are particularly famous: the first, exposed by the clarinet right at the beginning of the composition, follows the famous ascending *glissando* played by the same instrument, before being repeated by the muted trumpet and then, on more distinct rhythms, by the piano and orchestra. The second movement, with touches of Blues, introduced rather late, is first played by the violins with syncopated support from the trombones which alleviate the outrageously melodious tone.

Historical references

Composed originally (in 1924) for Paul Whiteman's jazz band, *Rhapsody in Blue* was orchestrated in 1926. It is this version that is most well-known today.

Serenades

In accordance with its etymology (*serus* = 'late'), the term *serenade* means 'evening music', just as *aubade* means 'dawn music'. Originally — from the troubadours and medieval minstrels to the Venetian gentlemen of the 17th century — serenade meant only a concert with voice and instruments played at night under the window of a person in order to honour or seduce them. Nevertheless, in parallel with this current meaning, musicians wrote, from the end of the 16th century, vocal and instrumental serenades of a celebratory nature and, in the first half of the 18th century, a *sereneta*, intended for the theatre, had developed.

In the classical era, composers used the term *serenade* for free-form instrumental works made up of several different movements and written for a relatively large orchestra. Usually written for specific occasions, and in a gallant style, the *serenade*, more worked than the divertimento but less tightly constructed than the symphony, falls somewhere between these two forms. Mozart was the primary 18th-century representative of the very orchestral serenade ('*Haffner*' Serenade, 1776 among others); but, after 1780 his serenade pieces were more like chamber music (*Eine kleine Nachtmusik*, 1787, is written exclusively for strings), while the symphony which dominated at the time virtually monopolized orchestral work.

In the Romantic era the instrumental serenade, almost entirely fallen into disuse, still resulted in several works (Brahms, Dvořák, Tchaikovsky and Hugo Wolf).

Among the composers of the 20th century, we must certainly mention the achievement of Arnold Schönberg, with *opus 24* for seven instruments (1923), which contains a movement that recalls the origins of the serenade, as it requires a voice.

Mozart, Wolfgang Amadeus

Serenade No.13, Eine kleine Nachtmusik, 1787

G major, K.525

The popular Mozart

Because of its relatively simple writing and melodic charm, Eine kleine Nachtmusik *has come to embody the finesse and clarity of Mozartian discourse to such an extent as to trivialize them.*

A composition for two violins, a viola, a cello and a double bass which plays in unison with the cello throughout, the *Serenade* K.525 comes across as a string quartet which is 'reinforced' in the low register by the double bass. Belonging, because of its instrumentation, to chamber music, it is an example of the genre of serenade because of its initial structure (five movements, one of which, a minuet with trio between the *allegro* and *andante*, has disappeared) and its sound, no doubt associated with an outdoor execution at an evening concert.

The first movement, *allegro*, begins with four bars (*intrada*) of a somewhat dry solemnity, which is quickly broken by the lively character of the first theme which achieves, due to the symmetric arrangement of its different parts, a lovely, rhyth-

mic, formal balance. It is followed by a second theme in D major which is very rhythmical and opens on a high-spirited phrase played by the two violins with the hushed accompaniment of the basses. Repeated alternately with its rhythmic thematic introduction, this phrase moves towards a simple, popular-style conclusion. After the repetition of the first four bars, the development appears, based on a modulation of the second theme and is followed by the successive reappearance of the *intrada*, the first theme and the second theme.

The second movement (*andante*: romance in C) has the smooth character of a reverie. But it also includes an abruptly stark change from C major to C minor representing the seriousness that is rarely absent even from Mozart's most apparently light-hearted works. But the return to the key of C major re-establishes the seductive appeal of the 'gallant' musical reverie.

Vigorous, and somewhat solemn, the brief minuet which follows is connected to a charming trio in D minor. This third movement precedes the final rondo built on a single theme whose alacrity conveys very well the mixture of almost folk merriment and bourgeois civility which is so typical of Mozart.

Historical references

Eine kleine Nachtmusik was composed in Vienna in 1787, the same year that Mozart produced some of his greatest works, including the *String quintets* in C major K.515 and in G minor K.516, and *Don Giovanni*.

Besides his *Serenades for strings*, Mozart also composed many serenades for wind instruments. The *Serenade No.10 in B flat major 'Gian Partita'* K.361 is one of his greater works. It dates from 1781.

Sonatas

At a relatively early stage in its development, in the 16th century, the *sonata* was no more than the 'sounded' (*sonare* 'to play an instrument') instrumental version of a vocal piece (cantata, from *cantare*, 'to sing').

In the 17th century, without adopting any well-defined form, but rather taking on aspects of the *ricercare*, a prelude or the overture, the sonata ultimately merged with the dance suite; 'a fusion which for a long time resulted in nothing but confusion' (André Hodeir). Around 1670–80, the Italians established a distinction between the *sonata da chiesa* (church sonata) in four movements and the *sonata da camera* (chamber sonata) in three movements, both of which were most often written for two types of instrumental formations: one solo violin and basso continuo (*solo sonata*), two violins and a basso continuo (*trio sonata*). The development of the trio sonata with G. Legrenzi, G. Bononcini and principally A. Corelli (opus 1 to 4, 1681–94) had repercussions on all European music (F. Couperin, J. S. Bach, G. P. Telemann, G. F. Handel) until 1760. It was accompanied by an evolutionary process which freed the *sonata da camera* from the dance suites — the names of which have been replaced by indications of movement — and established, at the beginning of the 18th century, the formal structure of the pre-classical sonata, called monothematic because each of its four movements (slow introduction, *allegro*, *adagio* or *vivace*) is constructed on the basis of a single theme.

Around 1750, when the violin was losing its pre-eminence over the harpsichord (as a result of the movement started in France in 1733), the dithematic sonata made its first appearance. The structure of this new form (three alternating movements 'fast-slow-fast' with two themes per movement) was established by C. P. E. Bach (*Sonatas with different repeats*, 1759). The dithematic sonata co-existed for a long time with monothematism. A bit later (1760) the dimensions of the dithematic sonata were expanded to four movements: *allegro*, *adagio*, *minuet*, *finale*. This was the classical sonata structure adopted, if not faithfully followed, by Haydn, Mozart and Beethoven. The first movement (exposition, development, recapitulation often followed by a coda) respected the sonata-form which became the 'typical structure' of most chamber music works (trios, quartets, quintets, etc.) and symphonic orchestra compositions.

In the Romantic era, the sonata was a piece reserved principally for the solo piano. The modifications introduced by Beethoven to the sonata-form encouraged Schubert, Schumann, Brahms, Chopin and Liszt to take liberties: 'The original two themes increased; to three or four in Brahms, and five in Liszt. In their defence, the composers did not shrink back from complexity. The vertical harmony of classicism gives way, at times, to polyphony, even to chromaticism' (Sylvette Milliot). Already presaged by Beethoven, Schumann, Liszt and Brahms, the cyclic form which César Franck was the first to use (*Sonata for piano and violin*, 1886) gave the sonata a new formal cohesion.

In the 20th century, from Fauré to Boulez and including Debussy, Ravel and Prokofiev, the sonata retained its appeal; it provided the opportunity of testing the impact of transgressing an aesthetic based on a fundamental structure (the sonata-form) of instrumental music.

Outline of the classical sonata

- FIRST MOVEMENT (sonata *allegro*)

Sonata-form

Exposition:
- — 1st theme in the principal key
- — modulation towards the key of the dominant
- — 2nd theme in the dominant
- — cadence in the dominant

Repeat of the exposition (almost always done)

Development: — fragmentation and modulation of the two themes, dramatically preparing the return to the tonic (or *re-entry* in the principal key)

Recapitulation:
- — 1st theme in the principal key
- — non-modulating transition
- — 2nd theme in the principal key

Optional coda

- SECOND MOVEMENT (slow movement)

Lied form

A: — initial theme moving towards the dominant
- — modulation, also towards the dominant
- — recapitulation of initial theme, concluding at the tonic

B: — modulating central section

A':— repeat of A, optionally modified

or

Theme and variations

- THIRD MOVEMENT

Minuet or Scherzo

A: — 1st section

B: — trio

A':— repeat of A, sometimes modified

- FOURTH MOVEMENT (finale)

Sonata-form (cf first movement)

and/or

Rondo-form (alternation of refrains and verses)

Scarlatti, Domenico

Harpsichord Sonatas, 1738–1757

The keyboard in a flurry of excitement

Influenced by the flamenco and heralding the Viennese classical style, Scarlatti's Sonatas *invented an extremely virtuoso instrumental style, specific to the keyboard.*

Although Scarlatti's *Sonatas* all contain only one movement, they are all divided into two parts. Each first half consists of taking its musical discourse from a principal key to a final key, with the assistance of a series of cadenzas; and each second half distances itself from the final key in order to re-establish the principal key. These fundamentally binary *Sonatas* are thus distinct from the classical sonata-form with its tripartite division (exposition, development, recapitulation). But they resemble it in their principle of modulating development which allows for the passing from one key to another. Furthermore, as Ralph Kirkpatrick pointed out, Scarlatti's sonata is similar, in its first half, to the classical exposition, and the first part of its second half foreshadows the sonata-form's development and the second part its recapitulation. 'It is the harmonic orientation which centres on a main tonal core, which is the distinguishing mark of Scarlatti's form.' This stability of tonal structure allows the musician to show 'a semblance of casualness in the distribution of thematic material', and even to produce the impression of great unpredictability. Moreover, many of these *Sonatas* are arranged into groups of twos, where the coupled pieces are just as likely to be opposing as complementary.

While in Spain, Scarlatti became fascinated by Iberian folklore. Thus the rhythmic complexity of his *Sonatas* and some of the features of their writing — such as 'the great dissonant chords, often evoking the guitar' (Marc Vignal) — come in part from the Andalusian flamenco. But this music is especially striking today due to its virtuosity and to the invention of a keyboard technique which combines interval leaps, crossing of the hands, and series of trills and arpeggios.

Historical references

Scarlatti's first 30 *Sonatas* were published in 1738, under the title of *Essercizi per gravicembalo*, and the composition of the entire collection of sonatas lasted until 1757. But they appear, for the most part, to have been written between 1752 and 1757.

Of the 555 *Sonatas*, no original copy remains, and we owe the knowledge of their existence primarily to copies made after 1752.

The first attempt at an exhaustive edition (*554 Sonatas*) was undertaken from 1906 to 1937 by Alessandro Longo. And the final edition, based on Kirkpatrick's numbering, finished in 1953, was produced in the 1970s by Kenneth Galbraith.

Mozart, Wolfgang Amadeus

Piano Sonata No.14, 1785

C minor, K.457

The darker side of Mozart's writing

The Sonata in C minor *K.457, without a doubt one of Mozart's most accomplished works, stems from a new 'Mozartian exploration of tragic feeling' (Charles Rosen).*

Too often thought of, due to its tonality and its dramatic nature, to be a pre-Beethovian work, the *C minor Sonata* K.457 has no real similarities with *Pathétique* (C minor), *Appassionata* (F minor) or any other sonata by the great German composer. Nothing in it, for example, foreshadows the rhythmic conflicts so typical of Beethovian style and so unlike Mozart's enharmonic modulations. The writing style and the formal dynamics of the *Sonata* K.457 are specifically Mozartian; but, and it is perhaps this that comes as a surprise, the mood of this composition breaks away from the gallant style (liveliness and vivacity whether apparent or real) which Mozart, grosso modo, adhered to until 1780, even though, despite its tonal dramatism, this Sonata ultimately remained true to the 'duty of remaining pleasant' (Jean Massin).

An impression of anxious tension emerges in the first movement, a rapid sonata-form *allegro* built on two highly-opposing themes, both of which express a restrained exaltation which proceeds to grow and reaches its climax with a coda which finishes on ten sibylline bars in a totally surprising, cursory manner.

The central movement, in E flat major (*adagio sotto voce*), is loose and lyrical and develops calmly. The overlapping of these vaguely melancholy melodies are enriched by cadenzas which evoke the Mozart of piano concertos. A demisemiquaver beat in the last bars of the piece, hints at the turbulent musical discourse to follow in the finale (*allegro assai*) whose form is a compromise between the sonata and the rondo.

Interspersed with many rests and broken up by pauses, this finale ends concisely, as though it had been cut short.

Historical references

Mozart composed this sonata in Vienna in 1784. The reasons for publishing this piece jointly with the *Fantasia in C minor* K.475 have never been made clear. Together, the two works were dedicated to his student and hostess at the time, the pianist Theresa von Trattner.

Haydn, Joseph

Sonata No.62, 1798

E flat major, H.XVI.52

An orchestral piano style

The group of Haydn's last three sonatas, to which this work belongs, represent an art in search of new values.

The pieces which make up this last series of Haydn's sonatas have a curious stylistic unity; 'the essential and shared characteristic of these sonatas is the instrumental writing: each begins with what *sounds* like a string quartet and many passages almost call for orchestral instruments' (Stéphane Goldet). This pianistically powerful writing which is fairly compact, almost symphonic and radically different from Mozart's, which is more distinguished by vocal music, discovered in the 19th century its logical extension not only in Beethoven but in Schubert and even Schumann.

Two other major sonatas

The very short *Sonata No.61 in D minor* with two movements includes an *Andante con moto*, 'a sort of pre-Schubertian impromptu followed by an extraordinary *presto* in half-tones with a persistent rhythm and notes linked together in Schumann's style' (Marc Vignal). There is also a pre-Schumann element in the rhythmic mood of the final *allegro molto* of the *Sonata No.60 in C major*, whose stunning initial allegro, based on a single theme embellished by a different countermelody at each of its three occurrences, foreshadows Beethoven.

With *Sonata No.62* (in three movements), Haydn gives evidence of his exceptional ability to create, in only a few bars, the extraordinary impression of sonorous blossoming. In its thematic work and on the level of tonal relations, the work establishes its innovative character; for example, during the initial *allegro moderato* the central development, exclusively a tributary of the second theme and beginning in C major, modulates abruptly into E minor in order to justify the choice of this key as the dominant key in the following movement which is a wonderful *adagio* with a central section in E minor. This *adagio*, reminiscent of Chopin in its ornamentations and its atmosphere of a nocturne, is followed by the final *presto* in sonata-form, a monothematic piece which nonetheless gives the impression of great melodic diversity.

Historical references

Haydn probably composed his last three sonatas during his second visit to London (1794–1795). The *Sonata No.62* was published in Vienna in 1798.

The catalogue of Haydn's 52 Sonatas compiled in 1918 by Anthony Van Hoboken (H = Hoboken) is today replaced by the classification done by the musicologist Robbins Landon who established a chronology of Haydn's works which included 62 sonatas, seven of which had been considered lost.

Beethoven, Ludwig van

Piano Sonata No.8 'Pathétique', 1799

C minor, opus 13

A collection of opposites

Integrating quasi-psychological values with pure music, the Pathétique *is a highly conflicting work.*

The first movement of the *Pathétique allegro di molto e con brio*, is preceded by a slow introduction marked 'grave' with an atmosphere and *tempo* that contrast with those of the *allegro* itself. This dramatic opposition is a driving force of this movement as it appears twice in the introduction. The *adagio cantibile* which follows has the shape of a rondo. Its refrain is a kind of 'romance without words' whose accompaniment is presented more rapidly each time. Alternating and contrasting with it, the verses' structures are less clear. With the aim of unification, the final *rondo-allegro* cites the first four notes of the first movement.

Historical references

Completed in 1798, the 'Pathétique' was published in 1799.

'Moonlight' Sonata for piano No.14, 1802

C sharp minor, opus 27, No.2

An autobiographical triptych?

Despite its unusual form, this sonata headed 'quasi una fantasia', received rave reviews.

The '*Moonlight*' *Sonata* joins together a piece in lied-form, a minuet and a sonata-form piece. The work owes its cohesion to the fact that its tempo accelerates in each of these movements. The first, *adagio sostenuto*, remarkable in its timbre effects, creates the impression of a continuous tone from which 'an imaginary viola' (Jörg Demus) is occasionally heard. The second, *allegretto*, is more tied to the music of the 18th century. The *Sonata* closes on a very rhythmically virtuoso *presto agitato*.

Historical references

The two sonatas of opus 27 were composed in 1801 and published in 1802. Beethoven later said of the second one that it was not his best.

The sub-title 'Moonlight' is an invention of the poet Ludwig Rellstab and does not signify anything.

Beethoven, Ludwig van

Piano Sonata No.23 'Appassionata', 1807

F minor, opus 57

A controlled excess

Displaying an entirely new musical strength and a concentration up to then unparalleled in Beethoven, the Appassionata *follows a rigid plan which keeps the power under control.*

Beethoven's *23rd Sonata* contains three movements. The first, *allegro assai*, vaster than any written previously by the composer, 'is divided into four clear sections all of which (exposition, development, recapitulation, and coda) begin with the principal theme' (Charles Rosen). But this very strict outline contains several irregularities for a sonata *allegro*: the second theme is a variant of the first, the conventional repeat of the exposition does not occur, and the development gives an almost preponderant role to the second theme, and recapitulation is more of a transmutation of the exposition than a simple repeat of it,

and the scope of the coda is unusually large. Furthermore, the musical discourse is interrupted in several strategic places by a motif of four notes which, amplified, runs throughout the *Fifth Symphony*. But this formal outline does not fully define the movement. Rather, it acts as a framework for the unfolding of a musical structure whose originality comes from the fact that Beethoven used sound parameters for dramatic ends. These contrasts of sound, which resulted in the production of a specifically musical 'suspense', have been extensively analysed by André Boucourechliev. These contrasts which affect the very nature of sound are principally caused by modifications of harmony, the use of rests, rhythmic changes and by the opposition of the low, medium and high registers (giving it timbre value), by abrupt variations in intensity, differences of mass (contrasts created between isolated notes and sonorous blocks) and finally by changes of tempo (particularly in the coda).

The variations of the second movement, *andante con moto*, take on, for the first time, 'the dramatic shape and spatial proportions of the sonata style' (Charles Rosen). The general form of the movement corresponds to an 'ascent by octaves from the lowest to the highest extreme'. When the theme finally returns to the low register it 'seems not like a *da capo* but like a true sonata recapitulation' (C. Rosen). But this movement also serves as the introduction to the final *allegro ma non troppo*, a kind of perpetuum mobile of great rhythmic violence.

Historical references

Drafted in 1804 and completed in October 1806, the *23rd Sonata* was published in Vienna in February 1807.

An acceptable sub-title

Beethoven supposedly accepted the sub-title 'Appassionata' which was given to his Sonata in a late edition.

From 1804 to 1810

Started at the same time as *Appassionata*, his *21st Sonata* opus 53, 'Waldstein' (1804) headed the series of Beethoven's 'second period' sonatas. The *26th Sonata*, opus 81a 'Les Adieux' (1810) was also part of this group.

Beethoven, Ludwig van

Piano Sonata, No.29, 'Hammerklavier', 1819

B flat major, opus 106

The impression of hearing the structure (C. Rosen)

A work which is excessive in its duration (45 minutes), its concentration and its difficulty of execution, the 'Hammerklavier' Sonata *owes its radical modernity to the clarity of its structure.*

Despite its undeniable originality, the 'Hammerklavier' *Sonata* follows the classical structure of four movements — but these are manipulated to Beethoven's requirements.

The first movement — *allegro* — contains four sections: an exposition immediately repeated, a development in *fugato*, a recapitulation profoundly transformed from the exposition, and a conclusion. One of the originalities of this movement lies in the fact that the same material determines both the details of the discourse (the melodic profile) and the harmonic structure of the whole (the modulations). Although this *allegro*, and certainly its development, is almost uniquely constructed on descending thirds, the sequence of keys in various sections is also determined by descending thirds, (for example from *B* flat major to *G* major). In other words, the thematic material and the large scale structure are derived one from the other and 'this results in Beethoven's greatest structural innovation' (Charles Rosen). Furthermore, the relations between these two levels — the part and the whole — are 'set off in such a way that their kinship is immediately audible' (C. Rosen).

The other movements of the sonata also respect this principle of unification, but generally in a much more relaxed way. The brief second movement, a scherzo — extraordinary in its timbre fluctuations — appears to be a parody of the first. This is followed by the third; 'the most beautiful slow sonata movement ever written' according to André Boucourechliev, an *adagio sostenuto* with hints of Chopin. The work finishes with a monumental fugue, introduced by the insertion of a striking section acting as a transition with the preceding *adagio* which gives the impression of being improvised and yet completely systematized at the same time. In effect, 'we are literally witnesses to a contrapuntal texture gradually taking shape and growing organically out of unformed material' (Charles Rosen). The fugue theme — coloured by the trill on its second note — is thus able to express itself and develop right up to the paroxysms of the very last bars.

Historical references

Composed between 1817 and 1819, the *29th Sonata* was published immediately after its completion.

This *29th Sonata* got its sub-title 'Hammerklavier' (German for pianoforte) from Beethoven having exquisitely written up his title-page in German. When his sonata was finished the composer declared 'Now I know how to write', but also said 'Here is a sonata which will give the pianists who play it 50 years from now a real challenge'.

Beethoven's last five sonatas, composed between 1816 and 1822, make up one of the peaks in the history of Occidental music.

Schubert, Franz

Piano Sonata, 1828

B flat major, D.960 (posthumous opus)

A 'static and unpredictable' extension *(A. Brendel)*

Schubert exploited the genre of piano sonata by indulging in melodic-harmonic experiments which were more original than they seemed. This work is one of the best examples.

Two themes are exposed in the initial movement *(molto moderato)* of the *Sonata in B flat major*. The first, in which Schubert's intimacy flows freely, is the object of extensive developments which could be considered repetitions — despite being treated with an uncommon sense of variation — giving the impression of an improvisation without rules. Shortly after the central development, the opposition between the first and second theme gives rise to a movement of violent emotional tension (D minor): however, the prompt return to a gentle melodic flow restores a calm which is sustained until the coda. This very long movement (about 14 minutes), typical of what Schumann called a 'heavenly duration', is followed by an *andante sostenuto* in C sharp minor, the most beautiful section of the work in which 'the *ostinato* formula of the accompaniment creates a hallucinatory or hypnotic effect which immediately plunges back into the tragic atmosphere of the lieder *Winter Journey*' (Brigitte Massin).

The scherzo marked *allegro vivace con delicatezza* contrasts, in its lightness, with the *andante*; its very tense trio, rich in harmonic subtleties and rhythmic precisions, is surprising in its extremely concise writing.

The piece concludes with a rondo of three themes, *allegro ma non troppo*, which emphasizes insistently its initial theme, now skilfully ornamented with many secondary motifs.

A triptych

Composed after the series of *sonatas D.958 in C minor* and *D.959 in A major*, the *Sonata D.960 in B flat major* forms, with these, what Schubert considered to be a triptych. There are many stylistic similarities which give this series the cohesion of a whole: the piano has orchestral overtones in the three pieces, each sonata makes almost orchestral use of the low register of the instrument, and all three put in relief important rests which are responsible for creating suspense amidst the melodic flow abounding in repetitive motifs, and for bringing out the chromatic harmonies used to create the effect of tension.

Historical references

Schubert completed his trilogy of *piano sonatas* in September 1828, barely eight weeks before his death. They were not published until 1838.

Chopin, Frédéric

Piano Sonata No.2 'Funèbre', 1839

B flat major, opus 35

An undoubtedly misunderstood work

Unlike Liszt (Sonata in B minor), *Chopin did not revolutionize the genre of piano sonata, but rather renovated it, especially with the Sonata No.2, 'Funèbre'.*

This composition, which comes across as a 'heterogenous construction' (Camille Bourniquel), begins with a solemn motif — 'grave' — of four bars, immediately giving the work a tension which the first theme, introduced by the *doppio movimento* passage, carries until the exposition of the second theme (in D flat). This theme is calmer at first, but leads progressively to the return of the general atmosphere of tension. Issuing from the first theme and motif, the development, from change of key to change of key, finishes off mingled with the recapitulation: this is one of the great formal audacities of

the work which had for a long time been interpreted as a blunder.

The scherzo, in E flat minor, accentuates the dramatic implications of the first movement. At its centre a somewhat sad but very melodic waltz of sorts takes the place of the trio.

A piece popularized by innumerable orchestra transcriptions (one of which was played at Chopin's funeral), the *Marche funèbre* (Funeral March) was composed before the rest of the sonata. The heroic-funereal figured highly in the comments about this passage describing a ceremonial of the acceptance of death. It also includes a pretty melody, repeated several times, which is ultimately more interesting than the relentless and imposing theme of the *March*.

A very surprising finale, astonishingly short (one minute and 13 seconds), serves as the fourth movement. In this section, we discover 'nothing solid on the melodic or harmonic level, but there are octaves played by both hands in a kind of dramatic quest which defies analysis'. The only indication given by the composer for this *presto* is *sotto voce e legato*. This is adequate for those who like to give meaning to the music making it represents 'the wind which whistles over the tombs' (Jacques Bourgeois).

Chopin's contemporaries who admired his work right from the beginning, were very critical of his *Sonata No.2*. Mozart hated the finale, Liszt felt that it contained 'more will than inspiration' and Schumann considered it a 'joke' that Chopin gave the name sonata to such a disparate work which started 'with discords', continued 'with discords' and finished 'in discords'.

Historical references

Completed in the summer of 1839, in Nohant, the *Sonata* No.2 was started in Mallorca where Chopin was spending the winter of 1838–9 with George Sand. It was published in Paris in 1839.

Liszt, Franz

Piano Sonata, 1853

B minor

A new type of sonata

Composed of a single vast movement in cyclic form, Liszt's Sonata in B minor *overturned the structures of the classical sonata.*

While the *Sonata in B minor* distances itself from the classical form in that it respects neither the structure nor the tonal ordering, it is nevertheless related in that it proceeds from the point to which Beethoven brought the classical sonata. Liszt exploits, on a piano treated almost orchestrally, the Beethovian principle of thematic dualism used for dramatic ends. And Liszt's developments, consisting of a complex entanglement of various themes, make use of a Beethovian process of variation.

The *Sonata*, due to its daring innovations, stunned the public at its first performance. Very few people appreciated it, except Wagner, who was full of enthusiasm.

Crossed dedications

Robert Schumann had dedicated his *Fantasia in C minor* (1839) to Liszt. So the latter dedicated, in exchange, his *Sonata in B minor* to Schumann. The chassé-croisé thus associated the main piano works of these two musicians, which were also two of the most important pieces of Romantic music.

One can detect in this sonata the concurrent superimposition of two structures: 'that of a big sonata-form in one movement and that of a great "cycle" of four linked movements' (François Lehel). It is clear that this formal dialectic rests on the 'systematic transformation' of a base material made up of five themes, three of which are principal.

The four sections can be presented in the following way: corresponding to the exposition of a sonata-form, the first section opens on a slow introduction announcing a first theme (A) before exposing the first two main themes (B + C) and opposing them in an *allegro energico* development. Next comes a *grandioso* section built on the third principal theme (D), then the piece progresses through an overlapping of the themes BCD, until reaching the coda.

Corresponding to the development of a sonata-form, the second section contains two movements; a lied-form and a scherzando. The lied-form expresses, *andante*, a new theme (E), and then repeats some of the preceding themes (D + A). The *scherzando* is a fugal *allegro* on two of the main themes (B + C).

The third section corresponds to a recapitulation. The themes B + C are also redeveloped (or varied), and then theme D is. Finally, after the coda which repeats all the themes one last time, the decidedly cyclical *Sonata* returns to its starting point, and finishes on a repeat of the slow introduction.

Historical references

Composed in 1852–3, the *Sonata in B minor* came only four years after Liszt moved to Weimar, and six years after he gave up his career as a virtuoso to become a composer.

Scriabin, Alexandre

Piano Sonata No.10, 1913

Opus 70

'Sonorous spatterings' (A. Lischke)

The Scriabin of the Sonata No.10 *is both a discover of atonality and the man of late neo-romanticism.*

The *Sonata No.10* links together its elements in a single continuous movement. Its prologue of 38 bars (*moderato*, 'very smooth and pure') is followed by a motif to be played with a 'deep and veiled ardour which lit-

Scriabin also called this *sonata 'of trills'*, the *'Insect'* sonata.

erally 'atomizes' itself with trills. A second fairly tense motif (*allegro* 'with emotion') which calls on the entire piano, combines with various fragments of previously exposed motifs. It is the main motif of the work. It finishes on a *presto* which reintroduces the prologue and dissolves it at the same time.

Historical references

Composed in the summer of 1913, the *Sonata No.10* was created as 'a sort of musical tribute to Nature and to the mystical Eros' (Manfred Kelkel).

Prokofiev, Sergei

7th Piano Sonata, 1943

B flat major, opus 83

A masterful rhythm

Second of the three 'War Sonatas', *this violent work marks the peak of Prokofiev's piano production.*

Considered to be the most radical of his sonatas, Prokofiev's *7th Sonata* is also the most concise of the three '*War Sonatas*'. Of its three movements, only the first is fully developed. It alternates an essentially rhythmic and strongly chromatic *allegro inquieto* with a more melodic *andantino*. This discordant, even atonal, first movement is

followed by a melodic and harmonic *andante caloroso*. The work ends with a brief toccata marked *precipitato*, whose 'massive blocks of chords, violent bassos ostinatos and powerful rhythms put the melodic aspects into the background' (Harry Halbreich), even more so than in the first movement.

Historical references

Started in 1939, the *7th Sonata* was completed in 1942 and performed by Sviatsoslav Richter on 18 January 1943.

Cage, John

Sonatas and Interludes for prepared piano, 1949

Innovative tinkering

Elaborated on the basis of a musing on the nature of sound and timbre, the Sonatas and Interludes for prepared piano *reveal the possibility of 'creating untempered sound spaces' (Pierre Boulez).*

The fact that the 16 sonatas and four interludes were composed for a 'prepared' piano means that these works contain a technique of modification of the natural sounds of an instrument, practised by John Cage himself, which consists of inserting, between the strings and inside the drum several 'foreign bodies' (nuts, wooden screws, rubbers, etc) in order to produce percussive tones.

This ballasting technique, accomplished 'in the way that we collect shells on a beach' (John Cage), indicates, in terms of the sound material, the role of chance. This chance is all the more active for given that each piece was written according to traditional musical notation, the breaking down of the keys does not lead to hearing the expected corresponding pure sounds, but rather creates, unexpectedly, muffled sounds often halfway between a note and a noise.

The unexpected character of the audible results increases with the possibility of altering the transformation elements of the original piano sounds; thus the *sonatas*, although of an invariable structure (a single movement in the style of D. Scarlatti's *Essercizi*) are capable of renewing the timbre melody supplied to them by the instrumental preparation.

The whole of this work based on particular qualities of piano sounds which 'has become a percussion orchestra for a single player' (John Cage) integrated by chance into the 'compositional make-up' of each piece, refers correlatively to a leading principle of composition which governs it, not in terms of a harmonic construction, but in relation to musical durations. It is the lapse of time occupied by a sound and divided by rests 'which creates the curious impression of statism, as if time had become space' (Claude Samuel) within an aesthetic ultimately aimed at transgressing the norms of Occidental music to approach an extremely oriental tradition which values the intrinsic qualities of each sound.

Historical references

Composed between 1946 and 1948, the series of sonatas and interludes for prepared piano is dedicated to Maro Ajemian. This pianist, after having presented a partial performance in New York in 1946, gave the first entire performance — around 70 minutes of music — at Carnegie Hall on 12 and 13 January 1949.

Boulez, Pierre

Third Piano Sonata, 1957

A union with probability

Integrating chance into the composition is at the root of this sonata. It is also a mobile work, offering the interpreter several possible 'paths'.

Pierre Boulez's *Third Sonata* — which does not have any particular shape except for some 'processes of opposition' (D. Jameux) — is mainly concerned with contrasting profoundly antagonistic material, either in writing style or in sound. The second concern of the work is completely directed towards the future, and has to do with the variable ordering of the five movements of the piece which are called *formants* and are entitled: 'Antiphonie', 'Trope', 'Constellation', 'Strophe', and 'Sequence'. The third formant must always appear in the middle and the four others may be permuted in certain combinations; so the sonata can thus be played in eight different orders. Furthermore, when movements four and five are placed before movements one

---

A contemporary Sonata

Written about the same time as Pierre Boulez's *Second Piano Sonata* (1948), Jean Barraqué's *Sonata* (1952) is also one of the major post-war serial pieces. The work, containing two connected movements (the first with a rapid tempo, the second a slow one), gets 'its dramatic intensity from the infiltration of empty spaces in the density of the material: masses, registers, blocks, bursting medleys, eroded by the anti-music which is the ultimate end … silence' (A. Féron).

---

and two, the central formant called 'Constellation-Miroir' is played backwards.

'Trope' deals with the principles of mobility which govern the general structure of the sonata. This formant contains four connected parts: 'Texte', 'Glose', 'Commentaire' and 'Parenthèse', which must be played in this order, but the interpreter is free to begin with any of the four pieces. The interpreter may also, in fact, permute 'Glose' and 'Commentaire' which creates a choice of eight possibilities. Of course, these combinations only make sense because 'the arrangement is assured by a very strict control over the initial and terminal zones' (Pierre Boulez) of each section; in other words all the conceivable transitions had been considered. But 'Trope' is also very original, pianistically.

Lasting about ten minutes, 'Constellation' contains five parts, three of which are called 'points' and the other two 'blocks'. The 'point' structures are 'based on pure isolated frequencies' and the 'block' structures correspond to 'continually varying' (Pierre Boulez) sound groups. Here again several possible paths are proposed to the interpreter. But the most interesting aspect is the exceptional exploitation made of the piano's resources: 'abandoned notes, muted notes associated with the harmonics, resonances, meticulous use of the pedal' (Claude Helffer).

Historical references

Composed in 1957, this *Third Sonata* was performed, with all five movements, in September of the same year in Darmstadt with the composer on piano. Only 'Trope' and 'Constellation' had been published at that time.

Bach, Johann Sebastian

Six Sonatas for harpsichord and violin, 1720

BWV 1014–1019

A manifesto of technical skill

Although this collection belongs to the Church Sonata tradition of the 17th century, Bach developed its concertante aspect and made the writing more contrapuntal.

In this collection, as in most of his works, composed for two instruments, J. S. Bach refers to the Italian sonata in two different ways. Firstly, five of his *Sonatas* — the 6th being an exception — respect the structure of four movements (slow-fast-slow-fast) of the *sonata da chiesa*. Secondly, their instrumental writing has traces of the trio sonata — an almost obligatory formation for the 17th-century sonata which brings together two solo instruments (usually two violins) and a basso continuo: the left hand of the keyboard takes over here the role of the bass, and the right hand 'is conceived of as the second violin part'. The harpsichord thus doubled creates a trio of sorts with the violin. This distribution is also based on the preponderant role of the harpsichord which 'directs the musical discourse, leaving the

violin to the task of acting as the often complementary ornament and reinforcement' (Alberto Basso).

Among the first five *Sonatas* BWV 1014–1018, of which the 5th is considered to be the most beautiful, one can detect constancies of movement construction from one to another. While the first movements, almost always of a unitary structure, demonstrate a rather 'cantabile' style, the second ones, on the contrary, manifest most clearly Bach's liking for counterpoint in that they are usually fugal and sometimes even actual fugues (*Sonatas* I, II, IV). The third movements restore the slow tempo of the first ones, and also have a unitary structure, but their writing is more differentiated. Finally, the fourth movements are either in the form of a fugue or a fugal-trio.

The *Sonata VI* BWV 1029, often considered to be the peak of the collection, must be examined in its own right, as it contains five movements, arranged symmetrically (*allegro, largo, allegro, adagio, allegro*) and the third, central, movement is played by the solo harpsichord.

Historical references

This collection of *Sonatas* was written when Bach was Kapellmeister in Cöthen, and we can assume that they were therefore composed between 1718 and 1722. But the *Sonata VI* is an exception for there are three versions of it, the first dating back to Cöthen, and the other two written in Leipzig. The definitive version does not seem to have been written until 1749.

As well as this collection, Bach composed several other harpsichord and violin sonatas, of which only two are definitely authentic. These are the *Sonata in G major* (BWV 1021) and the *Sonata in E minor* (BWV 1023)

Mozart, Wolfgang Amadeus

Sonata for piano and violin No.40, 1784

B flat major, K.454

An exchange between equals

The way in which this sonata creates a dialogue between the piano and the violin results in a perfect balance between the voices of the two instruments.

The *Sonata K.454* begins with a *largo* 'sequence of imperious and fresh accents' (J. and B. Massin) where the violin, after having cited note-for-note a very melodious phrase originally played on the piano, forms a 'great melody' leading towards a cadenza played with echo effects by the two instruments.

The free dialogue established by the following *allegro* is typical of this sometimes introverted, sometimes extroverted Mozartian musical discourse, in which the *cantabile* remains extraordinarily supple regardless.

An *andante* in E flat with three themes follows the *allegro*. This is one of Mozart's

When he composed the Sonata for piano and violin K.454 (April 1784) with the intention of having it played by the Italian violinist Regina Strinasacchi who was passing through Vienna, Mozart did not have enough time to transcribe — and perhaps not even to finish writing — the piano part which he was to play alongside the young virtuoso, and played it practically from memory the night of the concert (29 April).

most beautiful passages; it is grand and full of grace even in the formulation of what seems to most critics to be the expression of sorrow (second theme exposed by the violin). Preceded by a rest, the development by the violin (B flat major) of the main theme accentuates the dramatic tension of the piece: it creates a very tight dialogue between the piano and the violin, rich in echoes and modulations, and then returns entirely unexpectedly to the initial theme. The interchanges between the two instruments increase within very brief intervals (rarely more than two bars long), until coming to a cadenza which is not derived from any earlier motif and which follows the repeat of a fairly sombre ritornello (first section of the *andante*) modified on the violin by a new melodic line. The final bar gives this movement a conclusion tinged with solemnity.

In the third and last part of the work, an *allegretto* with all the characteristics of a rondo, the dialogues resume in a fluent and lively manner, giving the impression of 'a kind of mental drunkenness' (J. and B. Massin), in part based on the exceptional quality of the thematic links.

Historical references

Contemporary with his *Piano Concertos* Nos.17 (K.453) and 18 (K.456) as well as the *Quintet for piano and strings* K.452, the *Sonata* K.454 has several structural similarities with these compositions (the violin and piano alternatively play a concertante part).

Beethoven, Ludwig van

Sonata for piano and violin No.9 'Kreutzer', 1805

A major, opus 47

Piano and violin dynamics

A work from Beethoven's 'second period' (1800–1814), the 'Kreutzer' Sonata makes an essential contribution to the elaboration of the 'heroic' style.

Based on a rhythmic, harmonic and thematic unity, coming from the classicism of Haydn and Mozart, the *Sonata opus 47*, in its deliberately concertante style (Beethoven noted for the first edition: 'written in a *molto concertante* style, almost like a concerto'), represents a considerable expansion of this unity.

According to Charles Rosen, his first movement — a *presto* in A minor preceded by an *adagio sostenuto* in A major — 'is unequalled in formal clarity, grandeur and dramatic force by anything that Beethoven had yet written'. The rhythmic vigour of the violin gives the initial theme of this *presto* a striking depth; the theme in question, played afterwards by the piano, in melodic-harmonic figures with hints of the '*Appas-*

sionata' and '*Moonlight*' Sonatas, reappears as the stakes of a battle between two instruments compelled to engage in multiple attacks of virtuosity.

The second movement is an *andante* followed by four variations, which are not greatly modified from their theme: the first favours the piano, the second the violin, and the third balances the relation between these two instruments, while the fourth, after citing the theme, reveals a pre-romantic stylistic tendency 'in a very Schumann-like conclusion' (André Boucourechliev).

The work finishes on a brilliant light-hearted *presto* with the rhythm of a tarentella. The piano and violin engage in a renewed display of virtuosity.

Historical references

The first two movements of *Opus 47* were drafted at the beginning of 1803 (the third dates from 1802) and were finished in great haste by Beethoven who wanted to play his work as a duet with the famous English violinist George Bridgetower (1778–1860) at a concert on 24 May 1803 in Vienna. Originally offered to Bridgetower, the *Sonata No.9* was finally, at the time of its publication, dedicated to the French virtuoso Rodolphe Kreutzer who is said to have never played it in public, judging it to be 'unintelligible'. According to the critic of the *Allgemeine Musicalische Zeitung*, Beethoven 'pushed the concern with originality in this composition to the point of making it grotesque'.

Rodolphe Kreutzer (1766–1831), to whom Beethoven dedicated his *Sonata opus 47*, was a violin professor at the Paris Conservatory from 1795 to 1826. He was also known as the composer of the *42 Études or caprices*, written for teaching the piano and whose pedagogical value is so great that they are still used today.

Fauré, Gabriel

Violin and piano sonata No.1, 1876

A major, opus 13

When the sonata goes into extra time ...

With this work, Fauré endowed the genre of sonata with a pre-Debussyan formal flexibility.

Saint-Saëns praised this sonata for 'the originality of its forms, its studied modulations, its novel sonorities and the use of entirely unexpected rhythms'. To this he added that the charm of the work made the innovations seem natural. Of the four movements which

it contains, the third, an *allegro vivo* scherzo, is the most original in its rhythmic effects and the rare conciseness of its writing, among other qualities.

Historical references

Composed in 1875, the *1st Sonata for violin and piano* was published in 1876 and performed on 27 January, 1877. The second dates from 1916.

Debussy, Claude

Violin and piano sonata, 1917

G minor

Turning towards the past

As with his two earlier sonatas, Debussy referred to the old French Masters, out of a sense of nationalism.

The last of Debussy's three *sonatas*, this one for violin and piano is the most frequently played. It contains three movements: *allegro vivo*, a whimsical and light interlude, and a very lively finale. The music is very fluid and often marked with hints of Spain (the second theme of the interlude and some of the rhythms of the finale).

Of the two other *Sonatas*, the one for cello and piano comes the closest to the 'compartmentalized and fragmented discourse' (André Boucourechliev) of Debussy's *Études*, and the one for flute, viola and harp creates very sophisticated sound effects.

Historical references

Debussy's plan was to write six sonatas for various instruments in the style of Rameau's concerts. But he only managed to write three — the first two in 1915 and the last in 1917.

Beethoven, Ludwig van

Cello and piano sonata No.5, 1817

D major, opus 102, No.2

An outcome calling for a sequel

The last of Beethoven's cello and piano sonatas, Opus 102, No.2 *inaugurates, in its highly innovative writing, the last of the composer's styles.*

The two cello and piano sonatas of the opus 102 give evidence, firstly, of Beethoven's growing preoccupation with the principles of linking carried out by sound *masses*, and with the integration, within this balance, of increasingly marked contrasts. The second sonata of this dyptych is also unique in its presentation of a great variety of textures, going from the simple unaccompanied melody of the second movement to the complex entanglement of voices in the final fugue.

Of the three movements which make up this *Fifth Sonata*, the first, *allegro con brio*, is an epitome of musical concentration and tension. And the opposition developed between the two themes is pushed to a very high level of clarity because of their configuration: the rhythmic profile of the first is rather abrupt, and the second has a very melodic gentleness.

As Charles Rosen notes, this sonata contains the seeds of several ideas which are picked up and developed in the *Piano Sonata opus 106* 'Hammerklavier' — the most obvious being that the sublime slow movement, *adagio con molto sentimento d'affeto*, of opus 102 had already been linked to a final *fugue*.

Historical references

The years 1812–17 were, for Beethoven, a period of crisis when he hardly composed at all. Written in 1815, the two sonatas of opus 102 are among the rare works to have emerged from this period. They were published in 1817 and are dedicated to the Countess Marie Erdödy.

An Evolution

The route taken from Beethoven's first two sonatas of opus 5 to this *Fifth cello and piano sonata* is very impressive, especially if we consider that, with the first two attempts, he virtually invented the form by proposing, for the first time, an equitable alliance between the two instruments. At roughly equal distance from these two groups, is the *Third Sonata*, opus 69, written for cello and piano. Probably the most played of the five, it owes its celebrity to its scherzo, a curious example of the 'intrusion of the fantastic into instrumental music' (Olivier Alain).

The fugal finale of the *Fifth sonata* is the first occurrence of the synthesis — achieved by the later Beethoven — between drama and counterpoint. It foreshadows, besides opus 106, the *Piano Sonata opus 101* and the *Grosse Fuge for string quartet* opus 133.

To Schindler, his secretary had claimed not to understand the fugue finale of his Sonata, Beethoven replied: 'It will come'.

Bartók, Béla

Sonata for two pianos and percussion, 1937

Minute permutations of sound

Struck notes and a polytonal and discordant harmonic base make this Sonata Bartók's *most 'advanced' work, along with* Music for strings, percussion and celesta.

Slightly longer than the two other pieces of the work, the first movement of the sonata begins with a brief introduction, *assai lento*, which accelerates to the initial motif of the *allegro molto* (in C major) which is exposed in unison by the two pianos with the support of the kettledrums. This syncopated breathless motif, very skilfully renewed, is followed by a *poco più tranquillo*, a theme weaving into its complex rhythm a chromatic melody which is meant to enrich the episode before moving on to a new theme. Exploited with the help of very clever contrapuntal writing (from bar 105), this theme, after the subtle interlacings of the development (from bar

The percussive nature of all the instruments used (including the piano) make this sonata an essentially rhythmic composition. It puts the keyboards together with a fairly limited number of instruments which are struck (three kettledrums, a xylophone, two clear drums, a large drum, a suspended cymbal, a triangle and a gong), while still remaining within the framework of a classical structure: a *lento ma non troppo* movement framed by two *allegro* movements.

161), finds its logical expansion in the final fugue of the movement (from bar 332) where the initial motif and its rhythmic offshoots reappear.

With the second movement, a *lento ma non troppo* in F in lied-form, we discover the atmosphere of the 'Bartókian Nocturnes' (Michel Chion) in the fascinating murmuring effects. Its very melodic first theme gives way, in the middle of the piece, to an accompaniment (*pianissimo*) made up of a series of chromatic scales which present the piano with real problems of execution.

Somewhere between a sonata and a rondo, the third movement (*allegro non troppo*) changes the relation between the pianos and the percussion in favour of the latter. Nonetheless, the instrumental cohesion is preserved due to the fact that, all through the work, the instruments are treated equally. The xylophone, which exposes the main theme (C major), is used for its melodic possibilities. Far from ending like fireworks, the sonata finishes 'on *pianissimo* arpeggiato chords, separated by rests, and on an incessant rhythmic figure created by the clear drum which concludes by disappearing into space' (Pierre Citron).

Historical references

Commissioned to Bartók by the International Society of Contemporary Music, the *Sonata for two pianos and percussion* was composed in Budapest in the summer of 1937. It was performed in Basel on 16 January 1938, with the composer and his wife Ditta, respectively, on first and second keyboards; the percussionists Fritz Schiesser and Philipp Rühling assisted.

Suites

A *Suite* is a succession of dance movements whose *number, character*, and *relations* among each other are the three criteria which — fixed differently over the centuries — give this arrangement the status of a musical form.

The suite is the oldest of all instrumental forms: 'its origin goes back to the Middle Ages, when it was customary to group certain dances in pairs' (André Hodeir). However, it was not until the 16th century that this arrangement in twos took clear shape, where the first dance was usually moderate and of a binary rhythm and the second was fast and ternary as, for example, in the case of the pavane-gaillarde pair. But, simultaneously with this principle, and particularly with the lutists, rival suites appeared which contained as many as five dances, often linked by the same key.

It was not until the second half of the 17th century, with the great instrumental music movement, that the suite form stabilized, principally under the influence of German composers like Froberger, Kuhnau, Pachelbel and Buxtehude. The suite, from then on, had a structure of four movements: allemande, courante, sarabande and jig, to which other dances or an intro or prelude could be added, or which could be doubled by ornamental variants of a preceding dance. Corresponding to the standardization of the form, a normalization of the structure also occurred; whereby each movement tended to respect a binary division, the first part of which progresses from the initial key to the dominant, while the second then returns, by various modulations, to the principal key. At the end of the 17th century François Couperin's suites, entitled 'orders', counted among the major works of this type.

In the 18th century, it was Johann Sebastian Bach, once again, who brought the form to its highest level with, primarily, his *6 English Suites*, *6 French Suites*, *6 German Suites* or *Partitas*, all for the keyboards, *3 Sonatas and 3 Partitas* for solo violin, *6 Suites* for solo cello and *4 Suites* or *Overtures* for orchestra. But we must also mention — contemporaries of Bach — J. P. Rameau's *Pièces de clavecin* and G. F. Handel's Orchestral *Suites*. From the second half of the 18th century, the baroque form of the suite degenerated, to be more or less replaced by the divertimento and the serenade. The suite was eclipsed by the classical sonata and symphony.

However, in the 19th century and beginning of the 20th the suite reappeared in various forms, and principally in the form of stylistic pastiches such as those by Ravel (*Le Tombeau de Couperin*) and Schönberg (*Suite* opus 25). More frequently perhaps, the suite also consisted of the collection of pieces extracted from an opera, a ballet or stage music, examples of which abound; from Tchaikovsky to Stravinsky and including Bizet and Berg. The suite also sometimes took on the shape of a cycle of miniatures (Moussorgsky's *Pictures at an exhibition*).

Couperin, François

Second book of the harpsichords, 1717

The art of embellished melody

Couperin published the majority of his harpsichord music (240 pieces) in four books divided into orders, the Second of which showed a clear maturity of style and includes many outstanding works.

Eight pieces written in B flat major make up the first order (Sixth Order) of the *Second Book*. They almost all have a 'bucolic aim, as suggested by their titles, but the names given to the compositions are not "subjects"; they are more commentaries, poetic suggestions, allusions or hints' (Philippe Beaussant). *Les Moissonneurs*, a rondo with a chorus and three verses to be played 'gaily' and the famous *Barricades mystérieuses* (lively) are the most interesting pieces of the group, especially the latter with its enigmatic title, subtly interlacing lute-style rhythms which demand that the notes be played successively while remaining held.

The lute-style occurs in two pieces of the Seventh Order (eight 'gracious' pieces in G

major); *La Muse naissante* and *Les Amusements*.

The Eighth Order is composed of ten dances in B minor which, with the exception of *La Raphaële*, do not have proper titles. It includes *La Passacaille*, one of the greatest works written for the harpsichord in which tragic accents were introduced at a time when musical art was meant to amuse or to charm, not to stir the emotions.

With the ten pieces of the Ninth Order (in A major) we return to a gentle and gallant music, a homage to feminine grace: *La Princesse de Sens*, *L'Insinuante*, *La Séduisante*, etc.

In contrast, the Tenth Order (seven pieces in D major) is 'sparkling and lively, full of external splendour' (Georges Beck). The piece with which it begins, *La Triomphante*, divided into three parts, is a pastiche of theatrical depictions of the war.

A very beautiful composition, *La Castelane*, opens the Eleventh Order (five pieces in C major). It lets us appreciate Couperin's mastery in ornamentation, one of the fundamental elements of his style. The Order ends with *Les Fastes de la grande et ancienne Mxnxstrxndxsx*, a comical satire — on a falsely solemn tone — of the Ménestrandise and of the 'violists'.

As for the Twelfth and last Order of the *Second Book*, it contains eight pieces in E major. Couperin evokes equally well the merriment of a party (*La Galante*), the life of peasants (*La Fileuse*) and the figure of a mythological heroine (*L'Atalante*).

'Order' is the name which François Couperin 'Le Grand' and his disciples gave to the suite to designate a sequence of pieces composed in the same key: 'We can thus see the Order as a suite of a fairly free general structure, grouping together several often very lofty pieces' (André Hodeir). The first of Couperin's four harpsichord books contains orders one to five, the second six to 12, the third 13 to 17 and the fourth 20 to 27.

Historical references

The publication of the Four Books was spread out over 18 years: the first appeared in 1713, and the three others in 1717, 1722 and 1730.

Bach, Johann Sebastian

Partita No.2 for solo violin, before 1720

D minor, BWV 1004

The violin multiplied

In the use that they make of arpeggios and double strings, the Three Sonatas *and* Three Partitas *for solo violin succeed in producing polyphony on a monodic instrument.*

The *Partita No.2* contains, besides the usual succession of dances (allemande, courante, sarabande, jig), a monumental chaconne lasting almost half an hour, and on which the suite closes.

This Chaconne, 257 bars long, constitutes, with the fugue of *Sonata No.3* — the peak of the collection and one of the purple passages of all violin music. The illusion of hearing several instruments is particularly striking, as the 'broken chords of three and four notes create fleeting images' (Roland de Candé) but are sufficient to derive a polyphony from, containing up to four parts. The work is thus focused on technical achievement and baroque subterfuge.

This chaconne is a gigantic ensemble of variations on a thematic cell of four notes, whose development is almost completely continuous. 'To the theme itself are added other thematic representations ... each of which is varied in turn, and result in a "variation on variation"' (Alberto Basso).

Historical references

The date of composition of the *Three Sonatas* and *Three Partitas* is uncertain; but is probably prior to 1720, the date marked on the original score.

In the *Sonatas* and *Partitas*, the violin language is treated in a paradoxical way. The writing of this cycle is based on the adaptation of keyboard technique for the violin, and this transposition effort also partly explains the unprecedented — because plural — nature of the resulting sound.

Moreover, this collection is not a simple gathering of six autonomous pieces, but is highly structured. On one hand, the alternating sequence of sonatas and partitas shows that these are 'compositions which are divided into pairs, the second part of which is a corollary of the first' (Alberto Basso). On the other hand, the keys associated with each of these six pieces have been distributed according to a rigorous symmetrical system. Ultimately, while the *Three Sonatas* all respect the slow-fast-slow-fast structure, and all have a fugue as their second movement, the *Partitas* all have very varied structures.

The word 'partita' is the name that the Germans gave to the suite. However, the term also implies the idea of variation.

Achievement of polyphony on a monodic instrument by double strings and arpeggios. Extract of the chaconne *of the Partita No.2*

Bach, Johann Sebastian

Suite for solo cello No.5, around 1750

C minor, BWV 1011

The cello multiplied

The Six Suites BWV 1007 to 1012 *form a group of compositions both austere and seductive. From within this group, the* Suite No.5 *is one of the most representative.*

Written for an instrument whose highest string (A) has been tuned to one tone below normal (in G), the *Suite No.5* allows for the realization of certain chords in the key of C minor (gavottes I and II) which present significant difficulties of execution when they are played on a normally tuned cello.

More than the other pieces in the cycle, this one 'is very influenced by the French style' (Alberto Basso). The form of the prelude is that of a French overture whose second part begins with a rapid fugue theme, abundantly varied throughout the rest of the piece where it skilfully achieves a polyphonic effect. We discover the French style in the fairly solemn allemande and in

the courante (with a very lively *tempo*), while the sarabande, grave and slow, signals a pause before the bouncy gavottes and the final jig appear and accelerate the movement of the composition with dotted rhythm.

Historical references

Bach composed his *Solo Cello Suites* in Cöthen around 1718–23. The original manuscript was never discovered and the work has come to us from other copies, among which, Anna Magdelena Bach's copy is considered to have been the main source.

The *Solo Cello Suites* are founded on a less polyphonic musical writing than that used for the composition of his *Three Sonatas* and *Three Partitas for solo violin* (the strummed string instruments lend themselves less well to the exercise of polyphony than do the plucked instruments; a bow can only play two adjacent strings simultaneously). But Bach's skill is so great, and his knowledge of technical devices in terms of counterpoint so advanced, that anyone listening to the *Suites* feels that they are hearing more than one melodic line at a time. This natural proliferation of varied melodic figures, linked to the dynamics of a 'language essentially made up of phrases which are launched forward rather than being held back, and designed with great simplicity and a light-hearted spirit of invention' (Alberto Basso), seems to give the sound lines of a work like the *Suite V* their own driving force.

The *Six Suites for solo cello* all begin with a prelude followed consistently by four traditional dances (allemande, courante, sarabande and the jig, a double 'galanterie': Minuets I and II (Suites I and II), Bourées I and II (Suites III and IV) and Gavottes I and II (Suites V and VI).

Rameau, Jean-Philippe

New Suite of Pieces for the harpsichord or Third Book, 1728

The harpsichord diversified

With an undeniable originality, these New Suites each deal with a particular musical problem, like a collection of precursive études.

As was the case with the second, this *Third Book* does not respect the structure of the traditional suite. The dances (allemande, courante, sarabande, gavotte and minuets) alternate with genre pieces that have descriptive titles (*Fanfarinette, La Triomphante, Les Tricotes* ...). Furthermore, of the 16 pieces of the Book, 12 are divided into two parts, three are rondos and one is a variation piece. But it is interesting, that these three formal structures have, in Rameau's words, 'engendered different musical genres', being pieces with great variety in their writing. While some of the pieces are resolutely virtuosic and are even reminiscent of Scarlatti in their keyboard technique (*Les Trois Mains*, the *Doubles* of the *Gavotte*), others — generally the slow pieces — are more lyrical (allemande, *L'Indifférente*) or majestic (sarabande). Some pieces, of great dramatic force, seem to have been composed for the theatre (*La Triomphante, Les Sauvages, L'Egyptienne*) or for the orchestra which influenced their writing (*La Poule*).

In its entirety, this *Third Book* abounds in innovations of all kinds, as much in terms of its harmonic work and the rapidity of certain modulations, as in its rhythmic invention. However, there are certain pieces which stand out particularly from this collection. These are primarily the three initial dances, especially the allemande and the courante — for their arpeggios, their rhythmic contrasts, their counterpoint and their progressions — and the sarabande. But there are other pieces which deserve to be considered as pure music, that are equally important: *La Poule*, whose unique martellato theme and repeated chords are used for dramatic ends, and the rondo of *Sauvages*. Ultimately, it is *L'Enharmonique*, a piece intended to defend — as its title suggests — a musical theory issue, which is a passage of true classical development, long before classicism emerged.

Historical references

The date generally accepted for the publication of this *Third Book* is 1728, but in fact we only know that it was published between 1727 and 1730. There is also nothing that lets us know precisely — with one or two exceptions — when these pieces were composed.

Rameau's harpsichord works contain, besides this collection, a *First Book* (1706) consisting of a suite preceded by an unmeasured prelude, and a *Second Book* (1724) containing several major pieces ('Le Rappel des oiseaux', 'La Villageoise', 'L'entretien des muses', 'Les Cyclopes'). In 1741, Rameau also published his *Concert Pieces*, in which two solo instruments are added to the harpsichord.

Bach, Johann Sebastian

German Suites, or Partitas, 1731

BWV 825–830

A breach of the rules

In composing the German Suites, *better known as* Partitas, *Bach took great liberties with the traditional sequences of dances.*

Bach wrote the *Partitas* with apparent respect for a structure based on the sequence of four stylized dances that allowed for the alternation of slow (allemande), fast (courante), slow (sarabande) and fast (jig); but he went beyond this tradition by inserting pieces not directly related to dance. A framework thus enlarged and better adapted to vast fugal systems undoubtedly brought together these pure music compositions. They are divided into seven movements, except for the second which only has six.

Introduced by a melodic contrapuntal praeludium, *Partita No.1* (B flat major) is fairly orthodox; the dance nature of the concluding jig, is, however, hidden by the use of 4/4 time.

Bach departed much more from the spirit of the Suite in *Partita No.2* (C minor) whose last two movements, a French-style rondo and an Italian *capriccio* are complete strangers to this form.

Partita No.3 (A minor) stands out due to the presence of a French-style burlesque (fifth movement) and an Italian-style scherzo (sixth movement).

A French overture gives *Partita No.4* (D major) an orchestral character and a majestic tone which it maintains until its conclusion.

In *Partita No.5* (G major) Bach substitutes a *tempo di minuetto* (fifth movement) for the expected minuet: 'It is a subtle distinction, but one which conceals the effort to distance itself from the conventional suite and to conceive the rhythmic construction outside dance as a preconstituted form' (Alberto Basso).

The cycle ends with the *Partita No.6*, the longest of all, but also the most appealing and the richest in developed melodic figures, especially in the fundamental dances preceding the *tempo di gavotta* (fifth movement), a new 'act of reconciliation with dance proper' (Alberto Basso).

Historical references

The six *Partitas* were composed in Leipzig between 1725 and 1730. J. S. Bach published them himself, at first separately (the first in 1726, the second and third in 1727, the fourth in 1728, the fifth and probably the sixth in 1730), then grouped together to form the first book of the *Klavierübung* which was published in 1731. There was also a seventh Partita, of which no trace remains.

Handel, George Frideric

Water Music, orchestral suites, 1717

Dazzling music

A collection of three orchestral suites forming a fairly vast ensemble, the Water Music *was composed to add sparkle to a Royal water festival which took place at night on the Thames.*

The Suite in F major which opens the *Water Music* is written for horns, oboes, bassoons, strings and basso continuo. It begins with a French-style overture divided into six principal movements: a *largo* with dotted rhythm followed by a contrapuntal diptych using oboes and violins, as in certain concerti grossi; an *allegro* in triple time which allows for the entry of the horns whose timbre dominates until the end of the suite; a very noble *andante* in quadruple time; and a less lyric tune with the almost elegiac intervention of the horns; a bourrée to be played three times (by the strings alone, by the oboes alone, and then all instruments together); and finally, an *andante* preceded

by a 'hornpipe' (an English dance with folk origins) with a descending line and overflowing with spirit, also to be played three times. This overture is followed by an expansively-developed *allegro* whose noble sound seems to echo that of the *andante* in quadruple time. It closes the first suite.

Without horns or any other instrument from the brass family, the second Suite (in G major) is much more intimate. It is a piece of light-hearted orchestration (the strings are exclusively joined by flutes, piccolos and bassoons) which might have been intended to be played after the water excursion, during dinner. A minuet, a rigaudon (I and II) make up the various parts.

To the group of instruments of the First Suite, the Third Suite (in D minor) adds trumpets introduced to dominate the brilliant orchestration of the *tutti* and to create a joyful opposition to the horns. From the initial *allegro* to the final bourrée and including the famous hornpipe with its ascending theme (the most well-known passage of the *Water Music*), the minuet and the movement labelled 'slowly', all is dominated by the production of magnificent sounds evoking the Royal splendour.

Historical references

Early manuscripts put the last suite of the *Water Music* in second position and in many editions at the time, numerous variations of the order of the movements exist. The original manuscript is not known to us, it is usually replaced by the Fitzwilliam copy, established around 1740 by John Christopher Schmidt, Handel's secretary.

Handel composed the various pieces which make up the *Water Music* at different times, but we can be certain that the work, in its entirety, was almost finished by 1715. It was not published until 1732–3 (by John Walsh), sixteen years after its first public performance on 17 July 1717 for George I of England.

Bach, Johann Sebastian

Orchestra Suite No.3, around 1720

D major, BWV 1068

Elevated to the power of an orchestra

In writing his Four Orchestra Suites, *Bach gave a new symphonic power to a genre mainly devoted to ornamenting court occasions.*

While these *Four Orchestra Suites* are not organized as a cycle, all obey the same principles. Their first shared characteristic is their initial movement, a 'French-style overture'.

This type of overture, which originated with Lully who used it as an introduction to his lyrical tragedies, takes on the form of a contrasted movement in three parts. A central *allegro*, in fugal style is framed by two slow and majestic sections 'which are generally dominated by a dotted quaver-semi-quaver rhythm' (Roland de Candé).

This is the schema that Bach expanded considerably, as much in duration (each overture is about a third of the complete suite), as in orchestration (making them vast symphonic movements). This symphonic aspect is particularly convincing in the *Suites 3 and 4*, where the orchestra is more full.

The third is written for an ensemble including, besides the string instruments and the basso continuo, two oboes, three

trumpets and two kettledrums.

The significance of this overture is that, in its time, it gave its name to the suite as a whole. But this particular titling can also be explained by the fact that these suites did not respect the traditional structure (allemande, courante, sarabande, jig). Indeed, 'the slow sections of the four overtures were ..., for all their rigour, nothing more than stylized allemandes' (Nikolaus Harnoncourt). And the pieces which followed the initial movement only contained, for each suite, at most one of the obligatory four dances. Thus the *Suite No.3*, after an aria, two gavottes and a bourrée, finishes with a jig. However, regardless of their type, this series of dances 'gave rise to a dazzling display of rhythm and timbre' (A. Basso).

The most famous passage of the *Suite No.3* is its second movement, an *aria* for unaccompanied strings. It is a slow piece whose voice, as the title suggests, is very melodic.

Historical references

These four suites appear to have been written on Cöthen for a celebration given by Prince Leopold around 1720. Nevertheless, the instrumental complement of *Suites 3 and 4* being greater than the one Bach used in Cöthen, they may have dated from his first years in Leipzig, around 1725.

Bizet, Georges

First Suite of *L'Arlésienne*, 1872

Carmen foreshadowed

This suite demonstrates — three years before Carmen *— Bizet's ability to integrate folklore themes and forms.*

The purely musical quality of this suite, extracted from a piece composed for a drama by A. Daudet, suffices to show how Bizet renovated the genre of incidental music, by refusing to reduce it to a solely illustrative function. The suite contains four parts, 'Prelude', 'Intermezzo', 'Adagietto' and 'Carillon', and the 'Prelude' is itself divided into three sections. The first is a harmonic variation of an old Provençal Christmas carol, and the following two expose the themes of the two characters in the drama. With this 'Prelude', Bizet introduces, for the first time, a saxophone into the orchestra. Of the three other parts, the *adagietto*, played by the strings, is the most outstanding.

Historical references

Daudet's *L'Arlésienne*, with Bizet's incidental music, was performed in Paris on 1 October 1872. Bizet extracted this suite shortly afterwards.

Moussorgsky, Modeste

Pictures at an Exhibition, Piano Suite, 1874

A medley of tone colours

The ten pieces of this suite are particularly striking in their rhythmic liberty and the almost orchestral treatment of the piano.

Out of a concern for unity, Moussorgsky joined the pieces of his musical exposition with an interlude, or 'Promenade' which represents him going from one picture to another. However, this programme was not exactly realistic: in fact the interest of these ten pieces — from *Gnomus* to the *Great Gate to Kiev* — comes from a piano conception so grandiose that one almost forgets the instrument itself due to the overwhelming impression given of an actual orchestra. This impression is increased by the fact that a parallel stripping down of the writing helps to 'bring out the bitter taste of certain medleys' (C. Helffer).

Historical references

Moussorgsky composed his work in 1874, after the exhibition of pictures by Victor Hartmann, a friend of the composer who had died the year before.

The orchestration
A potentially orchestral work, *Pictures at an Exhibition* was orchestrated by Ravel in 1922.

Stravinsky, Igor

Pulcinella, concert suite, 1924

Stravinsky's phrasing adapted to Pergolesi

With Pulcinella *(the ballet and the suite), Stravinsky inaugurated his 'neo-classical' period, founded on the idea of building modernity on music from the past.*

This recomposition work based on 21 fragments of works by Pergolesi, or which were attributed to him, require a limited orchestral complement, both for the ballet and for the suite drawn from it: several wind instruments grouped in twos (flutes, horns, bassoons, oboes), a trumpet, a trombone and *concertino* strings (five) in opposition with *ripieno* strings (18). Clarinets and percussion are excluded. This orchestra, which has some of the characteristics of the 18th-century ensembles, also allows for numerous typically Stravinskian timbre effects achieved by unusual combinations (for example, the double bass and the trombone in the movement marked *vivo* or *duetto*).

While the ballet, divided into 18 instrumental or vocal parts, contains 21 movements, the suite only has 11 instrumental parts divided into eight movements: *sinfonia* (overture); serenade; *scherzino* (a), *allegro* (b), *andantino* (c); tarentella; toccata; gavotte with two variations; *duetto* (or *vivo*); minuet (a), finale (b). Taking into account the replacement of voices by instruments in the serenade and the minuet, these 11 parts of the suite are almost identical to the first five, to the twelfth and to parts 14 to 18 of the ballet.

Far from making up a series of isolated

musical sequences, *Pulcinella*, in its ballet or suite version, possesses a remarkable internal cohesion which gives it, besides its particular coloration, a rhythm (displaced accents, accentuated syncopation) and tonal relations like those, so characteristic, at work in *The Rite of Spring*. On the one hand, Stravinsky uses Pergolesian melodies and harmonics verbatim and on the other 'breaks the formal symmetry of the music of the 18th century by the elision, extension or repetition of parts of phrases, and obscures the traditional harmonic schema by the use of *ostinati* and the prolongation of certain harmonies' (Eric Walter White).

Historical references

Commissioned by Diaghilev, the ballet was composed in 1919–20 in Morges (Switzerland) and performed at the Paris Opera on 15 May 1920 by the Ballets Russes. The suite, started in 1920 (also in Morges), completed in 1922 and published in 1924 was performed in Boston on 22 December 1922. Pierre Monteux conducted.

'Returns to'

Among Stravinsky's other works, the following are recompositions made more out of a 'need to interact with history' (Pierre Boulez) than a desire to re-establish tradition: *The Fairy's Kiss* (a 'return to' Tchaikovsky), *Capriccio* for piano and orchestra (a 'return to' Carl Maria von Weber) and the arrangement of canonic variations by J. S. Bach on the Christmas Carol *Von Himmel Hoch* (1956).

Berg, Alban

Lyric Suite for string quartet, 1927

The feeling of calculation

Extremely constructed, but including many 'lyrical' connotations, Berg's first serial work seems dramatically governed, like a 'latent opera' (Adorno).

The general dramatic profile of this suite comes firstly from its organization into six movements. Alternately fast and slow tempos are unique in that the odd movements become faster and faster and the even ones slower and slower. Also, after the first two movements with relatively similar tempos, the gap grows progressively and in a sense speeds up at the junction of the last two. This point of maximum tension is clearly set in relief by 'the abrupt interruption of the fifth movement and the "theatrical" beginning of the sixth' (Dominique Jameux). Moreover, the progressive augmentation of this tension is intensified by the concomitant augmentation of atmosphere of each of the six movements, as indicated by their titles: 1. *Allegretto giovale*; 2. *Andante amoroso*; 3. *Allegro misterioso* (with its *trio estatico*); 4. *Adagio appassionato*; 5. *Presto delirando* (*tenebroso*); 6. *Largo desolato*.

Furthermore, this dramatic structuring of tempo derives entirely from the structure of the series adopted by Berg in which he applied 'the principle of *symmetrical complementarity*' (Stéphane Goldet) to the principal components of his work, and to the distribution of tempos. The partial use he makes of the series is also explained: the distribution within the *Suite* of strictly serial or freely atonal parts, obey the same principle of symmetrical complementarity. 'Thus we see right away Berg as the total opposite of what we had reproached him for being: far from indulging reluctantly in serialism ... he involves himself in it fully, with an *expansionary* spirit' (S. Goldet).

This 'combinatory turmoil' does not only give this quartet its cohesion, it also produces the very original beauty of its sound, helps to integrate the citations (such as those from *Tristan*) and makes possible the numerous references from one movement to another. But it is the details of each of these that must be commended, from the alternation of tempos in the first two, the mirror-image form of the third, the Bartókian trance of the fourth, the connected blends of the fifth, to the progressive invasion of silence in the sixth.

Historical references

Composed in 1925–6, *The Lyric Suite* was performed in Vienna in January 1927.

> The discovery in 1977 of a copy, annotated in Berg's handwriting which belonged to Hanna Fuchs, shed a new light on the piece which also proved to be a *programme work* — about the love, thwarted by convention, between Berg and the holder of the revealing copy. The initials of the two lovers (HFAB = B, F, A, B flat) appeared throughout it, and their symbolic numbers (10 for Hanna Fuchs, 23 for Alban Berg) governed, with others, the number of bars in each movement. But this is undetectable to the ear.

Berg, Alban

Lulu Symphony, Suite for orchestra and soprano voice, 1934

An abbreviated opera

Less a collection of extracts than an original composition, the suite which Berg pulled from his opera Lulu *testifies to the orchestral splendour it has achieved.*

As Berg wanted to give the five movements of his *Suite* a primarily symphonic balance, their arrangement does not follow the pattern of the opera. Thus, certain purely orchestral parts are sung in the opera, and others come from a detailed assembly of fragments from different scenes. In fact, movements one and five were entirely reordered, three and four increased by the addition of a new beginning or end, and the second is the only one which replicates a passage from the opera without changing it in any way. The balance achieved by this reduction for orchestra of the opera resembles that of Mahler's 7th symphony, 'with its two highly developed outer movements framing three shorter lyrical interludes' (Harry Halbreich).

Relatively unused instruments like the saxophone, the piano and the vibraphone give the first movement, a *rondo: andante* and *hymne*, a specific colour symbolizing a type of jazz. More subtly, this reference allowed Berg to 'situate by sound' the very 'fin-de-siècle' setting which he had dramatic need of.

The second movement, *ostinato*, contains two parts, the second of which is an exact reversal of the first, but beginning at the end. The inversion effect is striking and made completely evident by the very marked difference between the writing for the strings and the brasses. The listener thus gets the impression of being pulled backwards from the middle of the movement.

Although the third movement — *Lied de Lulu* — contains a vocal part of primary importance, the *variations* of the fourth are carried out by the orchestra alone. Their progression is centred around the contrast between the naive simplicity of the variation (a street song) on the theme and the sparkle of the orchestra. This principle allows the movement to evolve in very differentiated regions and to evoke the atmosphere of a casino as well as the sound of a barrel organ.

The final *adagio*, partly vocal, which ends with the murder of Lulu — a terrifying scream reinforced by a chord of 12 notes made of superimposed fourths — is, above all, a dazzling example of synthesis between two contradictory musical systems: serialism and tonal writing.

Historical references

Finished in the summer of 1934, the *Lulu-Symphony* was performed in Berlin the same year.

Symphonies

Five musical forms are at the origin of the *symphony* and mark its evolution before it adopted (around 1770) the four movement structure of the classical sonata: the *sinfonia* (identified in the Italian-style overture of the late 17th century), the French overture, the suite, the *concerto grosso* and the orchestra trio (or trio sonata).

In Italy, A. Vivaldi, T. Albinoni and especially G. B. Sammartini are responsible for emancipating the *sinfonia* with the aim of making it independent from the opera that it served as overture, and of giving it the status of an orchestral piece for concerts.

A parallel evolution took place in France where the symphony developed within the framework of public concerts such as the famous spiritual concert founded by A. D. Philidor in 1725. The French-style overture, an introductory piece to Lully's operas which also gave its name to the piece which headed the *Suite of Dances*, gradually established itself as an independent instrumental piece with the structure of a trio suite (Antoine Dornel's *Livre de symphonies*, 1709), and soon marked by the Italian instrumental style (L. G. Guillermain's *Symphonies en trio* opus 6, 1740). One could say that, 'after 1750, the influence of the foreign schools was such that a truly French influence in symphony had become impossible to detect' (Rémi Jacobs).

Austria (the Viennese School) and Germany (Mannheim and Berlin Schools) contributed greatly to putting the symphony on the path towards a more and more evolved independent musical form.

Experienced in the composition of works influenced either by the French overture or by the Italian sinfonia, and having attained a great mastery of the sonata-form, many Austrian musicians asserted themselves as precursors or contemporaries of J. Haydn with symphonies written in three or four movements. We have today rediscovered long forgotten Viennese pioneers of the classical symphony: G. M. Monn (1717–50), Carlos d'Ordonez (1734–86), Michael Haydn (1737–1806), J. B. Vanhal (1739–1811) and C. Ditters von Dittersdorf (1739–99).

The emancipating role played by the Mannheim School, which some musicologists underestimated in comparison with that of the Viennese School, is no less important. Johann Stamitz (1717–57) was its first and greatest representative. He applied to the nascent symphony the stylistic processes which originated in Italy (for example, the *crescendo*) and favoured orchestration work. His influence over F. J. Gossec (1734–1829) and the knight of St. Georges (around 1739–99), two great French symphonists of the time, was undeniable. Mannheim, in the domain of symphonies as well as symphony concertante, 'a kind of concerto with several soloists (usually two or three) and a symphonic style and structure' (A. Hodeir), also owes its reputation as an 'advanced' school to F. X. Richter (1709–89), J. C. Cannabich (1731–98) and I. Holzbauer (1711–83).

The Berlin School, dominated by Carl Philip Emanuel Bach (symphonies in three movements in sonata-form with two themes) is of lesser importance. Another son of J. S. Bach, Johann Christian Bach (1735–82), based in London, adopted the formal discoveries of the continental schools to create a style which privileged elegant melodic forms (six symphonies of opus 18, 1772–7).

From 1765 to 1770 J. Haydn, because of the fullness of his developments, the variety of his thematic work and the colour of his instrumentation, gave new formal dynamics to the symphony in a framework of a quadripartite structure:

a rapid first movement (*allegro*) sometimes preceded by a short, slow introduction, a second, slow movement (*andante* or *adagio*), a minuet and a fast fourth movement. Each of these movements is theoretically elaborated according to the structural principles of the sonata-form.

W. A. Mozart did not make any structural modifications to the symphony, but he did innovate on the harmonic level, (*Symphony No.40 in G minor* K.550, 1788), he introduced passages in fugato into a sonata form (finale of *Symphony No.41 in C major* K.551, 1788) and most importantly he created an equal dialogue between strings and wind instruments.

Beethoven's symphonies, which were all, at the same time, the outcome of the classical style, a synthesis of this style and a foreshadowing of the future, did not overturn the order or the nature of movements in the musical forms they belonged to (although the scherzo almost always replaced the minuet), but their proportions expanded and their content was radically new. Works of a fascinating skill which required an orchestra increased by many extra instruments to achieve mass sound effects, they gave timbre an essential musical value linked to the increasingly important role of percussion (*Ninth Symphony* opus 125, 1822–4).

Schubert, Mendelssohn, Schumann and Brahms 'composed symphonies in the tradition of their great predecessor and each of them resolved in his own way, the problems of the paternity' (Michel Chion). With Berlioz and Liszt, the symphony took on the narrative dimensions of programme music supported by an impressive orchestration: the structure of the sonata-form was subordinated to the musical theme and to extra-musical elements.

Constructed on the formal classical model, Bruckner's symphonies loosened this model from within, 'from its very fabric' (Michel Chion). Mahler, using the gigantic post-Wagnerian orchestra, did not only modify the number of movements (six for his third symphony, two for his eighth) and their order of succession, but he also exploded the formal framework of the symphony by almost completely abandoning the sonata-form.

Norms and 'classical proportions' were, on the other hand, respected by the French symphonists of the end of the 19th century and beginning of the 20th: Bizet (*Symphony in C*, 1855), Lalo, Saint-Saëns, Vincent d'Indy (*Symphonie cévenole*, 1886), Chausson (*Symphony in B flat*, opus 20, 1889–90), Dukas (*Symphony in C major*, 1896) and Roussel. César Franck's *Symphony in D minor* (1886) is also a classical symphony, but with a cyclical form.

R. Strauss allowed himself to be seduced (belatedly) by the idea of the programme (*Symphonia domestica*, 1904). Before him, many 19th-century composers who belonged to different 'national' schools had mingled with the international style some folkloric thematic material: Glinka, Tchaikovsky, Rimski-Korsakov, Balakirev, Borodin (*Symphony in B minor*, 1887) in Russia; Smetana (*Triumphant Symphony*, 1853), Dvořák, Janácek in Czechoslovakia; and Sibelius in Finland.

In the 20th century, the symphonic form lives on in neoclassical works by Prokofiev, Shostakovich, Vaughan Williams, Michael Tippett, Stravinsky (*Symphony in C*, 1940), Aaron Copland, and in the compositions by Charles Ives and Olivier Messiaen (*Turangalîla-Symphonie*, 1946–8). Neither Honegger, nor Darius Milhaud, nor André Jolivet, nor even Dutilleux really succeeded in renewing it. For Schönberg (two *Chamber Symphonies*, 1906 and 1906–39), Webern (*Symphony opus 21*, 1928), and more recently, Berio (*Sinfonia*, 1968) the symphony was nothing more than a conceptual tool of cultural reference to the past.

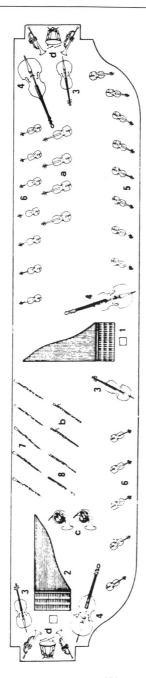

Arrangement of the Dresden Opera orchestra in the 18th century.

1. Kappellmeister's harps. 2. accompaniment harpsichord. 3. Cellos. 4. Double basses. 5. First Violins. 6. Second Violins, some with their backs to the audience. 7. Oboes (same). 8. Flutes (same). a. Altos (same). b. Bassoons. c. Hunting horns. d. A stand at each side for the kettledrums and trumpets.

Haydn, Joseph

Symphony No.45 'Abscheid' (Farewell), 1772

F sharp minor

The insurgent classical style

A work of great impetuosity, Haydn's Symphony No.45, called 'Farewell' because of its last movement, is also a farewell to the baroque style.

The *'Abscheid' Symphony* testifies to the 'romantic' crisis Haydn went through in the 1770s: this crisis was a direct result of the literary aesthetic of *Sturm und Drang* (Storm and Stress), the best-known example of which was Goethe's *Werther*. Musically, this aesthetic was conveyed by a style of great dramatic harshness, which Haydn almost immediately abandoned. The works written during this brief period are full 'of often brutal contrasts between a coarse but urgent regularity and an eccentricity often taken to the extreme' (Charles Rosen). But, undeniably, the most obvious manifestation

of this style was that Haydn, for the first time, wrote in the minor mode.

This crisis is also explained by the fact that Haydn sought to create new principles of continuity of musical discourse, without succeeding in freeing himself from the baroque technique of producing the illusion of movement by an arrangement of very differentiated sequences. In other words, there was a conflict between baroque persistence and the classical ideal, dimly anticipated by 'the large-scale balanced asymmetrical variation' (Charles Rosen).

In this respect the first movement, *allegro assai*, is particularly clear. In fact, 'only the beginning of the development uses the themes of the exposition and, at the end of roughly 30 bars, the musical discourse is brutally interrupted to make room for an entirely new theme in the form of a romance' (Karl Geiringer). In the following *adagio*, the strings are used with mutes and the tonal ambiguity between major and minor is very strong, which produces an undeniable effect of strangeness, increased by very daring modulations.

After a minuet, rich in syncopation, the finale opens with a very vigorous *presto*. But this last movement also contains one of the 'extravagances' typical of *Sturm und Drang*, and which gave the work its title. The *presto*, which appears to be about to finish, suddenly gives way — prepared by an unexpected modulation in unison — to an *adagio*. The instruments then begin, progressively, to cease playing, until only two violins remain in the last bars.

> By making the instrumentalists stop playing one after the other in the last movement of the *'Abscheid' Symphony*, Haydn simulates a resignation of the orchestra, and thus makes himself the spokesman to the Prince Esterházy for his musicians who wanted the season to end so they could rejoin their families. This request, it is said, was soon granted.

> Other Symphonies by Haydn from the *Sturm und Drang* period: the 44th, *'Trauer'* and the 49th, *'Passione'*.

Historical references

The symphony was composed in 1772 for the Prince Esterházy.

Mozart, Wolfgang Amadeus

Symphony No.35, 'Haffner', 1784

D Major, K.385

The sense of combined forms

Planned as a serenade, this work was written as a symphony; some characteristics of the former are retained.

The first movement of the *'Haffner' Symphony*, marked *allegro con spirito* and which Mozart wanted to be played 'with lots of fire', opens on an essentially rhythmic theme. This theme, the only one in the piece, develops with difficulty as it is interspersed with 'rapid ritornelli' (G. de Saint-Foix). It is introduced by the orchestra in unison, then picked up again by the basses and violas to create a brilliant series of contrapuntal figures, highlighted throughout the development.

After this fugal language, which is a result of the 'productive study' (N. Harnoncourt) of works by Bach and Handel in the spring of 1782 (a language which often shocked his Salzburg contemporaries who were used to the 'simplicities' of the style galant), Mozart returned, in the *andante* (second movement), to a more openly 'pleasant' writing. The reduced orchestral complement (strings, two bassoons, two oboes, two horns) and

the *andante* form both marked a clear return to the spirit of the serenade. Its main theme, light-hearted and tuneful, is followed by several secondary motifs with a lively melodic appeal.

Concise and animated, the minuet (third movement) is not quite a 'style galant' it represents the typical Mozartian minuet which, from then on, 'tended more and more to become the location where the main theme of the work is recapitulated' (J. and B. Massin). The trio which it includes has the nature of a song.

A finale (*presto*) to be played 'as quickly as possible' (Mozart), serves as the conclusion. It is built on a theme developed by the strings which is rich in counterpoint effects, and has an undeniable similarity with the tune of Osmin's triumphant fury in *Die Entführung aus den Serail* (The Abduction from the Seraglio), an opera composed shortly before, in 1782. This relationship was described by N. Harnoncourt as a striking example of a 'specifically Mozartian fusion of theatre music with instrumental music'.

Historical references

Mozart composed the *Symphony No.35* in Vienna between 20 July and 7 August 1782. He had received a commission, with his father Leopold's help, for a serenade which Sigmund Haffner, a rich burgomaster of Saltzburg, wanted to hear for the occasion of his son's ennoblement. But the work, according to Mozart's correspondence, immediately qualified as a symphony. It was published in Vienna in 1784.

The *Symphony No.35* was not the first work Mozart wrote for the Haffner family; it followed the *Serenade No.7 in D major* K.250, and the *March in D major* K.249, both composed for the Burgomaster's daughter Elizabeth's wedding.

SYMPHONIES

Mozart, Wolfgang Amadeus

Symphony No.38 'Prague', 1786

D major, K.504

A language with a new opulence

Less brilliant than imposing, the 'Prague' Symphony *admits a gravity in many places which brings the Mozartian symphonic language to the level of the tragic.*

Symphony No.38 demonstrates Mozart's recently acquired ability to conceive his works in terms of full and dense sound masses with the aim of giving them maximum impetus and accentuating their magnificence in sombre contexts. This idea translates, on the instrumental level, as a close interdependence between the strings and the woods and brasses, with the two latter groups of instruments losing their 'old-fashioned' ornamental stylistic function.

Lacking the traditional minuet, the *'Prague'* has three movements, each one constructed with the symmetrical strictness of a sonata piece; it thus achieves its balance in a ternary division which also extends to the structure of its developments. The first movement, indicated *adagio* and *allegro*, 'contains without a doubt the richest and most complex slow introduction, before that of Beethoven's introduction to his *Seventh Symphony*' (Charles Rosen). With the modulations of its theme in *gruppetti* and the rests which punctuate its powerful chords, it evokes the atmosphere of dark solemnity which marks the entrance of the Commander in *Don Giovanni*. The first and principal theme of the *allegro* (a lively and impetuous piece, but slightly tinged with anxiety) seems very like an outline of the *fugato* of the overture to *The Magic Flute*.

In the *andante* (G major), which subtly combines chromatic roulades with counterpoint, the second theme takes on the shape of an orchestral variant of the duet between Don Juan and Zerlina (*Andiam, andiam, mio bene*). Here, the always present tragic tone 'is overcome without it being entirely evaded' (J. and B. Massin).

The rapid and seemingly lively finale (*presto*) picks up on a motif from *Il Nozze di Figaro* (the little *allegro assai* duet between Cherubin and Suzanne in the Second Act). With *'Prague'*, Mozart easily made the transition from the instrumental style to the theatrical dramatic style and vice versa, allowing the symphony of the classical age to complete one of its most decisive evolutions.

Historical references

Completed in Vienna in December 1786, the *Symphony No.38* figures in the catalogue of Mozart's works under the name *'Prague'* because it was played for the first time in the city at a concert organized in his honour. In Prague, where *Il Nozze di Figaro* attained a great success in 1786, the *Symphony in D minor* got an equally enthusiastic reception.

A numerical symbolism
According to some musicologists, such as Jean and Brigitte Massin, the fact that the 'Prague' Symphony is in a sense governed by the number three, relates to Mozart's intention (he had been a Freemason since 1784 and was invited to Prague in 1786 through the efforts of one of his lodge brothers) to base this work on masonic principles, specifically the idea of universal harmony.

154

Mozart, Wolfgang Amadeus

Symphony No.41, 'Jupiter', 1788

C major, K.551

The reconciliation of opposites *(L. Finscher)*

Mozart's last symphony 'Jupiter', *forms a triptych with the* 39th *(in E flat major, K.543) and the* 40th *(in G minor, K.550); musically* 'Jupiter' *is the most skilful of the three.*

It is not impossible that Mozart's intensive study and partial reinstrumentation of C. P. Emanuel Bach's oratorios exerted an influence over the majestic orchestral nature of '*Jupiter*'.

From the beginning of the first movement, *allegro vivace*, the appearance of two highly contrasted motifs, one rhythmic and the other melodic, indicate that we are entering into a sound space with clearly marked *forte-cantabile* oppositions, and from within which the themes, far from being removed from the complex network of motifs that they created, merge completely with it. The initial theme, whose constituent elements emphasize the heroic dramatic nature of the beginning of the work, is followed by the second theme which is recognizable by its more intimate resonances. This second theme, after the return of the first, gives way to an opera-buffa tune, the arietta *Un bacio di mano* (K.541) which Mozart wrote in May 1788 and which gives its melodic substance to the immense concluding development of the grandiose *allegro*.

Violins and violas fitted with mutes open the *andante cantabile* (second movement) whose structure is reminiscent 'but more clear and more ardent' (J. and B. Massin) of the andante of the *Symphony No.39*. The kettledrums, well-represented up to this point, are no longer heard. Abrupt 'darkening' tones alter the general tonality of F major.

A single theme with pre-Wagnerien coloration fragmented by lively trio motifs animates the third movement (*menuetto*), which also conceals subtle counterpoint effects.

The famous finale (*molto allegro*) is in sonata-form; it integrates fugato passages which amiably combine the four principal contrapuntal motifs of the movement.

The execution of *Symphony No.41* requires a fairly small orchestra. The same is true, with a few exceptions, for the *Symphonies No.39* and *40*: a string quartet with cello distinct from the basses, a flute, two oboes (replaced by two clarinets in the *39th*), two bassoons, two horns, two trumpets and two kettledrums. These last four instruments are absent from the *40th*, which instead includes (in the definitive version) a part for two clarinets and a part for two oboes.

Historical references

Like the first two sections of the great triptych to which it belongs, the *Symphony No.41* was composed in Vienna in 1788. None of the three symphonies, except perhaps the *40th*, was performed in Mozart's lifetime. The dates of the first publication are unknown. As for the subtitle '*Jupiter*', it emerged around 1820 from J. P. Salomon, Haydn's impresario.

Haydn, Joseph

Symphony No.92 'Oxford', 1789

G major

The classical style at its height of glory

A brilliant synthesis of construction and humour, the 'Oxford' Symphony *is perhaps the most elegant example of the ideal of the classical style: 'artful simplicity' (Charles Rosen).*

The first movement of *Oxford*, an *allegro spiritoso*, preceded by a slow *adagio* introduction, is 'Haydn's most massive expansion of sonata form until then' (Charles Rosen). The exposition-development-recapitulation formula is somewhat overturned here, as the three parts contain, respectively, 62, 42 and 76 bars; in other words the recapitulation is longer than the exposition — a very exceptional occurrence. More precisely, the recapitulation only takes up the first 24 bars of the exposition then goes on immediately to a completely unexpected new development which is as long as the preceding one. This skilfully calculated formal imbalance also gives the

The title *Parisian Symphony* was given to the six symphonies (82–7) composed by Haydn at the request of the Olympic Lodge Concert in Paris. The best-known are the *82nd ('Bear')*, *83rd ('La Poule')* and *85th ('La Reine')*, but the most beautiful is, without a doubt, the *86th* in D. After this group, Haydn composed between 1787 and 1789 another five symphonies for Paris; the famous *88th* and *89th*, and finally a group of three (*90*, *91*, *92*), the last of which is *Oxford*.

movement the impression of great size, all the more apparent as Haydn had compressed his phrases as much as possible in the exposition. And, although the recapitulation, in a sense, 'seems to be made, like a mosaic, out of fragments of the exposition', these 'separate small bits' nonetheless succeed in creating a whole for having been put together by 'a tough, dynamic conception of the total controlling rhythm' rarely achieved before then (C. Rosen). A coda concludes the movement.

The *adagio* which follows, a long melody interrupted in the middle by a more lively section, is especially remarkable in the value given to the wind instruments.

For the third movement, an *allegretto* minuet, Haydn composed one of his most stunning passages, and its central trio in particular is highly ironic. On first listen, it is impossible to figure out where the first beat is, and 'the orchestration is part of the joke, as the winds and strings seem to have different down-beats' (Charles Rosen). Haydn later makes very unusual use of silence to throw his listener off again.

Following this musical trick, the finale, marked *presto* is a 'marvel of spirit, wit and skill' (Jean Dupart). It is as though Haydn had wanted to conclude with the message that he was capable of composing in a completely clever style, without making it obvious.

Historical references

'*Oxford*' was composed in 1789. As Haydn did not have a new work to present, he played it in Oxford on 7 July 1791, the night before receiving a doctorate *honoris causa* by Oxford University (hence its name).

Haydn, Joseph

Symphony No.103 'Drumroll', 1795

E flat major

A learned popular style

Haydn's penultimate symphony, the 103rd shares with the twelve London Symphonies *a taste for experimentation and a perfect assimilation of popular style.*

The first movement of Haydn's 103rd *Symphony* begins with a slow introduction marked *adagio*. But to open this introduction with a blatant drumroll and to connect it with several bars played in unison by the bassoons, cellos and double basses is more unusual and attests to how Haydn, in his later years, achieved a modern conception of timbre in its own right. But the value of this slow introduction is far from being limited to a study of instrumentation. While the bars which immediately follow the drumroll — which contain an evocation of *Dies Irae* — have such a slow tempo that it is impossible for the ear to discern the rhythm,

their accelerated reappearance makes up a passage of the principal *allegro* and here they sound like a popular melody. The beginning of this first movement has more of a generative role than simply an introductory one, and shows the extent to which Haydn's popular style is fabricated. Furthermore, the beginning of the slow introduction is repeated verbatim at the end of the *allegro*, but only to be immediately followed by its transformation into a popular melody which creates an extremely bold musical contrast.

The second movement (*andante piuttosto allegretto*) is in the form of double variations, alternating on two slow march-like themes. But as these two themes of folklore origins, whose popular nature had been emphasized elsewhere by Haydn, are very similar, the overall form of the movement is more like a monothematic rondo. As the principle of variations modernizes the orchestration, a division gradually develops between the popular profiles of these two themes and the increasingly worked timbre effects within. The resulting impression is one of a progressive distancing from the source material. The following minuet proceeds in a similar fashion.

For the finale, Haydn composed an *allegro con spirito* which is a tour de force also seen in Beethoven. Resolutely monothematic, this movement manages not to repeat itself and thus gives the impression of a never-weakening dramatic force.

Historical references

Composed in 1795, this symphony was produced on 2 March of the same year.

Haydn's last twelve symphonies (*Nos.93 to 104*) are called the *London Symphonies* because they were first performed in London, on two visits the composer paid to the city between 1791 and 1795. Some of these twelve very great works were given subtitles: the *94th (Surprise)*, the *96th (Miracle)*, the *100th (Military)*, the *101st (Clock)* and the last, the *104th (London)*. But Haydn created two more great orchestral works with the overtures to his oratorios, *The Creation* (1799) and *The Seasons* (1801).

Beethoven, Ludwig van

Symphony No.3 'Eroica', 1806

E flat major, opus 55

The constructive functions of the orchestra

In its innovative timbre structuring and its extra-musical involvement, Eroica *alters the formal order of classical symphonic style.*

An *allegro con brio* forms the initial movement of the third symphony. Its size (almost 700 bars) immediately indicates Beethoven's desire to implement the formal extension process which would allow him to break away from the model, half the size, inherited from Haydn and Mozart. Far from leading to a loose melodic-harmonic construction, this size amplification resulted in a proliferation of motif cells and a thematic tightening, which sometimes makes it difficult to distinguish precisely the dominant theme; the listener may even get the impression of a writing without themes, which only makes use of the energetic force of the rhythm and the varied resources of a harmonic language. The *allegro con brio* does, however, expose several themes, the most characteristic of which is introduced by a horn call not repeated in solo until the recapitulation.

For the traditional *adagio*, the second movement substitutes a funeral march whose two outer sections (in C minor) frame a central part in C major. As was the case with the allegro, 'the timbre enters directly into the musical architecture' (André Boucourechliev), by joining the elements of 'a complex rhythmic network' to create a very strong dramatic tension.

The scherzo (third movement), which replaces the old minuet, is a composition with a lively and regular rhythm whose main theme Beethoven borrowed from a popular song. Its central trio is a dialogue between three horns (this is the first use of a third horn in Symphonic orchestra).

Built principally on a theme that had been used at the end of the ballet *The Creatures of Prometheus* and developed, *ostinato* like a passecaille, the finale (*allegro molto, poco andante, presto*) links together twelve variations on this theme with an astounding freedom of invention.

Historical references

Started in Heiligenstadt in 1802, *Eroica* was completed in Vienna in 1804.

The work, first performed at the An der Wien theatre (7 April 1805), received scattered applause; the critics said it was 'interminable, overloaded, incomprehensible and much too noisy' (Czerny's account).

Beethoven disillusioned by Bonaparte
Beethoven had originally dedicated *Eroica* to Bonaparte, Prime Consul at the time, who he felt to be a defender of the republican ideal. The day after his coronation, disillusioned, Beethoven changed the title of his composition to *'Heroic symphony to celebrate the memory of a great man'*, and thereafter dedicated it to Prince Lobkowitz.

Beethoven, Ludwig van

Symphony No.5, 1809

C minor, opus 67

When 'the work creates the theme'

Successive metamorphoses of a very simple theme in itself, the Fifth Symphony *draws from this principle its extraordinary unity.*

The main theme of this work reduces itself to a rhythmic figure of three quavers and a crotchet. But this simplicity,

giving rise to 'innumerable possibilities of expansion', allowed for the release of 'for-midable energy potentials' (A. Bou-courechliev). Almost omnipresent in the *allegro con brio* and hardly heard in the *andante* at all, the main theme reappears in the scherzo and also controls the mysterious transition leading to the triumphal march with which the finale begins. As for the last movement, it finishes with a very long cadence needed 'as an outlet for the extreme tension accumulated throughout this immense work' (C. Rosen).

Historical references

Composed between 1805 and 1808, the *Fifth Symphony* was produced in 1808 and published in 1809.

Symphony No.6, 'Pastoral', 1809

F major, opus 68

The intrusion of the descriptive

Although it is an evocation of rural sentiments, the Pastoral *nonetheless retains features of the classical symphony.*

In an attempt to evoke a series of varied atmospheres, Beethoven indulged in an unusual kind of thematic development. Far from resorting to short generating motifs, this work presents a succession of 'vast themes with finely chiselled melodic and rhythmic contours, intended to remain unchanged, and to reveal one after the other their tranquil beauty' (A. Bou-courechliev). The instruments are used for their imitative effects (bird songs). These features give the symphony a very relaxed and somewhat naive character, with the only exception being the fourth movement ('The Storm').

Historical references

The *Pastoral* was composed, produced and published at the same time as the *Fifth Symphony*.

Beethoven, Ludwig van

Symphony No.7, 1816

A major, opus 92

Beethoven's eulogy to rhythm

Generating a persistent force, the base rhythms of the Seventh Symphony *also assure its internal coherence.*

Considered by some to be a 'Dionysian' work and nicknamed 'apotheosis of dance' by Wagner, and classified by others as pure music, the *Seventh Symphony* 'defies all exegesis' (A. Boucourechliev).

A long and slow introduction (*poco sostenuto*) contains the seeds of the vigorous rhythmic elements of the *allegro vivace* which follows. Played with a balanced rhythm, the *allegretto* (second movement) is based on a lovely theme which undergoes many variations, one of which is the *fugato*; its obsessive processional mood has made it well known. The third movement, marked *presto*, is a lively and brisk scherzo, followed by a double appearance of the trio (*assai meno presto*). As for the finale (*allegro con brio*), it seems literally to go beyond the rhythmic violence of the scherzo.

Historical references

The *Seventh Symphony* was composed in 1811–12. Beethoven conducted the first performance on 8 December 1813 in Vienna where it was a huge success.

Symphony No.8, 1816

F major, Opus 93

A tribute to the classical style

Unlike the gloominess of the Seventh, *the* Eighth Symphony *almost has the character of a divertimento.*

Marked *allegro vivace e con brio*, the first movement (without an introduction) develops two clearly defined main themes, successively brought out by skilful contrapuntal combinations. The second movement replaces the ritual *adagio* or *andante*, with an *allegretto scherzando* made up of a humorous syllabic canon composed in honour of J. N. Maelzel, the creator of the first patented metronome. After a minuet in place of the usual scherzo, the long finale ends with a *fortissimo* which insistently reaffirms the original key of the work.

Historical references

Finished in 1812, the *Eighth Symphony* was played for the first time in Vienna in 1814 but was only a moderate success.

Schubert, Franz

Symphony No.8 'Unfinished', 1822

B minor, D.759

The flow of pathos *(M. Schneider)*

The Eighth Symphony *marks a break with the post-classical style of Schubert's first symphonies. It is called* 'Unfinished' *because it only contains two movements.*

A rather enigmatic work due to the organization of musical figures which it develops, the *Eighth Symphony* originally presented musicologists with the problem of its unfinished status. They were not all of the opinion that it should have contained a 'sequel'. Some of them, such as Brahms, felt that Schubert, in working on the scherzo, considered the first two parts to form a completed whole; he did not feel obliged to follow the traditional quadripartite division.

On the side of those who felt it was unfinished were Brigitte Massin, who justly remarked that it was not an exceptional Schubertian creation, and Alfred Einstein who presumed that Schubert, losing hope of ever finishing such an ambitious work, simply abandoned it. Another theory was that Schubert underestimated the value of

his work, considering it to be too close to Beethoven's style.

Some on the other hand, put forward the hypothesis of a finale which he had intended to extract, whole or in part, from the first interlude of *Rosamonde*, once the scherzo was finished.

As it stands, the *'Unfinished'* begins with an *allegro moderato* in B minor with two themes. After the appearance of a kind of 'epigraph-theme' (Brigitte Massin) introduced *pianissimo* in the low register by the cellos and the double basses in unison, the actual theme appears suddenly over a string tremolo, also played in unison by the oboes and clarinets. Less tense, the second theme (in major), at first played by the cellos, evokes a pastoral or a ländler. Its syncopated accompaniment gives it the general dramatic atmosphere of the whole movement; it then gets brutally interrupted by a rest followed by a *fortissimo* in a minor key by the whole orchestra.

Marked *andante con moto*, the second movement (E major), relatively more serene than the *allegro*, also contains two themes. 'Part of the richness of this *andante*, besides the succession of its melodic motifs, comes from its often contrapuntal writing' (Brigitte Massin).

Historical references

The *'Unfinished' Symphony* was probably composed in the summer of 1822. Only discovered in 1860 (the manuscript was in the possession of the head of the orchestra, Anselme Huttenbrenner, who had taken it from his brother), it was played for the first time in Vienna on December 1865; Schubert had been dead almost 40 years.

The theory that the work had been duly finished was also supported, in 1939, by Arnold Schering who felt that the *Eighth* was an almost literal transposition of a very strange two paragraph story written by Schubert himself in 1822 and entitled *Mein Traum* (my dream). Today, Nikolaus Harnoncourt acknowledges Schering's theory.

Beethoven, Ludwig van

Symphony No.9, choral 'Hymn to joy', 1826

D minor, opus 125

The making of a hymn

A magnificent synthesis of classical forms, Beethoven's Ninth *and last* Symphony *also succeeds in integrating vocals into the orchestra in the final hymn.*

Opening on a sequence of open fifths by the horns, second violins and cellos, the beginning of the first movement (*allegro ma non troppo, un poco maestoso*) gives the impression of being disorganized, but serves as the basis for the progressive emergence of the first theme, and thus makes it come across even more forcefully. Rigorously constructed in sonata-form, this movement eliminates all the conventional repetitions, as the exposition is not repeated and the recapitulation is profoundly transformed. This transgression of convention gives this *allegro* the nature of an immense development and an extraordinary power.

Placed, exceptionally, in the second position, the scherzo is more of an apology for the rhythm. The drum beats which are in

---

In 1792, inspired by Schiller's poem *Ode to Joy*, Beethoven came up with the idea of setting it to music. The musical theme of the hymn appeared in various versions in some of the composer's earliest works. The best-known example is the *Fantasia* opus 80 for piano, chorus and orchestra, whose theme and formation presage the finale of the *Ninth Symphony*.

---

evidence from the first bars and are frequently repeated by the following ones, confirm this impression.

The slow movement (*adagio molto e cantabile*), which entangles, during variations on its main heme, a fairly similar *andante* theme, becomes more meditative. But the end is disrupted by trumpet sounds.

The introduction of the choral finale, noted *presto*, does not clear up this turbulence. For, after its tremendous initial discord, and alternating with a cello and double bass recitative (whose function is to introduce the vocals), the three preceding movements are evoked, only to be dismissed soon after.

Thus the theme *Hymn to joy* is the only one left in a position to make itself heard, at first timidly and then steadily amplified by its many repeats, to the point of gradually invading the entire movement, whose structure is one of the most complex created by Beethoven. The finale respects the sonata-form, the variation formula and the four movement structure of the symphony (*allegro*, scherzo, *andante*, finale). The *allegro* of the finale exposes to the whole orchestra and the chorus the theme of the hymn, and leads towards a military scherzo with Turkish music. Then the andante exposes a second theme, which is mixed with the hymn by the end of the finale, resulting in a triumphant double fugue preceding the frenetic bacchanale which concludes the work.

Historical references

Composed between 1822 and 1824, this work was performed in Vienna on 7 May 1824 and published in 1826.

Schubert, Franz

Symphony No.9 'Great', 1828

C major, D.944

An irresistible rhythmic flow

Influenced by the Beethovian model, the Ninth Symphony *establishes its independence through its orchestration, its themes and its incessant beat.*

Of impressive length (more than 50 minutes), Schubert's *Ninth Symphony* also has an imposing instrumental complement (flutes, oboes, clarinets, bassoons, horns and trumpets in three pairs, three trombones, kettledrums and strings).

The first movement, *allegro ma no troppo*, is preceded by a slow andante introduction which has two functions. The long phrase of its theme, initially introduced by the solo horns, consists partly in taking over the entire orchestral mass gradually, and partly in generating the principal motifs of the *allegro*. This *allegro*, despite its rigorous sonata-form construction, is unusual in that its themes, far from clashing, develop side by side almost to the point of becoming superimposed. The produced effect is not at all the result of the Beethovian classical conflict, but rather gives the impression of a continuous approach that encircles, in the conclusion, the return of the *andante*, now expanded to almost hymnal proportions.

The second movement (*andante con moto*) first exposes two highly contrasting themes: the first is melodic and supported by a regular rhythmic beat, and the second, much fuller, is almost liturgical in places. The two themes, varied in these ways, become entwined and progressively attain a maximum level of tension played *fortissimo*, which is almost immediately interrupted by two bars of rests. Then a new theme emerges with the strings playing *pizzicati*. This dramatic effect leads to a skilful transition which brings back, the two main themes for one last time.

The most impressive part of the third movement, a scherzo, is the opposition of its central trio, introduced by the horns, 'between the static lyricism of the theme and the forward thrust of its accompaniment' and 'its enrichment of sound, its abrupt minor passages and its permanent modulations' (Brigitte Massin).

With the finale, *allegro vivace*, which contains no less than 1154 bars, the rhythmic fever is picked up again, even more strikingly than before, and the work ends in a victorious atmosphere.

Historical references

The date of the composition is uncertain. Some feel it was not finished until 1828, while others think 1826 a more likely date. Discovered by Schumann in 1839, it was played the same year under the direction of Mendelssohn and published the following year.

Berlioz, Hector

Symphonie Fantastique, 1830

Opus 14

'My life is a novel' (Berlioz)

Many of Berlioz's works echo his emotional concerns. The Fantastique, *an instrumental drama with dreamlike scenes, is exemplary in this regard.*

The arrangement of *Fantastique* into five parts follows the outline of a detailed explanatory 'programme'. But what stands out today is not the somewhat outdated story of this drama, but its instrumental writing. It displays wonderful skill in the variations on the theme of the 'fixed idea' (image of the loved woman) which occurs in the first movement and reappears modified, within each movement: 1. 'Rêveries — Passions'; 2. 'Un bal'; 3. 'Scène aux champs'; 4. 'Marche au supplice'; 5. 'Songe d'une nuit du sabbat'.

In this first great composition Berlioz brilliantly explores the specific possibilities

Along with Liszt's *Symphonic Poems* (1848–81) whose way was paved by it, the *Fantastique* marks an important step in the evolution of 'programme' music. Despite being entitled a symphony, it can be seen as nothing more than a symphonic poem which Liszt, in transcribing it for the piano, greatly helped to popularize.

of each instrument of the orchestra, with the aim of combining their timbres (strings and two harps blended to represent a ball; cor anglais and oboe together to create the country scene and so on). This instrumentation marked a real formal progress, as it was not decorative in any way. As Pierre Boulez remarked, it was about 'instrumental inventions' which 'make up an integral part of the composition, particularly as they are not merely a superficial gloss'.

The *Fantastique* is also innovative in terms of its rhythmic elaborations. And, finally, it has transformed the compositional schema of the classical symphony by following a method of thematic exploration which presupposes that 'the purpose of themes is not necessarily constrained to a single development divided up by the sectioning of the movements' (Claude Ballif).

Historical references

Written when Berlioz was 26, the *Symphonie Fantastique*, symptomatically sub-titled 'Episode from the life of an artist', is the sometimes happy, sometimes nightmarish evocation of the conflict-ridden love between Berlioz and the Irish actress Harriet Smithson who he met in 1827 and married in 1833. The work, whose 'programme' was published in *Le Figaro* on 21 May 1829, was acclaimed by the romantic youth on the night of its première on 5 December 1830.

The 'fixed idea,' the main theme played by the flute and then by the clarinet and bassoon.

Mendelssohn, Felix

Symphony No.4, 'Italian', 1833

A major, Opus 90

A melodic extension

The 'Italian' Symphony *is strongly dominated by a melodic brio which is responsible for this symphony being Mendelssohn's most popular.*

Some people saw the *Italian* as an essentially descriptive work depicting four scenes from a Roman carnival: 1. 'Carnival'; 2. 'Procession'; 3. 'In the Roman rooms'; 4. 'Carnival dance'. It is unlikely, however, that Mendelssohn would have followed this descriptive plan of an overdone image that he had never shown any interest in whatsoever. On the contrary, just as he had found in Walter Scott's novel certain folk themes and images of Scotland that he used as extra-musical sources for his '*Scottish' Symphony*, it is likely that he turned to his personal experiences of Italian ruins and

countryside and a Neapolitan dance as the compositional sources for the creation of the *Italian*.

The lively and 'vigorous sound of the violins which open the first movement create a tone of heroism' (Rémi Jacobs) in the *allegro vivace* whose second theme, not radically different from the ardent first theme, completely tempers the rhythmical-melodic exuberance and mood of *perpetuum mobile*.

From the beginning of the second movement (*andante con moto* in D minor) the oboes, bassoons and violas expose the fairly solemn melody of a choral repeated by the violins and constantly supported in the background by the *staccato* playing of the cellos and basses. Slightly livelier, the central part of the piece momentarily puts the clarinet into relief before returning conclusively to the theme based on the choral melody.

In the third movement, a *Con moto moderato* in A major with a trio in E, Mendelssohn gives a very fine example of his melodic extension skill. The orchestral coloration of the trio (horn calls) is reminiscent of Weber.

As for the finale, marked *saltarello (presto)*, but whose rapid rhythm is more that of a tarentella (a dance from the south of Italy), it develops its melodic motifs in a lively manner over the foundation of a stylistic *ostinato* of sorts.

The other symphonies

Besides the 12 symphonies for string orchestra composed when he was very young (1821–3), Mendelssohn created five other symphonies, only three of which are particularly interesting: the *Italian*; the *Symphony No.3 in A minor, Scottish*, opus 56 (started in 1829, finished in 1842) and the *Symphony No.5 in D minor, 'Reformation'*, opus 107 (begun in 1829, completed in 1830), the epitome of the 'choral symphony' which was the object of scorn by Debussy (Mister anti-dilettante Quaver).

Historical references

Started during a trip to Rome (1 November 1830 to April 1831), the *Italian* was finished in London in 1833. This city was also the location of its first performance (13 May 1833, conducted by the composer).

Berlioz, Hector

Harold in Italy, symphony with principal viola, 1834

Opus 16

A very carefully laid out sound set

The indifference displayed by the character of Harold, represented by a solo viola, towards the scenery he passes through gives Berlioz the pretext for superimposing very different sound patterns.

Berlioz's second symphony, *Harold in Italy* has a unique structure. On one hand, the chosen solo instrument — a viola — is one of the least 'resonant' instruments there is, and Harold's theme is hardly 'brilliant', especially in comparison with the themes of the other four movements which are very strong. According to Berlioz, the 'unpreponderant' viola is only 'combined with the orchestra' and 'does not deprive the orchestral mass of any of its force'. In actual fact, the leitmotiv of Harold proves, on analysis, to have generated all the thematic material of the symphony. And the relations thus established allow it to merge into the midst of the material that it has been largely responsible for organizing.

Although Harold is inspired directly by Byron's *Childe Harold*, the scenes, through which Berlioz has him travel, are based, according to the composer, on 'the poetic recollections of my peregrinations in the Abruzzes'. *Harold in Italy* was originally called *The Last Moments of Mary Stuart* so we must, therefore, refrain from 'giving up' on his 'programme' music.

The slow introduction, *adagio*, which takes up half of the initial movement, *Harold in the mountains*, is remarkable mainly in its beginning, displaying spectacular contrapuntal skill, there gradually emerges Harold's theme, at first played in minor by the winds then replayed in major by the viola. The *adagio* then moves towards an *allegro* full of rhythmic junctions and orchestral *tutti*.

'The Pilgrim's March' which follows evokes the passing of a cortège whose litany, in each verse, is punctuated by a C natural played by two horns and a harp, simulating a distant bell. The force of this effect comes from Berlioz's success in economically halving the sound space.

While the middle section of this second movement consists in superimposing three different levels (arpeggios played by the viola, rhythmic beat by the double basses and choral by the violins and woods), the third movement, '*An Abruzzo Highlander serenades his mistress*', of folklore origins, also succeeds, in the last part, in distributing various thematic elements over its three sound levels. The effect is all the more original as the polyphony achieved is 'complicated by an interesting polyrhythm' (Henri Barraud).

The last movement 'Brigand's Orgy' is an orchestral orgy which contains the seeds of many future innovations.

Historical references

Harold is the result of a commission by Paganini, who wanted a viola concerto. But due to the very limited role given to the soloist, it was Urham rather then Paganini who performed the work in 1834.

Berlioz, Hector

Roméo et Juliette, dramatic symphony, 1839

Opus 17

The orchestra in all its forms

More loyal to the dramatic plot taken from Shakespeare than to the structure of the classical symphony, Roméo et Juliette *inaugurates an unusual musical form.*

Berlioz, in his symphony 'with chorus and solo singers', abandons the voice as soon as it comes to dealing with love, preferring to leave his central extra-musical theme to the orchestra alone; thus the work manages to transmute its literary subject into a purer musical representation. This immense composition is divided into four parts, each one containing several narrative sections.

A brief fugal introduction followed by a prologue with recitatives and chorus — a kind of vocal outline of the principal scenes of the drama — constitutes the first part.

The three purely instrumental sections of the second part ('Romeo alone'; 'Sorrow'; 'Distant sounds of a ball and concert'; 'Feast at the Capulets') begin the actual musical plot. Because of its bold chromatic writing, the first section gives the impression of Berlioz as a 'breakaway musician' who then spectacularly confirms his skill of superimposing themes and tempos in the famous feast at the Capulets.

The chorus and orchestra introduce the third part, with three sections ('Serene Night', 'The Capulets' gardens silent and deserted', 'The Young Capulets leave the Palace singing') which is followed by an instrumental *adagio* called 'Love Scene'. This passage is one of the most beautiful in the work: a 'tune which generates itself in inexhaustibly renewed rhythmic and melodic figures' (Michel Chion).

A no less remarkable episode is 'Queen Mab's Scherzo' (orchestra alone) which begins the fourth part. Here Berlioz displays a prodigious sense of instrumentation by weaving a network of 'microscopic sounds' developed *pianissimo* on a lively saltarello rhythm. Next comes the alternately instrumental and vocal fugal march of Juliette's funeral, itself linked to an orchestral piece (Romeo at the Capulets' tomb) which is alternately pathetic, spasmodic and exalted. Far less convincing, the finale for solo bass ('Father Lawrence's Aria'), chorus ('Fight and Reconciliation between the Capulets and the Montagues') and orchestra, is reduced to nothing more than a fairly conventional opera scene.

Historical references

The work was composed between January and September 1839. The Poet Émile Deschamps, a translator of Shakespeare, wrote the words. Dedicated to Paganini, it was played for the first time on 24 November 1839.

After Berlioz, several composers used the story of *Romeo and Juliet* as a theme: Gounod (*Roméo et Juliette*, opera, 1867); Tchaikovsky (*Romeo and Juliet*, fantasia overture, (1880); Prokofiev (*Romeo and Juliet*, ballet, 1935–6). Bellini's opera *The Capulets and the Montagues* (1830) was written nine years before the work of the great French Romantic.

Schumann, Robert

Symphony No.3 'Rhenish', 1851

B flat major, opus 97

Romanticism under the scrutiny of classicism

With his symphonies, Schumann attempted to achieve a 'new unity of genre' (Boucourechliev) by adapting the romantic instability of his writing to a more classical construction.

Schumann's symphonies received a bad press for a long time. They were criticized for being poorly constructed, badly orchestrated and for occupying a hybrid position between the symphony and the symphonic poem. Today, despite, or because of, these faults, they are regarded as being the first attempt at the extension of a form, for having tried to integrate into one coherent whole extremely disparate elements. In the way in which their various movements are organically interdependent, they also seem to foreshadow the later Sibelius and, in the extent that they represent 'the point of all musical and imaginary confluences' (Dominique Jameux), prefigure Mahler's aesthetic.

One must see the subtitle *Rhenish* as indicating less a precise musical programme

Schumann composed his four symphonies over a period of just ten years (1841–51). The first, in B flat, *Spring*, opus 38 was written in 1841; the *Second*, in C major opus 61 in 1846. As for the *Fourth*, in D minor opus 120, Schumann wrote a first version in 1841, and then rewrote it in 1851; its four movements are connected without interruption, and its particularly striking formal unity makes it, in fact, the most successful of the four.

than an allegiance to German Romanticism, as symbolized by the image of the Rhine. For this reason, in the composer's own words, the 'popular elements' predominate here, even though the work also exhibits extremely accomplished counterpoint.

The first of the five movements, 'Lebhaft' (lively), in its method of developing its two highly antagonistic themes — one being very rhythmically energetic and exposed by the whole orchestra, and the other which is lyrical but secondary to the first — is the movement which most clearly displays a concern for almost Beethovian formal construction. It also hardly prepares us for the diversity of scenes which are to come.

First, a scherzo varies a popular song inspired by a Ländler, and contrasts with its trio section which is played mainly by wind instruments. Then, in third position, is a slow movement 'Nicht Schnell' (without haste), which is characterized by the continual changing of its orchestration and by the way in which a solo instrument occasionally breaks away, for a brief moment, from the overall texture.

The fourth movement 'Feierlich' (solemn), also with a slow tempo, serves to introduce the finale. With the mood of a choral and played by the trombones and the horns, the theme develops according to an orchestral polyphony whose magnificent counterpoint testifies to Schumann's knowledge of Bach's works. A fifth and last movement, 'Lebhaft' (lively) closes the work in an atmosphere of a country fair.

Historical references

This work was composed in 1850 and performed in 1851, under the direction of the composer.

Liszt, Franz

Faust-Symphony, 1857

A pre-Wagnerian principle

The themes which represent the three characters of the Faust-Symphony *and continuously combine with each other throughout the work, are a foreshadowing of the Wagnerian leitmotiv.*

The original title of the work (*A Symphony about Faust in three psychological portraits*) suggests that Liszt, with his three movements respectively devoted to Faust, Margaret and Mephistopheles, does not follow the development of the story, but rather creates a musical picture of the three main protagonists of Goethe's text. While the intention of the *Faust-Symphony* was to characterize certain figures by a certain number of thematic elements which prefigured Wagner, its realization reveals an orchestral effort which, in following Berlioz's model, is no less exemplary.

The slow introduction of the first movement, '*Faust*,' is particularly striking in this

The *Faust-Symphony* was expanded by the addition of an epilogue for tenor and men's choir at the time of its first performance.

Another symphony by Liszt: The *Dante-Symphony*. Composed in 1855–6, it contains two movements 'Hell' and 'Purgatory', linked together on a choral magnificat. First performed in Dresden in 1857, it is dedicated to Richard Wagner.

respect. The instruments, often solo, which follow each other smoothly, produce undeniable timbre melodies or merge into sonorous blends, very unusual for the time. But this introduction also has the function of exposing the first two themes attributed to Faust: the chromatic, almost atonal theme of 'anxiety' and the theme of 'love', played by the oboes. Mingling with each other, they move towards a rapid section where we hear the two other themes of Faust: the first tumultuous and played by the strings, the second heroic and played by the brasses. Undoubtedly in order to stabilize a character who is fairly perturbed by the presence of four antagonistic themes, 'Faust' is the only movement of the work in which Liszt refers to a classical form with the use of the sonata-form.

Although 'Margaret' — the following movement with a slow tempo — only has one theme, it is soon after combined with Faust's themes and gives rise to orchestral innovations such as the harp *glissandi* heard in the middle section.

The principle underlying the third movement, 'Mephistopheles' (*allegro vivace-ironico*), is perhaps the most original of the work. For this 'nihilistic character' Liszt did not compose any new themes, being content to reuse Faust's themes and caricaturing them. The devil is thus depicted here as the metamorphosized image of the 'Self', and such a conception allows this magnificently orchestrated dance to show once again Liszt's 'cyclical spirit'.

Historical references

Composed in 1853–4, the *Faust-Symphony* was first performed in 1857. It is dedicated to Berlioz.

Lalo, Edouard

Spanish Symphony, 1873

D minor, opus 21

A skilfully 'characterized' style

This work combines two forms (symphony and concerto) and abounds in 'effects' intended to highlight the solo violin.

The first of five movements of the *Spanish Symphony*, an *allegro non troppo* in D minor built on the model of the symphony *allegro* with two themes, develops from a very rhythmic phrase followed by a habanera. In the scherzando (G major), the melody, put into relief by the soloist, is played on a seguidilla rhythm. We return to the rhythmic structure of the habanera with the *intermezzo* in A minor. The *andante* (D minor) is constructed around a melodic figure inspired by the tsigane style, while the final rondo, marked *allegro*, introduces several Spanish themes played on a foundation of basso ostinato.

Historical references

Composed in 1873, the *Spanish Symphony* was performed in Paris on 7 February 1875. It was an immediate and great success.

Franck, César

Symphony in D minor, 1889

A strictly symmetrical machine *(M. Marnat)*

The Symphony in D minor *is a lyrical work which synthesizes the German romantic style with the French-style 'classicism'.*

This composition in three movements begins with a piece which alternates a dramatic initial *lento* with an *allegro non troppo* which are rich in complex but haphazardly organized thematic material.

The simpler *allegretto* is also more rational: 'two themes in minor make up its skeleton, each of these — the main innovation of this work — once finished, are followed by a secondary motif contrastingly exposed in major' (Jean Gallois).

Built around two principal themes, the final *allegro non troppo* brings back the essential themes of the symphony according to one of Liszt's favourite principles: the cyclical form.

Historical references

Started in 1886, the *Symphony in D minor* was completed in 1888 and produced in Paris on 17 February 1889.

Bruckner, Anton

Symphony No.7, 1886

E major, opus 110

For the 'heavenly duration' *(67 minutes)*

Bruckner's Seventh Symphony *marks the apogee of an incontestably original symphonic work, but one which is less revolutionary than 'evolutionary' (J. Gallois)*

The *Symphony No.7* is built on the traditional plan of four movements. Its initial *allegro moderato* in expanded sonata-form, exposes three essentially melodic themes: the first, introduced by cellos and horns under a string tremolo, is immediately striking in its richness of sound and is fairly tense. The second, which is calmer and developed from the melody of the oboes and clarinets, has a very distinct Wagnerian character which the third theme obscures by overlapping on a persistent rhythm by the strings, several complex melodic-harmonic combinations.

Started when the premonition of Wagner's death was haunting Bruckner and finished under the blow of the news that he had died, the *adagio molto lento e maestoso* (constructed as a rondo) is very like a funeral ode with two themes, one in C sharp (conveying overwhelming calamity) and the other in F sharp (giving the pacifying mood of a requiem); the theme in minor is introduced by an impressive tuba quartet.

This emotionally charged passage (the most famous of the composer's) is followed by a rhythmic scherzo (general key of A minor) marked Nicht Schnell. Built on a single theme made up of three distinct motifs, it contains a trio in F major to be played 'a little bit slower' in which the melody predominates.

The finale, an *allegro ma non troppo*, is structured like a sonata movement with two themes. From the beginning of the piece, the initial theme, exposed by the first violins, breaks through from under a tremolo of second violins; it derives from the theme with which the *allegro moderato* (first movement) begins. As for the second theme, it is handled by a string choral introduced by the violins on a *pizzicati* base (cellos).

Historical references

The composition of this work occupied Bruckner from 23 September 1881 until 5 September 1883. First performed in Leipzig on 30 December 1884 by Arthur Nikisch for a benefit concert given as a memorial to Wagner, this symphony (dedicated to King Louis II of Bavaria) aroused enormous enthusiasm and finally made the name of Anton Bruckner (at the age of 60) known to the public. The success in Leipzig was replicated in Munich, Karlsruhe, Cologne, Hamburg and elsewhere. Only Vienna reacted negatively: on the night of the Viennese premiere (21 March 1886) the critic Hanslick spoke of a musical 'boa constrictor'.

The writing of *Symphony No.7*, resolutely tonal, while still being 'very modulating', often chromatic and rich in contrapuntal ornamentation, summarizes well the Brucknerian symphonic art, an art which is otherwise a stranger to timbre work experimentation. The orchestration reflects a concern with putting in relief different parts of a musical discourse based on the principle of unity and on the law of contrasts, and in which silence, as with Schubert and later Mahler, plays an important role.

Saint-Saëns, Camille

Symphony No.3 'with organ', 1886

C minor, opus 78

A well-balanced consequence of Romanticism

By applying, in a thoroughly classical spirit, the general principle of variation inherited from Liszt, Saint-Saëns' Third Symphony *avoids academicism through its instrumentation.*

The *Symphony 'with organ'* is unique, firstly, in having been divided into only two parts, even though it certainly contains the traditional four movements. For, as Saint-Saëns himself indicated, the first movement, *allegro*, 'arrested in its development, serves as the introduction to the *adagio*, and the scherzo is linked by the same process to the finale'. The composer also adds that he had 'sought, by this means, to avoid to a degree the interminable repeats and repetitions that tend to disappear from instrumental music'.

The second unique feature of his work has to do with its orchestration. Thinking, 'that the moment had come, for the symphony, to benefit from the advances of modern instrumentation', Saint-Saëns did not hesitate to use a very well-stocked orchestra with no less than three flutes, two oboes, one tenor oboe, two clarinets, one bass clarinet, two bassoons, four horns, three trumpets, one tuba, three kettle-drums, one organ, one piano (played sometimes with two hands, sometimes with four), one triangle, one pair of cymbals, one bass drum and a string quartet.

After a brief slow introduction, the highly structured first movement, *allegro moderato*, develops, with the involvement of the entire orchestra, a theme descended from *Dies Irae*

which continues to be heard throughout the piece. Played immediately after the first, the second movement is an *adagio* whose quasi-religious mood comes from the selected orchestration: the organ, supported by the string quartet.

The scherzo (*allegro moderato*), first movement of the second part, which marks the appearance of the piano, consists primarily of the varied repeat of *Dies Irae*, stressed vigorously this time. A calmer section, acting as a transition, leads to the finale (*maestoso*) which opens with a chord struck on the organ and immediately produces the effect of a solemn march. Next, the music, becoming louder and faster against a background of arpeggios played on the piano, comes to a close in a bombastic atmosphere in which the combined efforts of the organ and orchestra converge completely.

Historical references

Composed in 1886 at the request of the London Royal Philharmonic Society, Saint-Saëns' *Symphony No.3* was first performed on 19 May of the same year. It is dedicated to the memory of Franz Liszt, who was too ill to participate in the performance. He died shortly after, on 1 August 1886.

> At the first French performance by the Conservatory Concert Society, Gounod pointed out the composer and declared 'I present to you the French Beethoven'. Saint-Saëns, being more modest and more clear-headed, simply said of his symphony, 'I gave it all that I could give'.

Brahms, Johannes

Symphony No.4, 1886

E minor, opus 98

The romantic panegyric of polyphony

The Fourth Symphony *is a skilful contrapuntal work in which Brahms effects a return to Bach in the elegiac mode characteristic of many of the pieces written towards the end of his life.*

With a wealth of harmonic and rhythmic innovation, the first movement, a sonata-form *allegro ma non troppo* in E minor, contains two themes and four secondary motifs. The first theme, introduced by violins and punctuated by rests, plays an essential role in the structure of the whole composition. It undergoes a system of melodic variation which allows Brahms to present it as a genuine chacone theme: the whole work, from then on, is dominated by this musical form, which we know Bach made use of in his time (*Chacone from Partita No.2 in D minor* for solo violin). Played on wind instruments with a string accompaniment, the second

theme does not have the same structural importance; it contrasts with the first only in its much more energetic character.

Four introductory bars played in unison by the horns and the woods, mark the beginning of the *andante moderato* (in E major) which plays on the alternation of two principal themes, one of which is typically elegiac and the other blatantly lyrical. Here, 'the spirit of the chacone' (Claude Rostand) is only found in a diffuse state, mainly in the rhythmics of the first theme with which the whole piece is tinted.

The *allegro giocoso* in C major which follows, although it has the exuberant nature of a scherzo, is constructed in sonata-form. A complex process of thematic generation implying during the development, the return of the themes of the first movement, preserves the 'spirit of the chacone'.

In the finale, a rather tense *allegro energico e passionato* in E minor treated exactly like a chacone, Brahms introduces a theme of J. S. Bach taken from the *Cantata 150* 'Meine Tage in den Leiden'. Barely modified, this theme of eight bars repeated in the form of 31 variations constitutes the polyphonic framework of the whole movement. Added to this finale are a coda *poco più allegro* with four variations and a final cadence of six bars.

An instrumental form which comes from an old (16–17th century) dance of Spanish origin, the *chacone* (or chaconne) is very similar to the *passacaille*. Like this dance, it 'consists of a series of expositions of the same theme; but here the fundamental pattern is not only varied in its accompaniment, it undergoes transformations which simulate its own contours according to the system of variations called thematic amplification' (André Hodeir).

Historical references

Composed in 1885 in Mürzzuschlag (Styria), the work was first performed in Meiningen on 25 October of the same year. The enormous success it gained at its premiere was not replicated in Vienna on 17 January, 1886, however.

Tchaikovsky, Piotr Ilyich

Symphony No.6 'Pathétique', 1893

B minor, opus 74

The impression of a secret agenda

The first unique feature of the Pathétique is that is does not respect the traditional order of movements. But it is also innovative in its orchestration and rhythm work.

The development of the symphony and the unusual placing of its slow movement in last position creates the perception of a drama carried out in four sections: Exposition, Diversion, Precipitation, Lamentation, but without revealing enough for us to know what drama, other than musical, it is.

Preceded by a slow *adagio* introduction in which the low register is taken even lower by the use of a bassoon, the first movement, *allegro non troppo*, first exposes its two main themes; one rhythmic and hurried, the other melodic with a more restrained tempo. The last bars of the exposition are

A questionable theory

Tchaikovsky died one week after the first performance of the *Pathétique*, on 28 October 1893. Many critics believed that the cryptic programme of his symphony must be biographical, and that the composer had described in it his imminent death. This theory has recently been seriously weakened: Tchaikovsky was, in fact, driven to suicide after appearing before a jury looking into a scandal regarding his homosexuality. History, however, considers it kinder to say that he died from cholera.

played *pianissimo* by a solo clarinet. The contrast with the *fortissimo* entry of the development is one of the most striking there is. Especially as the orchestral mass, playing in jerky motifs, and unexpectedly distributed on very differentiated levels, gives the impression of an expansion of the entire sound space. The orthodox funeral motif played by the horns and tuba seems to recede into the distance. Once the melodic theme has been recapitulated, the movement finishes in a relaxed atmosphere created by the regularity of the *pizzicati* in the coda.

The second and third movements are both based on pre-arranged musical material; the first (*allegro con grazia*) is a kind of waltz which Tchaikovsky, demonstrating a great rhythmic subtlety, wrote in quintuple time; the second (*allegro molto vivace*) a march. While the waltz creates the pleasant atmosphere of a ballet, the march is almost diabolical and certainly the most modern movement of the symphony. Skilfully orchestrated and rearranging some of its layers in such a way that they are perceived as textures, it includes polyphonies whose rhythmic organization still has the power to amaze.

The work finishes with a slow movement (*adagio lamentoso*) that also abounds in orchestral innovations which are picked up later by Gustav Mahler.

Historical references

Composed in 1893, Tchaikovsky's *Sixth Symphony* was performed on 16 October the same year, under the direction of the composer. His brother, Modeste, suggested the title *Pathétique*.

Dvořák, Anton

Symphony No.9, 'From the New World', 1894

E minor, opus 95

A medley of folklore

Influenced by many different folklores, the Symphony 'From the New World' *is presented as a musical patchwork made homogenous by a solid orchestration.*

Opus 95 is the first of the compositions written by Dvořák during his visit to the United States (1892–5). Less based on a descriptive style conveying the impressions created by the liveliness of a big city like New York or the vastness of the scenery on the other side of the Atlantic, this work is distinguished by certain unique features of its writing: the use of modal scales with five notes (pentatonic), the frequent recourse to dotted rhythm, rests and syncopation. For many musicologists these peculiarities show the influence of the 'black spirituals' and popular Indian songs; others think the work only has connections with Czech (or Slavic in general), Austrian or Scottish popular music.

Composed in the general key of the symphony (E minor), the first movement begins

The title 'From the New World' gives the symphony the sense of an address to friends, to the music lovers of his country; in short to the 'Old Europe' which the composer had left with regret.

with an *adagio* linked to a very animated and essentially rhythmic *allegro molto*. This is the only movement of the work which maintains the structure of the sonata form intact.

At the beginning of the second movement (a *largo* in D flat major), after choral chords played by the brasses, the solo cor anglais exposes the famous melody — main theme of the piece — which was probably inspired by Dvořák's reading of Longfellow's *Hiawatha* (1855). Whether or not it is evocative of an Indian funeral scene, this theme is nonetheless an excellent example of Dvořák's art of 'pentatonization' ...

To be played *molto vivace*, the third movement (general key of E minor) is a brilliant and lively scherzo built on the basis of a small worked motif in canon.

The finale, an *allegro con fuoco* in E minor, alternates in the framework of a kind of fantasia. Clear, succinct and very rhythmic, the first of these themes contributed significantly to the immense popular success of this work.

Historical references

Started in the winter of 1892–3 and finished in May 1893, the *Symphony 'From the New World'*, was triumphantly performed on 16 December 1893 at Carnegie Hall in New York by Anton Seidl with the New York Philharmonic Orchestra. Dvořák conducted the European performance on 13 October 1894 at the National Theatre of Prague.

Mahler, Gustav

Symphony No.7, 1905

E minor

In praise of heterogeneity

A work which places great demands on the listener, created with the aim of making 'the ductility of musical time' (P. Boulez) perceptible, the Seventh Symphony *generates 'celestial lengths'.*

Directed mostly towards the future, even though Mahler always shows respect for the traditions of the 19th century (Beethoven, Brahms), the *Seventh Symphony* seems not only like a new exploration of Wagnerian melodic and harmonic innovation, but also and primarily like a work aimed more or less consciously at overtaking an entire musical language 'sick' with its tonal system. It is made up of a purely instrumental ensemble (symphonies two, three, four and eight bring in one or two voices) divided into five movements.

The initial *allegro* ('Langsam': slow; *allegro risoluto ma non troppo*) is actually a slow movement in sonata-form, very darkly coloured (use of tenor horn, trombones, etc), less tragic than epic and in which

In the *Fifth, Sixth* and *Seventh Symphonies*, the Mahlerian technique of sound montage and of folklore citation is refined by developing more and more in line with an original procedure of re-creation of polyphony, following which, according to Mahler, the themes which depict the sounds of a fun fair 'must come from all sides and remain totally different in their rhythms and melodies', with the composer intervening 'to organize' and put together all the pieces into a coherent whole'.

different sections link together to form a 'perpetual variation' (Adorno) which is often close to atonality because of its super-imposition of fourths.

The first nocturne ('Nachtmusik' of the composition is the second movement (*allegro moderato*) and has the form of a rondo Mahler returns here to the medieval 'military' spirit of some of his *Wunderhorn Lieder* (1892–8).

In the bold discontinuity of its timbre, the third movement, a *scherzo* in D minor marked 'Schattenhaft' (shadowy), lets a feeling of anxiety show through, associated with the almost fantastical evocation of night.

The fourth movement and second nocturne, an *andante amoroso* in F major not without humour, belong to the genre of serenade. Admirably orchestrated, it brings in the guitar whose timbre, according to Schönberg, was at the origin of the conception of the entire movement. This is followed by the finale (*rondo allegro ordinario*), an excellent illustration of the Mahlerian concept of a polyphony inspired by the superimposition of sounds creating the din of a fun fair.

For many musicologists, such as Karl Schumann, this piece was created as a 'huge mockery of the accepted aesthetic of the times, like a resounding satire of the vulgarity of the world and a commentary of the pompous style of the turn of the century'.

Historical references

Begun in the summer of 1904, the *Seventh Symphony* was finished the following summer. Its first performance was in Prague (19 September 1908) where the work, conducted by the composer, was praised only by the critics.

Schönberg, Arnold

Chamber Symphony No.1 for 15 instruments, 1906

Opus 9

A necessary contraction

The reductions in length and of instrumental complement made to this work only serve to better focus 'the emancipation of the discord' attempted by Schönberg.

A product of the composer's first period, the *Chamber Symphony No.1* is full of innovation. Firstly, it reduces the symphony orchestra to a group of 15 soloists. But the instruments chosen (flute, oboe, cor anglais, bassoon, double bassoon, two horns, two violins, viola, cello and double bass) and the importance accorded to the low registers paradoxically create 'a more extensive range' (J. P. Derrien). The second innovation is that the symphony has only one movement. But it is made up of five discernible parts: sonata exposition, scherzo, development, quasi adagio, and finale, the

Immediately after completing his *Chamber Symphony No.1*, Schönberg began writing a second. Started in 1906, then returned to in 1911 and 1916, he did not finish it until much later, 1939, when he was exiled in the United States. It is, in a sense, the traditional opposite of the first; tonality is hardly threatened at all, and its instrumental formation is that of Haydn's symphonies.

arrangement of which is based both on the structure of a symphony in four movements and that of a sonata-form.

It is impossible not to see, in this overlapping of two structures, a consolidation attempt intended to channel the most destabilizing innovation of the work and of historical importance as it consists in overturning tonality. From the fifth bar, introduced by the horns on a very rapid tempo there is a succession of *consecutive fourths* which is one of the foundations of the piece. The melodic formations derived from the whole tone scale also appear in the principal figure of the first theme, exposed by the cello. Whereas, the interval of a fourth and the whole note scale have, with regards to tonality, the function of demolition. To build a work on the basis of discordant elements prepared the route towards atonality, a stage which Schönberg was to pass through with *String Quartet* opus 10. The writing of opus 9 also displays a new kind of 'coherence' (Schönberg). The intervals of fourths, while they are used melodically are also used harmonically (in the form of chords). In other words, Schönberg begins here to reduce melody and harmony to a common denominator, and this principle of economy foreshadows the future serialism.

Consecutive fourths of the Chamber Symphony

Historical references

Composed in 1906, it was performed the following year in Vienna where it caused a great scandal.

Mahler, Gustav

Symphony No.9, 1912

Symphonic substance metamorphosized

The modernity of Mahler's Ninth
Symphony *comes from the fact
that it is associated less with the
assembly of preconstituted musical
forms (ländler, fugues, citations)
than with their continuous
transformation.*

The basic unit on which Mahler organized
his music was not the theme, but the pre-
constructed *block*. Although this *block* made
use, in the first works, of pre-existing
musical entities such as the waltz, march or
ländler, it gave way, in his later works, to
genuine 'thematic complexities' (Adorno).
This change of scale of the base cell (going
from the theme to the block) explains why
Mahler's works are so long (the *Ninth* lasts
$1\frac{1}{2}$ hours) and also assumes that 'the listener
must arrange his memory in blocks, if he
hopes to understand musical relationships'
(Claude Malherbe).

The Tenth Symphony

In 1910 Mahler began writing his *Tenth
Symphony* which was to contain five
movements. The first and third movements
which are the most accomplished, an *adagio*
and a *purgatorio*, were published in 1924 by
Ernst Krenek and the work was completed in
the 1960s by Deryck Cooke. Only the initial
adagio is frequently played today for, even
though it was strictly speaking only a sketch, it
is one of Mahler's most radical passages.

In this respect, the first movement of the
Ninth, *andante comodo*, marks the successful
outcome of this problem. The motifs 'are
tirelessly varied, increased, reduced, put
together, taken apart and superimposed'
(Henry-Louis de La Grange), to the point
that the technique of progressive development has to do with 'the variant, as opposed
to the variation' (Adorno). The symphonic
material used does not appear to be pre-
established, but rather produced by its own
organization. As for the general profile of
the movement, it progresses through many
sequences, alternately, of tension and relaxation, the former ending with striking
orchestral *tutti* and the latter in segments of
'collapse' (Erwin Ratz), where the music,
left to pursue its own course, gives the
impression of floating. These segments are
the most original of the piece, particularly
in their conception of the orchestra, which
in treating it like a group of soloists, is
already the conception found in modern
music.

The two central movements, dominated
by humour, both set out to deconstruct
worn-out musical material. The scherzo
goes to work on a popular type, the dance;
while the burlesque rondo, in a hallucinatory display of virtuosity, restructures
the most complex form there is: the fugue.

The finale *adagio* occupies an intermediate position, for while its main material
is a simple *gruppetto*, its immense development gives rise to innumerable variants.
And in the coda, the music slowly falls
apart, as if sentenced to silence.

Historical references

Written in 1908 and 1911, this work was
performed in Vienna for the first time on
20 June 1912, under the direction of Bruno
Walter.

Sibelius, Jean

Symphony No.5, 1919

E flat major, opus 82

The art of fusion (M. Vignal)

A controversial figure for a long time, due to his conservatism, Sibelius is today considered, especially with Opus 82, *to be an important renovator of the symphonic form.*

Symphony No.5 conveys a desire for formal restructuring in the complex treatment of its first movement (*tempo molto moderato* and *allegro moderato*); which brings out, over four joined episodes, a genuinely original 'synthesis of slow Wagnerian rhythm and Beethovian dynamics' (Marc Vignal).

The exposition, first of the four episodes, begins with a horn call of eight notes played on a muffled drum roll: this is the initial theme of the section. Soon interwoven with three others, it forms a 'first group of themes' which only uses wind instruments and the support of the drums. The introduction of the strings, in the 17th bar, marks the entrance of a 'second group of themes' (principal key of G major) with even more pathos than the first. The second episode returns to the thematic material of the preceding one with orchestral variants which give it an extra touch of brio. At the beginning of the development (third episode), a

very striking passage, the musical discourse which is gradually losing its thematic direction and its driving force, suddenly appear to be static, as if it must remain immobile on the brink of silence. It abruptly rediscovers its dynamism after an intervention by the brasses followed by the emergence of a powerful theme leading to a *crescendo* which creates a strong dramatic tension. This tension, after a skilfully handled transition (going from slow to rapid tempo), culminates in the fourth and last episode which is distinguished by its hymnal scherzo nature.

Much simpler in conception, the second movement, an *andante mosso quasi allegretto* in G major, is a series of variations developed from a single theme.

Marked *allegro molto*, the finale (in E flat) is based on three major themes initially exposed together then played in isolation; the first in the development, the second during the recapitulation and the last in coda.

Historical references

The object of three different versions, this work, begun in 1914, was played for the first time in its definitive version (1919) on 24 November 1919 in Helsinki. It had been performed in its original version (four movements) in the same city on 8 December 1915, the composer's 50th birthday.

Prokofiev, Sergei

Symphony No.1, 'Classical', 1918

D major, opus 25

A famous 'in the style of'

Symphony No.1 marks less a 'return to' Haydn than it pays tribute to him via a modernized pastiche.

Created as a parody, the famous and very short *Classical* was also considered by Prokofiev to be a necessary exercise in learning how to compose without a piano. It resulted in this piece which is not lacking in old-fashioned charm and whose many parts attest to a great writing skill.

An *allegro* in sonata-form with two lively and rhythmic themes is followed by a more melodic *larghetto*. The little gavotte which follows, substituted for the traditional minuet, is marked by a great harmonic fluidity. Taking up again many of the thematic elements of the *allegro*, the turbulent finale (*molto vivace*) creates the sense of a perpetuum mobile.

Historical references

Composed in 1916–17, the *Symphony No.1* was played for the first time in Petrograd in 1918 under the direction of the composer.

Shostakovich, Dmitri

Symphony No.2 'October', 1927

B major, opus 14

A modernized celebration

A committed work, Symphony No.2 *participates nonetheless in the contemporary modernism movement.*

In this composition, Shostakovich abandons the traditional quadripartite division in favour of a single musical mass without any 'classical' thematic development. It is divided only in the second half by the intervention of the chorus (a hymn on the class struggle which finishes with a salute to the October Revolution and to Lenin). This chorus unfortunately is much less boldly written than the instrumental part which is often atonal and takes its best effects from a post-Schönbergian and post-Stravinsky melodic and harmonic distortion.

Historical references

A commission by the Soviet Government, who wanted to celebrate the tenth anniversary of the October Revolution, *Symphony No.2*, composed in 1927, was performed in Leningrad the same year.

Janácek, Leos

Sinfonietta, 1927

Opus 60

Fanfare for the birth of a nation

Although the Sinfonietta, *a tribute by the septuagenarian Janácek to the young Czechoslovakian state is naïve in its plan, the innovations of its writing belong absolutely to the 20th century.*

Full of intentionally raw colour and calling on Czech national folklore tunes, the *Sinfonietta* contains five movements.

The first, *allegretto*, is a fanfare for nine trumpets, two tubas, two bass trumpets and kettledrums. It is resolutely monothematic and unfolds according to a favourite technique of Janácek's consisting in mixing variations of a theme with its continuous repetition.

The second movement, *andante*, contains two themes; the first has the nature of a popular dance and the second lyrical. These two themes, played respectively on the oboe and on the flute and oboe, give way to five variations.

After a *moderato* using strings with mutes alternately crossed over by a trombone choral, a country dance and another fanfare, the fourth movement, *allegretto*, initially develops a polka theme and finishes with an extremely rapid stretta which soon after involves the whole orchestra.

The fifth movement, *andante allegretto*, opens on a bucolic theme played by three flutes at first, and then developed on a base of basso ostinato. But this calm is quickly disrupted by the reappearance of the initial fanfare whose role is to put the final end to the work.

But it is the boldly innovative musical treatment that should be emphasized. The orchestra, first of all, 'is not considered to be a monolithic mechanism, but rather a multitude of chance formations which come together in its midst, cross over, collide or come together' (Guy Erismann). The rhythmic superimpositions are often highly complex. The harmony, finally, with its unresolved chords, its intervals of fourths and its whole-note scales, is very like the harmony found in many works from the beginning of the 20th century.

Historical references

Composed in 1926 for the Sokol Federal holiday, the *Sinfonietta* is reminiscent of a military style music which Janácek had heard in a park in Pisek. This music, which he saw as a symbol of the new Czechoslovakia (independent since 1918) inspired him. However the following year, when the work was published, the composer specified that it was his city of Brno that had inspired him; and this statement was corroborated by the subtitles which his movements had at the time of the first performance, in June 1926: 1. 'Fanfares', 2. 'The Castle', 3. 'The Queen's Monastery', 4. 'The Street', 5. 'The Town Hall'.

Webern, Anton

Symphony, 1929

Opus 21

A mathematical sound

Mastering the serial technique rigorously, the Symphony *opus 21, making use of an equally calculated counterpoint, released a completely new sound.*

Written for a fairly limited orchestra (clarinet, bass clarinet, two horns, harp and strings), the *Symphony* opus 21 contains two movements. This unusual division is derived from the structure of the series which generated the work. For the twelve notes of this series are also divided in two, and the last six even follow the sequence of the first six, but reversed and transposed. The first movement, with a slow tempo, pushes this idea of reflection even further as it itself has two parts, each played twice. As for the very solid organization of this movement, it presents the problem of perceptibility. The use, already rigorous, of the series is then combined with a double canon in four voices.

In the first part of this movement, while the figures which seem to be responding, show through this canonic structure, what is most obvious, besides the use of rests and great disjointed intervals, is the impression of immobility. Such an effect comes from the fact that each instrument takes on a certain number of pitches which it maintains throughout the first part. In other words, when a pitch reappears, the timbre work which is associated with it also reappears. But, on top of the static impression created, each musical line moves frequently from one instrument to another according to a principle of 'transferal of tone-colours' (Henri-Louis Matter) which, although it systematizes the old timbre melody, also foreshadows spatial music.

With the first part of this movement, Webern's aim is not so much to camouflage the canonical structure behind audible elements, as to keep it in reserve. This is proven by the first bars of the second part, which produce very distinctly the successive entries of four voices, even though this unveiling of the canonical structure is undoubtedly meant to put the sound material, up until now very static, into the movement. The second movement 'Theme and variations', which has a very rapid tempo is thus able to give way, thanks to 'subtle modifications of the sound scenery', to a 'constant renovation of the acoustic aspects' (H. L. Matter).

Historical references

Composed in 1928, this work was first performed in Philadelphia in 1929.

Roussel, Albert

Symphony No.3, 1930

G minor, opus 42

A departure from the descriptive

The Symphony No.3 *which belongs, in Roussel's own words, to the period of his 'definitive mode of expression', is founded on the dynamics of rhythm.*

The *Symphony in G minor* gives formal evidence that the Rousselian evolution is leading steadily towards a 'music which is satisfied in itself, and which seeks to free itself from any pictorial or descriptive elements' (A. Roussel), in short, which leads to what we call pure music.

The work, composed of four traditional movements, united by a motif of five notes played by the brass in the development of the *allegro vivo* (which reappears in each of the four parts), can be considered 'cyclical'.

Less melodic than rhythmic, this *allegro vivo* is dominated by the lyrical force of its first theme (in G minor) which is powerful, very emphasized, indeed almost 'mechanized', as opposed to the much calmer melody of the second theme (in B flat major).

From the beginning of the second movement (*adagio*), one is aware of the 'cyclic' motif of five notes which is handled differently in the three parts of the piece, and takes a fugal form in the central *più mosso* section.

Marked *vivace*, the third movement is a brilliantly coloured 'scherzovalse' (A. Roussel). It plays on two themes: one played by the strings in unison and the other by the woodwinds.

In the popular-style rondo (*allegro con spirito*) which makes up the finale, the 'cyclical' motif brought back by a brief development separates from the rest to be played *andante* by the solo violin. We encounter it one last time, amplified, acting as the central point of a long and exuberant coda which makes use of the entire orchestra.

Historical references

Composed in 1929–30 for a commission by Serge Koussevitzky to celebrate the 50th anniversary of the Boston Symphony Orchestra of which he was head, the *Symphony No.3* was first performed in Boston by the orchestra on 17 October 1930. It was a great success. Its European premiere, in 1931, by the Lamoureux Concerts in Paris, received the same enthusiastic response from the public, the critics as well as from many composers, including Francis Poulenc.

Messiaen, Olivier

Turangalila-Symphonie, 1948

An arrangement of smooth rhythms and melodies

Compared to its fairly simple melodic flow, the Turangalila-Symphonie *reveals a more complex organization on the level of its essential component: rhythm.*

This work whose title, taken from Sanskrit, means both the passage of time, movement of rhythm (*Turanga*) and the divine action of the cosmos (*Lila*), is intended for a gigantic orchestra with 103 musicians and two solo instruments (piano and Ondes Martenot). It is divided into ten movements linked together by the return of several themes and mostly by the reappearance of four cyclic themes essential to the melodic and rhythmic framework.

Two of these four themes are heard in the *introduction* (first movement): the 'statue-theme' (heavy and slow, played here by the trombones *fortissimo*) and the 'flower-theme' (slow, played *pianissimo* by the clarinets). The third cyclic theme, called the 'love theme' introduced in the *Chant d'amour I* (second movement) and replayed in the

Turangalîla I (third movement), *Chant d'amour II* (fourth movement) and *Joie du Sang des Etoiles* (fifth movement), does not undergo its complete development until the sixth movement (*Jardin du sommeil d'Amour*) where it is played 'very moderato, very gently' by the Ondes Martenot and the muted strings. Finally, the fourth cyclic theme, audible from the beginning of the sixth section of the seventh movement (*Turangalila II*) establishes itself with a clear rhythm on the piano in the introduction of the eighth movement (*Developpement de l'Amour*); hardly audible within the ninth movement (*Turangalila III*), it is then combined with the first theme of the finale where it is repeated in the coda.

In many places Messiaen introduces into *Turangalila* what he called 'rhythmic characters'. An example (second part of *Turangalila I*) is the large drum with crossed rhythm representing a person who acts; others include the maracas with an uncrossed rhythm = a person 'acted upon by the first one'; and the wood-block with invariable rhythm = an immobile character. He also uses 'non-reversible rhythms' (identical whether read forwards or backwards).

Always present, the Ondes Martenot produces multiple effects, some of which are overly emphatic. As for the solo piano 'sometimes treated as percussion ... it clothes, varies and embellishes the orchestration' (O. Messiaen).

The Ondes Martenot

Maurice Martenot (1898–1980) is the inventor (1918) of this radio-electric musical instrument introduced to the public in 1928. Many times perfected, this instrument with two parts (keyboard and rhythm) like a loudspeaker system, allows one to get spectacular effects of metallic resonances, spatialization and atmosphere.

Historical references

Composed between July 1946 and November 1948, the work was performed in Boston in December 1949; Leonard Bernstein was at the podium, Yvonne Loriod on piano and Ginette Martenot, the sister of the inventor, on the Ondes Martenot.

Berio, Luciano

Sinfonia for eight voices and orchestra, 1968

A montage based on Mahler's 'lost property' *(Berio)*

An analysis of the relationships between various musical forms from the past, and between the spoken and the sung, accompany the elaboration of this complex intertextual system.

Intended to make voices and instruments 'sound together', the *Sinfonia* only remotely resembles a symphony. It is divided into five parts with subtle interconnections. The musical development which structures the first part suddenly becomes suspended (at the moment where the piece takes on the tone of a concerto for piano and orchestra) not to be returned to and played out to their logical conclusion, until the fifth and last movement. A montage using citations from texts (*Sinfonia* is a total stranger to collage), works in the first movement on the relationship between the musical discourse and a reading of short pieces from Claude Levi-Strauss' *Le Cru et le Cuit* (The Raw and the Cooked).

In the second part the voices only play on phonetic elements responsible for introducing, gradually, from the vocative 'O', the name of the Reverend Martin Luther King.

Considered by Berio to be spontaneously proliferated, the music of the scherzo of Mahler's *Symphony No.2* serves as the 'support structure' for the third movement, and as the centre and 'model in miniature

of the whole work' (Berio), enriched by references to Bach, Berg, Schönberg, Debussy, Beethoven, Boulez and others, themselves integrated into the harmonic structure of Mahler's scherzo. Here, in the style of Mahler's 'text' which develops in parallel with them, extracts from Samuel Beckett's *The Unnamable* proliferate; these extracts produce, in their turn, new citations: slogans from May 1968, phrases from everyday language and so on.

The fourth part, the shortest of the five, begins with a brief allusion (two notes and two words) to the beginning of the fourth movement of Mahler's symphony; it then gathers together several text fragments from the first three movements.

Even more complex than the others, as it is presented both as 'the support structure' of all which precedes it and as its analytical summary, the fifth part, where the spoken text is not clearly perceptible, appears to be a movement which 'dreams the elements of the preceding ones . . .; it is almost — in a Freudian sense — about *the interpretation of a dream*' (Berio).

Historical references

A first version with four movements was composed in 1967–8 and performed in 1968 in New York. The first French performance was at the Royan Festival in 1969. It was played for the first time with its fifth movement at the Donaueschingen Festival of 1969.

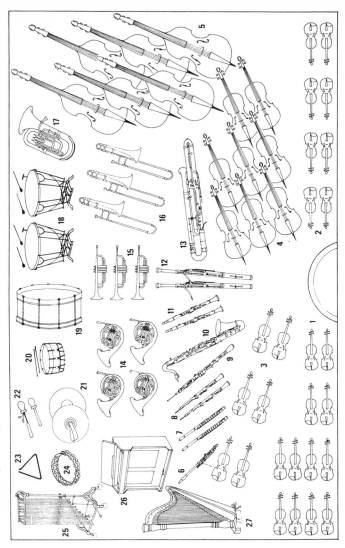

Usual arrangement of instruments in a Symphony Orchestra.

1. First violins.
2. Second violins.
3. Violas.
4. Cellos.
5. Double Basses.
6. Piccolo.
7. Flutes.
8. Oboes.
9. Cor Anglais.
10. Bass Clarinet.
11. Clarinets.
12. Bassoons.
13. Double Bassoon.
14. French Horns.
15. Trumpets.
16. Trombones.
17. Tuba.
18. Kettledrums.
19. Bass Drum.
20. Drum.
21. Cymbals.
22. Castanets.
23. Triangle.
24. Tambourine.
25. Glockenspiel.
26. Celesta.
27. Harp.

Toccatas

In its generally accepted sense, the word '*toccata*' (from the Italian *toccare* 'to touch') designates a musical form without a precise structure, to which belong pieces for keyboard instruments composed with the intention of emphasizing the fingering of the interpreter.

The origins of this form are little known; it is possible that there is a link, as suggested mainly by the arpeggiato chords, between the toccata for harpsichord, organ and piano and the primitive toccata from the Middle Ages played by trumpets during the hunt and in war time, which also turns up, in an evolved form, in the works for the beginning of the 17th century, such as Monteverdi's *Orfeo* (1607) which begins with a toccata *con tutti li stromenti*. From the 16th century, the era of the oldest known specimens of the keyboard toccata (pieces by Andrea and Giovanni Gabrieli, Claudio Merulo, and others), the harpsichord and the organ almost completely monopolized the form in question. In the 17th century, under the influence of Girolamo Frescobaldi (Fiori musicali collection, 1635), the toccata took the form of a musical piece in which homophonic sections and fugal passages are linked together (toccatas by Jan Pieterszoon Sweelinck, Johann Jakob-Froberger, Samuel Scheidt, Georg Muffat), but it was Dietrich Buxtehude (1637–1707) 'who proved himself to be the incontestable master, before Bach, of the great toccata form, inserted in or preceding a fugue' (Jean-François Labie).

A clearly marked distinction between organ toccatas and harpsichord toccatas was established at the beginning of the 18th century, which also witnessed a certain confusion between authentic toccatas and works labelled as such but whose characteristics are more those of a sonata ('toccatas' by Leonardo Leo, Domenico Scarlatti, and others). J. S. Bach, author of seven toccatas intended for harpsichord and four others for organ such as the famous *Toccata and Fugue in D minor* BWV 565, accentuate the epic appeal of this form by alternating recitative fugatos and non-arpeggiato chords. After Bach, the toccata fell rapidly into disuse. It reappeared occasionally in the 19th and 20th centuries, treated as pieces of great virtuosity for the piano by Muzio Clementi, Karl Czerny, Schumann (*Toccata* opus 7), pastiched (Max Reger, Prokofiev), arranged rhythmically like motu perpetuo (Debussy's *Pour le piano*, Ravel's piano version of *Le Tombeau de Couperin*), or adapted to the classical style which inspired in certain composers the more or less explicit attempts at a 'return' to Bach: Eugene Gigout's organ toccatas, Charles-Marie Widor (toccata from the *Fifth Symphony*), Louis Vierne.

Bach, Johann Sebastian

Toccata and Fugue in D minor, around 1708

BWV 565

In competition with Buxtehude

A great classic of the repertoire, the Toccata and Fugue in D minor *is a brilliant, powerful, even effervescent composition, but with a much less complex structure than the skilled fugal choral.*

This piece of work by a composer and organist still young, in search of an unrestrained declamatory effect, and little inclined towards the intimacy which prevailed at the time among the Italian disciples of Frescobaldi. But this fairly short tripartite work, which seems to be heading towards developing itself entirely within the framework of a formal liberty which allows him to remain as close as possible to the 'art of improvisation which here turns its back on contrapuntal structure' (Alberto Basso) is not actually as freely expansive as it appears.

By integrating a fugue into its centre, it overcomes the disadvantages of an overly exclamatory language of broken rhythms, whose repetition is by necessity monotonous. The fugue in question (97 bars) with very few indications by the composer, also reinforces the thematic unity of the composition, for its seven notes — except the repeated 'A' — are identical to the initial notes of the toccata. Almost paradoxically, it establishes with its jerky introductory 'prelude', thanks to its continuous rhythm, the necessary contrast for the breaking up of a series of excessive uniformity of supporting volcanic tones. Beyond the 'need to reign by bedazzlement' (Luc-André Marcel), the great Bachian art of staging tightened by the constitutive elements of the work, begins to take shape.

The *Toccata and Fugue in D minor* begins suddenly with a piece of 29 bars treated at first in a grandiose style which, after an impressive *decrescendo*, gives way, from the beginning of the *prestissimo* to the purer style toccata with roulades played over the keyboards in octave intervals.

The fugue, linearly developed, lacking in polyphonic combinations, opens with a concertante tirade connected to a passage (bars 59 to 85) which reintroduces the toccata form.

In the final section Bach returns to the epic style with the work finishing on a series of sound medleys intended to convey the dynamics of the contrasts which emphasize their respective opposite indications: *adagissimo, presto, adagio, vivace, molto adagio.*

Transcriptions

A work 'endowed with a musical frankness within the reach of everybody' (Alberto Basso), the *Toccata and Fugue in D minor* BWV 565 was the object of several piano transcriptions, the best-known of which, by Karl Tausig (1841–71) and Ferruccio Busoni (1866–1924), added to its popularity without really adding anything new.

Historical references

The *Toccata and Fugue in D minor* was probably composed around 1708 in Weimar, where Bach occupied the post of organist at the ducal chapel until 1717.

Trios

From around 1750, the term *trio* came to signify any instrumental formation made up of three solo musicians, and the works thus entitled generally respect the formal structure of sonatas, in three or four movements.

From the classical ear to the present, several kinds of groupings were envisaged, but the one for piano, violin and cello, the first example of a trio, is also the most common. Although with Haydn — who wrote the first trio of this type — the piano was still clearly dominant over the violin and the cello, with Beethoven, who composed nine trios, the three instrumentalists have equal value. Throughout the 19th century and until the beginning of the 20th century, many composers have made use of this formation: Schubert, Mendelssohn, Schumann, Franck, Brahms, Tchaikovsky, Fauré and Ravel.

Less common, the string trio (violin, viola, cello) has tended to create high level works like, in the classical era, Mozart's *Divertimento*, the five very beautiful works by the young Beethoven; and, in the 20th century, Weber's *Trio opus 20* and Schönberg's *Trio opus 45*, which was one of his last works.

But this chamber music formation can also have other groupings, such as the reed trio (oboe, clarinet, bassoon), and can even have a blatantly heterogenous combination like the *Trio for clarinet, viola and piano* by Mozart or the *Trio for piano, violin and horn* by Brahms.

Mozart, Wolfgang Amadeus

Divertimento for string trio, 1788

E flat major K.563

A pre-Beethovian conflict

A late work by Mozart, this Divertimento, *combining with the popular divertimento, form a highly complex counterpoint, foreshadowing Beethoven's late quartets.*

While the polyphonic writing of this string trio is exceedingly skilful, the succession of its six movements (*allegro, adagio, minuet, andante, minuet, allegro*), returns to the form of the old divertimento, in order to transform it for the better.

And although the work owes its exemplary character to this stylistic contradiction, its two slow movements, respectively in second and fourth position, stand out from the rest as Mozart has, in these, outdone himself. It is in the use of double strings on the violin and on the viola which gives the adagio in A flat an almost Beethovian richness.

As for the andante in B flat, while the exposition of its theme evokes at first the atmosphere of a divertimento or a serenade, the four variations which follow display an entirely different scope. With the fourth in particular, the theme, supported by demi-semiquavers on the violin and semiquavers on the cello, is suddenly reduced to a cantabile firmus played by the viola, and the power of the effect is once again entirely Beethovian.

Historical references

This Divertimento was only composed by Mozart in 1788, soon after his last three symphonies, to thank his friend, the merchant Michael Puchberg for having generously consented to lend him money.

The *Divertimento for string trio* benefits from the experience acquired by Mozart in writing his *Six Quartets dedicated to Haydn* (1782–5) and his *String Quartets* K.515 and 516 (1787). The trio doubtlessly owes the fact that it is one of the great peaks of Mozart's music to its late chronological position.

Problems with the trio

One of the fundamental principles of tonal language at the end of the 18th century has to do with the dramatic use of discord, in relation to a perfect chord of three notes. Such a principle, in order to succeed, must have at its disposal a minimum of four voices, which explains the primacy of the string quartet at that time. It follows that to write a trio in 1788 would necessarily be a tour de force, as it would have to simulate the four voices of a quartet. More precisely, for such a simulation to be produced, 'non-discordant voices must play two notes of the chords, either by double strings, or by rapidly alternating the two notes' (Charles Rosen). This technique allows us to understand how Mozart — who tended to prefer the second method, that of alternation — was able to endow his divertimento with such a richness of tone.

Haydn, Joseph

Trio for piano, violin and cello, 1797

E major H 28 (L 44)

A glimpse towards romanticism

Belonging to a group of three pieces of exceptionally virtuosic piano technique, the Trio in E major *may well be the 'strangest of all Haydn's late works' (Charles Rosen).*

The *Trio in E major* contains three movements. The pianistic colour given to the main theme of the first movement, an *allegro moderato*, is unusual as, even without the accompaniment by the two stringed instruments playing *pizzicati*, the piano on its own gives 'a general impression of *pizzicato*' (C. Rosen). As for the structure of this movement, Haydn skilfully organized the balance around its very strong modulation, heard throughout the development in the distant key of B flat major.

Baroque in the relentless rhythm of its bass and in its sequential construction, classical in its progression and its dynamic accents, the strange slow movement which follows is already romantic 'to the extent that romantic style means the reintroduction of baroque processes and textures modified by a classical sense of climax' (Charles Rosen). Exemplary, in this respect, is the series of brilliant features making up the final cadence which manages to postpone the resolution of the tension until the very last chord of the movement, struck, for this reason, with all the more force.

Most of the finales of Haydn's trios are of a ternary ABA form, and their central section, which is an actual development, serves as the climax. This one is no exception, and moreover presents, in its third section, unexpected glimpses of the violin and even, at the end, of the cello.

Historical references

Published in London in 1797, the three trios 27, 28 and 29 according to Hoboken's numeration system (43, 44 and 45 in Robbins Landon's) were composed for Thérèse Jansen, a German pianist based in London. As a compliment to the great technical skill of this interpreter, Haydn made his three trios extremely virtuosic.

Haydn's trios for piano, violin and cello — numbering 45 after their last edition — constitute the third major collection of works by the composer, along with his 104 symphonies and his 68 string quartets. As suggested by their titles, these trios are actually 'sonatas for piano with accompaniment by violin and cello'. That is to say, the piano parts are clearly dominant and should even be considered with those of Mozart's concertos, the most brilliant created, before Beethoven.

The 45 trios for piano, violin and cello composed by Haydn can be divided into three groups. A first grouping contains his early works (written before 1770), the next one corresponds to the 1780s and the last one to the 1790s; these two contain, respectively, 14 and 15 trios.

But of all these trios, a good number from the 1780s and the majority from the 1790s, which count among Haydn's best productions, only one is well known, due to its finale, a 'rondo all'ongarese': it is the *Trio in G major* H 25 (L 39); its only fault is that it has eclipsed the others.

Beethoven, Ludwig van

Trio for piano, violin and cello, No.7 'The Archduke', 1816

B flat major, opus 97

'The will for courage' (Schindler)

More inventive on the thematic, harmonic and tonal levels than all his preceding trios with piano, The Archduke *is a highly skilful work from Beethoven's middle period.*

The introductory allegro moderato of the *Archduke Trio* is a sonata-form piece constructed on two main themes. The first, played by the unaccompanied piano, then repeated by the violin, is based on a melody with a vigorous rhythm broken up by rests which, from a smooth initial dolce, goes on to a crescendo with heroic overtones. Presented in a contrastive manner (chords close together on the piano), the second theme, in G major, then brings in a fairly gentle and very melodic motif played by the strings, and whose melodic relationship with the first theme gives the entire piece a great unity. The development, which carries out an extreme decomposition of the initial theme, as well as the recapitulation within which this theme makes a brief appearance to serve as a triumphant con-

clusion, also contributes to the reinforcement of this unity.

In the second movement, a scherzo (*allegro*) with bold rhythmic and melodic innovations, a striking contrast is established between the dance-like mood of the beginning, developed from an ascending scale in B flat major, and the almost gloomy mood which melancholically drives the middle part and to which the coda returns.

A theme in lied form is the starting-point for the series of five free variations which it generates, making up with them the entire third movement (*andante cantabile ma pero moto*). We arrive here, in the key of D major, at the great Beethovian art of variation allowing — in the fifth variation — the piece to go from a 'disjointed, broken-up and engrossed theme emerging sporadically like bits of fog' (André Boucourechliev) to its explicit return.

Joined *attaca* to the preceding movement, the final, *allegro moderato*, in rondo form is expressed around a refrain whose theme, perhaps inspired by a dance rhythm, gradually gives the entire piece a tonal liveliness which continues to increase until arriving at a presto in A major whose accelerated rhythm results in a triumphant *più presto* coda.

Historical references

Started in 1810, composed between the 3 and 26 March 1811, the *Archduke Trio* (so named because it is devoted to Archduke Rudolph of Austria) was played for the first time on 11 April 1814 in Vienna, for an evening performance of chamber music. Beethoven was on piano, accompanied by Schuppanzigh (violin) and Linke (cello).

Created within a structurally large framework (four movements totalling 1200 bars) which has resulted in the piece evoking 'a symphony in trio form', *Opus 97* depends on this structure to bring together the three solo instruments.

Schubert, Franz

Trio with piano, No.2, 1828

E flat major, D.929

With the aim of equalling Beethoven

The Trio No.2 *displays an obvious concern for structuring based on thematic relations which support its movements. Its proportions confirm the Schubertian tendency to expand forms.*

In its thematic richness and its many modulations, the *allegro* of the *Trio No.2* is remarkable. It develops around three themes. The first, very flexible, gives itself to variation. The second, in B minor, maintains, by its hesitations, the doubt over the course of the movement. Played three times in three different colours, a third theme feeds the central development which is 'a stunning voyage across a dozen tonalities' (Brigitte Massin). The conclusion, thanks to an unexpected return of the second theme, admits a rhythmic transition towards the following movement.

With the andante con moto in C minor, the piece distances itself from the Beethovian model and nears the lieder *Winter's Journey*, of which this movement appears to be the instrumental appendix. The melody — a Swedish tune — is played by the cello before being taken up by the piano. After two appearances of a section in a major key only just dispelling the funeral connotations of the march in a minor, a coda leaves the theme suspended implying its imminent return.

The scherzo (*allegro moderato*) returns to E flat major. Its theme evokes, in its form, the initial theme of the *allegro*. It is exposed in a canon of two voices, one on the piano the other on strings, while the modulations so typical of Schubert alter the discourse at the beginning of the second part of the movement. The following trio has very clear contours. But after a prolonged rest and a furtive return of repetitions of the scherzo, the cello plays a melody which picks up on the theme played by the strings in the first movement.

Recalling the second movement of Beethoven's *Trio No.2 opus 70*, the finale has the same structure, a chassé-croisé of two opposing sections (a first theme played by the piano in a dance rhythm, and a second, very light and exposed in an instrumental order which inverts a new appearance). But this long movement distinguishes itself primarily in the singular intervention of the *andante* theme which changes into minor to become the centre of the conclusion.

Historical references

The *Trio No.2* was composed in November 1827 and published the next year in Leipzig. Performed by the violinist Schuppanzigh on 28 December 1827, it was exceptionally fortunate: not only was it the pivot of the only concert Schubert gave in his life, on March 26 1828, but the *Trio No.2* was also established as the model of a chamber music work with piano, for the next three decades.

The Trio No.1

In 1827 Schubert wrote another trio (No.1 in B flat major, D.898). Schumann, in a thorough study devoted to the two trios, declared the first 'more suffering, feminine and lyrical' and the second 'more active, virile and dramatic'. He preferred the latter.

Brahms, Johannes

Trio with piano, No.3, 1887

C minor, opus 101

The time for concision

The Trio *opus 101 is an example of Brahmsian composition built up on itself. It is complex on the level of the writing but its internal structure remains relatively simple.*

Typical of Brahms's renunciation of very elaborate developments, the first movement of the *Trio in C minor*, an *allegro energico* built in sonata-form, calls on three themes. The initial theme is of a heroic and vigorous quality which dominates the whole movement by creating secondary themes (bars 1–80). In contrast, the second theme plays on the increase of a melodic tension produced by the strings which emphasizes the arpeggiato punctuation of the piano. After an allusive return of the principal theme during the third of the secondary themes (a method specific to Brahms of fusing the sonata-form with the form of the variation), the third theme is brought in, in the very last movement, to serve as the conclusion to this part of the work, before the development (bars 81–131). In this development, a model of conciseness, Brahms hardly explores more than the first theme, albeit in different forms. The fairly brief recapitulation (bars 132–92) precedes a coda where only the initial theme and its first motif are used.

Composed of briefly rhythmically complex motifs, the second movement, *presto non assai* (C minor), assumes the form of a scherzo. It contains at its centre a stunning passage in F minor during which the curious *pizzicati* (which resemble arpeggios) punctuate long chords held by the piano.

With the third movement, marked *andante grazioso* (C major), Brahms wrote a very bare piece, of an almost Mozartian lightness and smoothness. It only contains two melodic motifs, the first of which, falsely popular in its style and beginning on the strings without piano, establishes an effective dialogue between the instruments.

The work finishes on an *allegro molto* (C minor) in sonata-form, of great rhythmic diversity and with a thematic richness surpassing that of the *allegro* and the *presto assai*, but which obeys with less rigour the principle of economy which governs the preceding movements.

Historical references

The *Trio No.3* in C minor was composed during the summer of 1886. It was played publicly for the first time in December of the same year, in Budapest. Brahms was on piano, Jenö Hubay (1858–1937) on violin and David Hopper (1843–1913) on cello.

Variations

Originally describing a technical process of ornamentation allowing a piece to be played in a way which is not identical to its original configuration, the word *variation* has come to refer to a musical form which emerged in the 16th century (Cabezón's *Differencias* for organ, John Bull's and William Byrd's *Pieces* for virginal) and which, as a mix of the varied and the homogenous, often also established itself as a 'formula of tribute' (Michel Butor) from one musician to another.

This form respected a rather complex principle of melodic, rhythmic and harmonic modifications of an initial theme intended to be exposed, and then repeated several times and modified in different ways throughout the composition. The different presentations of a single theme within one of the parts of a work makes the variation not a form, but a writing process which has participated in the structural elaboration of almost all musical forms (for example Beethoven's *Fifth Symphony* could well be considered a composition whose structure is elaborated from variations on the famous rhythmic motif of four notes).

The 17th century saw the emergence of variation based on the principle of *cantus firmus* (a fragment of a medieval liturgical melody acting as the unifying base for a polyphonic composition), a principle which primarily governs, other than numerous organ verses, two offshoot forms of the variation: the chaconne and the passacaille. Here, 'the melodic model is maintained in full (sometimes in modified values) and surrounded by various covering layers by the other parts' (Jacques Chailley).

In the 18th century the ornamental variation (also called the varied aria) prevailed, in which the theme, although altered, is still recognizable throughout the piece, whose melodic line changes with the addition of ornaments (trills, anacruses, appoggiaturas and so on). J. S. Bach, with his *Goldberg Variations* BWV 988, brought about a skilful synthesis of the ornamental variation and the passacaille, while Rameau, Handel, Mozart (*Ah! vous dirai-je maman*, K.265) and Beethoven with his *Variations on a theme in F*, opus 34 explore the variation in an even more brilliant manner with the help of techniques which nonetheless quickly become stereotyped.

Even before it reached its end after having too many easy successes in the 19th century (Schubert, Schumann, Brahms and César Franck were all exceptions as they became involved with the post-Beethovian amplifying variation), the genre had been abandoned by Beethoven in favour of a kind of variation which was revolutionary as it no longer applied itself directly to the modification of the melody, but rather to that of a harmonic archetype (*Diabelli Variations* opus 120).

With Max Reger, Fauré, Dukas, Stravinsky and others, the 20th century, which showed an interest in the mixing of same and different, innovated primarily with the continuous variation, a technique of exploitation of the series of twelve sounds introduced by Schönberg (*Orchestra Variations* opus 31, 1926–8) and Webern (*Piano Variations* opus 27, 1936; *Orchestra variations* opus 30; 1940).

Bach, Johann Sebastian

Goldberg Variations, around 1741–2

BWV 928

Co-ordinated intelligence *(Glenn Gould)*

First of the great contrapuntal cycles of Bach's last creative period, the Goldberg Variations *achieve a magnificent balance between the mathematical and the musical.*

In the *Goldberg Variations*, actually entitled *Aria with variations for harpsichord with two manual keyboards*, the canon-style and fugue-style passages avoid the somewhat solemn character which is generally found in canonic and fugal polyphonies, for they borrow from a subtle art of interwoven motifs — evoking in places Domenico Scarlatti's style — clearly intended to make them less austere.

The work, described as 'caustic and incisive' (Glenn Gould), nonetheless has a very intriguing sound. It contains 32 pieces, each of a bipartite division: a very simple aria appearing already as a sarabande in Anna

According to Johann Forkel (1749–1818), the first biographer of J. S. Bach, the *Goldberg Variations* resulted from a commission by the Count von Keyserlingk. He was suffering from insomnia and wanted his personal harpsichordist, Johann Gottlieb Goldberg, a student of Bach's to play a long piece capable of overcoming the boredom of his involuntary sleeplessness. Thus, it is perhaps better to think, like many contemporary musicians, of the work as simply the execution of a personal project of Bach's.

Magdelena Bach's *Petit Livre de Clavier* (1725) in which the basso ostinato — much more than the melody — serves as the theme; 29 variations; a quodlibet and the repeat of the aria from the beginning.

From this global division, Bach organized his composition following an extremely rigorous and very clear principle of ordering: the aria (theme) and the first two variations form an initial group of three pieces followed by a group of nine 'triads' (each 'triad' being made up of a canonic variation, a free variation and a third virtuoso variation) which precede the two concluding pieces (quodlibet and repeat of the aria). The base key, G major, only changes after three repeats in variations 15, 21 and 25 all written in G minor, which means that 'the diversity of tonal levels, a characteristic feature of the *Well-Tempered Klavier*, is here abandoned to give way to a "specificity" of writing entrusted to the calculated diversity of the rhythmic figures … and the contrapuntal combinations' (Alberto Basso).

These 'rhythmic figures' play a contrasting role which is even more evident in the pieces where Bach retains dance features, as in variations 3 (canon on a Sicilian rhythm), 7 (a rapid forlana), 13, 25, 26 (three sarabandes) and 27 (canon on a jig rhythm).

The quodlibet (30th and last variation) combines two amusing popular songs with the bass of the aria in an ingenious and humorous way. We get the impression of a purely homophonic piece treated as a choral.

Historical references

The Goldberg Variations, fourth and last part of the Klavierübung, were composed between 1741 and 1742 in Leipzig.

Beethoven, Lugwig van

Diabelli Variations for piano, 1823

Opus 23

The irruption of a modernist logic

Variations, not on a theme, but on the components of a theme, the Diabelli Variations *constitute the first 'inquest' into the elements of a musical language.*

The material on which these *Variations* are based — a waltz composed by Diabelli — is musically rudimentary. Beethoven did not take the waltz's melodic line or its rhythm (the elements which make up the 'tune' of a theme), but was interested only in its skeletal structure. This included the general harmonic functions of the waltz (relations between the tonic and the dominant), the symmetries of its division (two parts of 16 bars each), the mirror-image effects created between the two sections (the first goes from the tonic to the dominant and the second from the dominant to the tonic), and, finally, the rhythmic spread — or anacrusis — with which the work opens.

It is the exploitation of this fairly simple, but scrupulously respected with very few exceptions, structure which allows a related tune to weave itself through all the variations, and allows each of these, displaying a 'specific state of sound matter' (A. Boucourechliev) to succeed in establishing autonomy.

But it is primarily the availability of the *Diabelli Variations* 'system' which must be commended, as well as its aptitude for integrating the most distant melodic lines (that of the 31st variation, in particular, foreshadows Chopin) as well as the most a priori restive musical forms (the fugues from variations 29 and 32). By adopting, instead of the 'generating principle of musical structures' (A. Boucourechliev), Beethoven overturned the very notion of variation. Not content just to bring about such an overturning, he indulges in the luxury of pointing it out, as is the case in at least two of the 33 *Variations*. The first, because it is a march and because by proposing as the first variation of a waltz a piece in quadruple time, Beethoven could not have better expressed its distance from the traditional variation; and the 22nd because it borrows, not without humour, another theme — an aria by Leporello in Mozart's *Don Giovanni* — which indicates Beethoven's abandonment of the thematic variation.

Historical references

After a proposal in 1819 by the publisher Anton Diabelli to write variations on one of his waltzes, Beethoven, who had at first refused, wrote his 33 *Variations*. Composed in 1822, at the same time as the *Ninth Symphony*, they were published in 1823.

Other piano variations by Beethoven: six *Variations in F major*, opus 34 (1802); 15 *Eroica Variations* opus 35 (1802); five *Variations on 'Rule Britannia'* (1803); 32 *Variations in C minor* (1806); six *Variations on a theme from 'Athenian Ruins'* opus 76 (1809).

Brahms, Johannes

Variations on a theme by Haydn, 1873

Opus 56a

An ascending trajectory

Opus 56a, with well-worked orchestral tones, demonstrates Brahms's exceptional mastery in the genre of the variation.

The '*Haydn' Variations* are considered to be the first truly symphonic piece by Brahms. The work is made up of a very simple theme, admittedly not Haydn's (*andante* in B flat major), modified by eight successive and contrasting variations (change of tempo and so on) and a finale with variations based on a basso ostinato figure from the first five bars of the initial theme. 'Highly declaimed and gifted with a richly ornamented accompaniment' (Claude Rostand), this finale emphasizes the ascensional nature of the composition.

Historical references

Brahms wrote the '*Haydn' variations* in 1873. He conducted the first performance in Vienna on 2 November of the same year.

Franck, César

Symphonic variations for piano and orchestra, 1886

An uncommon meeting

This work, at the same time variations and concerto, marks the return of Franck to the keyboards.

An adaptation, according to Vincent d'Indy, of two classical forms (the variation and the concerto) to the 'new piano technique', these *Symphonic Variations* are based on two themes. The first is dramatic and played on the strings in unison, while the very melodic second one is first heard on the woodwinds and strings playing *pizzicato*, then on the piano. Next come five variations of the second theme and an interlude. Finally, the first theme reappears in a brilliant finale with a liveliness uncommon to the author of the *Beatitudes*.

Historical references

Composed in 1885, the Symphonic Variations were performed on 1 May 1886.

Miscellaneous

'The sonata seems finally to have reached the end of the line. This is very good because we cannot repeat the same forms for centuries' (Robert Schumann). From the emergence of the romantic style, the classical forms have been contested on two main grounds. Firstly, in terms of works which refer explicitly to existing forms in order to better be able to shake them up (eg Liszt's *Sonata in E minor*); or in music which appears to want to distance itself from all formal references, as suggested by their titles which either represent 'genre pieces' ('impromptu', 'intermezzi', 'nocturne') or are specific to a particular work (Schumann's *Kreisleriana*, Liszt's *Années de pèlerinage*). What gradually emerged was less the abandonment of forms considered outdated, than the rejection of all previously accepted forms in the composition of a work.

While Brahms was the last great defender of classical forms, Debussy — with whom modern music came into being — was the first composer to believe that each work should engender and define its own form. However, this division was not quite so clear-cut, as there were numerous composers (Schönberg, Berg, Webern and very recently, Ligeti) who, as well as composing works which created their own forms, continued to refer to old structures (symphony, concerto . . .) even though they usually retained only a few of the structural features.

In fact, it was not until after World War II that the rejection of all pre-existing forms was adopted by almost all composers worthy of the name. Among those who broke new ground were: Luciano Berio, Pierre Boulez, Bruno Maderna, Luigi Nono, Karlheinz Stockhausen and Iannis Xenakis.

Schubert, Franz

Piano impromptus, 1827

D.899, opus 90; D.935, opus 142

When the lied gets by without the text

Although Schubert did not create the genre of the free-form short piano piece — nor that of the impromptu — he did, due to his accomplished art of the lied, enrich the formula.

The two series of four pieces which make up the *Impromptus* obviously form a group. The similarities between the two are striking: the same use of flattened tonalities and a similar arrangement of tempos. Moreover, the transition from one to the other goes from a major key to its relative minor. These pieces, which display a 'feeling of freedom in terms of form' (Brigitte Massin) are written in a manner akin to the lied, with the development of a melody on an accompanying bass.

The *Impromptu No.1* of the first series is an *allegro molto moderato* in C minor; its theme, with the false tone of a funeral march, undergoes accompaniments. *No.2*, an *allegro* in E flat major, is characterized by a fluidity created by the quaver triplet scales which use almost the entire keyboard; a rhythmically emphasized central section contrasts greatly with it. *No.3, andante* in G flat major, proposes only one theme which is constantly repeated in different colours; only the bass breaks the rules of the game. *No.4*, an *allegretto* in A flat major, is somewhat reminiscent of the *No.2* in the lightness of its arpeggios played in the higher register and in its ternary form inherited from the lied.

The second series opens on an *allegro moderato* in F minor; it is the longest and most complex of the *Impromptus*; it has an A–B–A–B–A structure. The *allegretto* in A major which follows in much simpler; it is presented as a minuet with a limpid theme; the trio turns once again to a play of argeggios in triplets which supports the syncopated bass. *No.3*, an *andante* in B flat major, is a virtuoso movement of variations which Schubert judged harshly. This last piece, an *allegro scherzo* in F minor, is the most abrupt of the series; of A–B–A form, it contrasts the vehemence of the first theme, full of trills, off-beats and breaks in the rhythm, with the calm of a great central section soon overcome by the neighbouring turbulence.

The 'form' of the *Impromptu* was not invented by Schubert. A Czech composer, Vorísek, published in 1822 the first piano impromptus. Another Czech musician, Tomásek, created pieces of this genre as early as 1810. Schubert, himself, before the *Impromptus*, devoted himself to this type of writing with his *Musical Moments*.

Historical references

Very little time separated the composition of the two series of *Impromptus*. The first dates from the summer or autumn of 1827, and the second from December. *Nos.1* and *2* of the first series were published in the same year, but *No.3* and *No.4* did not appear until 1857.

Schumann, Robert

Kreisleriana for piano, 1838

Opus 16

To compose the unforeseeable

A key work of German romanticism, the Kreisleriana *owe their appearance of improvised music to the unpredictability of their melodic, rhythmic and harmonic sequences.*

The *Kreisleriana* are composed of eight interconnected pieces. Pieces two, four, and six are slow and the other five are fast, but most of them contain central sections or are crossed over by sections which contrast with their atmosphere or tempo. The longest piece of the collection, the second, which is 'very internalized and not very fast' is broken by two faster interludes; and the seventh, 'very fast', after its section, gives way to a *fugato*, soon interrupted by a slow coda. This technique of construction, based on intrusions, which gives some of *Kreisleriana*'s passages their improvised nature, is further increased by the fact that many of these insertions, when they are not whole pieces, seem 'to begin in mid-course and to finish without any real conclusion' (Charles Rosen). While the third piece is worthy of attention for its persistent triplets, the fourth and fifth pieces are, from a melodic point of view, the most innovative of the collection. And, finally, the eighth is exemplary in the gap attained between its two voices, the melody played by the right hand being completely independent from the left-hand accompaniment.

Historical references

The *Kreisleriana* were written in the space of only a few days, at the end of April 1938. As Marcel Brion suggested, the external circumstances of Schumann's life influenced his identification with Kreisler, or rather his 'possession' by Hoffman's character. More than one thing brought them together: the failure of their music, their battles in vain against the detractors of modern music, and their isolation. These motives were added to by the obstacles put in the way of Schumann and Clara Wieck's love by her father.

Schumann composed *Kreisleriana* because he identified with the character of Johannes Kreisler, a fantastical, passionate and mad musician from a novel by E. T. A. Hoffman. The subtitle of the *Kreislerian*, '*Phantasien*' — in the romantic sense of the word, more nightmare than fantasy — was also a reference to the author of the *Contes Fantastiques*. But this musical evocation allowed Schumann to demonstrate his rhythmic ingenuity and to introduce new melodic complexities.

Besides the *Fantasia* opus 17 and *Three Sonatas*, Schumann composed many piano cycles in the *Kreisleriana* genre, including *Papillons* opus 2 (1830), *Davidsbündlertänze* opus 6 (1837), *Carnaval* opus 9 (1835) and *Kinderscenen* opus 15 (1838). Most of these works had two versions and the second of these are the ones that are played today, but the first ones, according to Charles Rosen, are much more innovative.

Chopin, Frédéric

Nocturnes for piano, 1827 to 1846

Legato above all else

In the Nocturnes, *Chopin gave free rein to his taste for chromatic harmony and long ornamented melodic phrases, in order to refine the contours of his musical aesthetic.*

The Irish composer John Field (1782–1837) to whom we owe the application of the term 'nocturne' to this type of pianistically free composition, of an intimate and mono-thematic nature, had a profound influence on Chopin, who was then only 17 (*Nocturnes* Nos.1, 2, 3, 9): the same style of accompanied melody, same fio4rituras inspired by the Italian *bel canto*.

In writing the triad of opus 15 (*Nocturnes* 4, 5, 6), Chopin broke away from his model before fully asserting his personal conception of the nocturne in the two pieces (Nos.7 and 8) of opus 27. The first (C sharp minor), of A–B–A form like almost all of the *Nocturnes*, begins with a dreamlike *larghetto* which contrasts with a rhythmically tense and sombre central section. The second

(D flat major) develops a skilfully orna-mented melody on a base of arpeggios col-oured by very varied harmonies. The two *Nocturnes* of opus 32 (Nos.9 and 10) are less brilliant. Of higher musical quality, No.11 in G minor opus 37 No.1 allows the stylistic progress to be assessed (it is, in effect, a new version of No.6 opus 15 No.3); No.12 (G major) opus 37 No.2 alternates two themes (the second with the rhythm of a barcarole) on a formal A–B–A–B–A–B pattern. With the *Nocturne* No.13 in C minor opus 48 No.1, Chopin creates one of the most original pieces, superbly worked in the transition between the very sombre *lento* with which it begins and the rhythmic *agitato* of its middle section. Written in F sharp minor, No.14 opus 48 No.2, while it does not have all the merits of the preceding one, is no less remarkable on the level of melodic innovation. Much more interesting than the very popular No.15 (F minor) opus 55 No.1, No.16 (B flat major) opus 55 No.2 'reflects the general increase of contra-puntal activity in Chopin's late music' (Max Harrison).

Due to the complex arrangement of their melodic lines, the sophistication of their chromatic harmony and their rhythmic fluidity, the *Nocturnes* No.17 in B major opus 62 No.2 establish themselves as two of Chopin's major compositions, they give a pre-Fauréan conclusion to the *Nocturne* cycle.

Historical references

The composition of the *Nocturnes* was spread out over a period of twenty years (1827–46).

Nocturnes Nos.19 (opus 72, No.1), 20 and 21, published posthumously, are really early works composed on the Fieldian model.

The Nocturne No.10 was the object of a famous orchestral adaptation for the ballet *Les Sylphides*

Liszt, Franz

Années de pèlerinage for piano, Third Book, 1883

The very near future

Belonging to Liszt's last period and working towards the elimination of tonality and its forms, the Third Set (or Book) *of pèlerinage is an impressive piece of music.*

The 26 pieces of this summary of romantic music which makes up the *Années de pèlerinage* are alternately descriptive and evocative, and the pieces of the *Third Book* are no exception, as suggested by their titles: *Angelus, Aux cyprès de la villa d'Este,* 1 and 2, *Les Jeux d'eau à la villa d'Este, Sunt lacrymae rerum, Marche funèbre, Sursum Corda.* One sees in this music an attempt to compensate for the relinquishment of classical forms.

This is particularly true of the pieces from the *Third Book* which, musically speaking, have abandoned all traditional references, to the point of sometimes appearing almost bare, despite the aspect of grandeur that they retain. Liszt, in going directly from one key to another without modulation, appears to be the composer 'to attempt a dissolution of tonality' (Alfred Brendel); and this dissolution brings with it the abandonment of classical/romantic developments, symmetries and repeats. Also, the pieces of this *Third Book* follow one another in often very contrasting blocks, with 'colour' acting as the linking device. Finally, the rhythm is often obsessive and any sign of 'tuneful' melody banished.

But this music, of 'archaic' and 'impersonal force' (A. Brendel), which appears to lament the loss of a distant world, contains the seeds of much of the 20th century, as is particularly evident in *Les Jeux d'eau à la villa d'Este,* which foreshadows Debussy and Ravel, or in the *Sunt lacrymae rerum,* and the *Marche funèbre* which heralds Bartók.

Historical references

The composition of the whole collection of the *Années de pèlerinage* was spread over 40 years. The first two *Books* recall a trip taken with Marie d'Agoult to Switzerland and Italy. Most of the pieces of the *First Book (Switzerland),* published in 1855, come from a collection entitled *Album d'un voyageur,* composed around 1835 and revised between 1848 and 1853. Published in 1858, the seven pieces of the *Second Book (Italy)* were written between 1846 and 1849, and in 1861 Liszt added three more pieces called *Venezia e Napoli.* The *Third Book,* composed mainly in 1877, was published in 1883.

Les Années de pèlerinage.
While the *Third Book* foreshadows, in many ways, the music of the 20th century, the two preceding *Books,* written much earlier, are more the last phase of Liszt's symphonic poems. Of the nine pieces of the *First Book (Switzerland),* the sixth, *Vallée d'Obermann,* is the most interesting. As for the *Second Book (Italy),* the pieces were somewhat eclipsed by the longer and more dazzling piece which closes the collection: *Après une lecture de Dante (Fantasia Quasi Sonata)*

Chabrier, Emmanuel

Pièces pittoresques for piano, 1888

An instinctive modernism

Especially innovative on the harmonic level, the Pièces pittoresques *show signs of Debussy, Ravel and Satie.*

'Admirably crafted and of a good-natured tone' (Francis Poulenc), the music of the ten *Préces pittoresques* display the allusive, impulsive and sometimes humorous side of Chabrier, but also show his obvious loyalty to sound.

The collection opens with *Paysage*, fol-lowed by *Mélancolie, Tourbillon, Sous-bois* (much admired by Ravel for its harmonics), *Mauresque, Idylle* (with new harmonic dis-coveries), *Danse villageoise, Improvisation* (a homage of sorts to Schumann), *Menuet pompeux* (orchestrated by Ravel in 1918) and *Scherzo-Valse*.

Historical references

Composed in 1881, the *Pièces pittoresques* were played for the first time by Marie Poitevin at the National Society on 9 August the same year.

Chausson, Ernest

Concert for piano, violin and string quartet, 1892

D major, opus 21

A darkly affected cyclicism

A work which is highly structured with slightly turn-of-the-century subtleties, the Concert *stands out between César Franck and Debussy.*

Divided into four movements, the *Concert* has, as the base theme of its cyclic form, an idea played by the solo violin in the first movement. This first movement, sometimes calm, sometimes lively, is followed by an unhurried Siciliano whose rhythmic and melodic charm evokes Fauré. The third movement (marked grave), at first funeral, then tragic and melodic, returns to finish with the lugubrious opening theme. As for the finale (very lively), it restores the prin-cipal themes of the other movements on a dynamic mode.

Historical references

Composed between 1889 and 1891, the *Concert* was performed by Eugene Ysaÿe's quartet in Brussels on 4 March 1892.

Brahms, Johannes

Intermezzi, 1892

Opus 117

An economical and miniaturist romanticism

The last of Brahms's piano music, the Intermezzi *of opus 117 are amazing in their brevity and their restrained aesthetic with neither Hungarian nor Viennese references.*

These three *Intermezzi*, by virtue of their structure, belong to the genre of lied which was a favourite of Brahms who, shortly after their completion, undertook the publication of popular German songs. Their ternary composition is in A–B–A form.

Intermezzo No.1 is an *andante moderato* in E flat major, and then E flat minor. It is expressed around two themes, the first of which uses an old Scots song. The uniqueness of this piece comes from the allocation of its melody to an intermediate voice. Brahms, who seemed to be very fond of it, called it the 'lullaby of my troubles'.

The second, in B flat minor, marked *andante non troppo e con molto espressione*, has a middle part in D flat major, more melodically and formally straightforward, framed by two sections with elusive arpeggios. A coda, *più adagio* combines the two themes while according primacy to the first.

The third piece — *andante con moto*, then *poco più lento*, then *più moto e espressivo* — in

C sharp minor and A minor begins *pianissimo* in unison with the octave, on a march-like section. The central part contrasts greatly with its syncopation and restless movement. The final repeat of the initial theme creates a somewhat funereal atmosphere in this last passage.

With this minimal music, which seems sometimes to hover on the edge of silence, we have come a long way from the flamboyant Brahms of the 'symphonic' period and from all technical ostentation.

Historical references

These three pieces were composed in Ischl during the summer of 1892 and published soon after.

Opus 117 represents, after the seven *Fantasias* of opus 116 and before the ten pieces of opus 118 and 119 which were composed in the summer of 1893, the second of Brahms's last four solo piano cycles.

The failure of the orchestration of the *Intermezzo No.1*, despite its immediate public success, testifies to the degree to which this music is really intended for a specific instrument.

These four works should be considered as Brahms's pianistic legacy. Over the remaining few years he was to live, the composer never felt the need to add a codicil.

Debussy, Claude

Nocturnes for orchestra, 1901

Three considered visions (A. Robbe-Grillet)

Abandoning almost all traditional development structures, the three Nocturnes *are an undeniable affirmation of Debussy's language.*

Musical reflections — and not descriptions — of three visions whose unfolding they transpose, Debussy's *Nocturnes*, called *Nuages, Fêtes* and *Sirènes*, renounce all traditional frameworks. From a structural point of view, the plan of the work, a kind of 'inverted symphony' (Marcel Dietsch), proposes two slow movements framing a lively piece. From a thematic perspective, Debussy, intensifying the 'second incarnation' of *Prélude à l'après-midi d'un faune*, abandons the classical principle of development, replacing it with a method of writing consisting of the linking and superimposition of various motifs, indefinitely repeated and varied.

This technique is particularly evident in the first *Nocturne, Nuages*, whose motif,

Debussy's three *Nocturnes*, whose titles come from the pictures by the English painter Whistler, are the work which marks the transition from *Prélude à l'après-midi d'un faune* (1894) to *La Mer* (1905). While the cor anglais of *Nuages* continues the flute from *Faune*, 'the trumpet calls repeated many times (in *Sirènes*) have an undeniable relationship with the trumpet call at the beginning of *La Mer*, also repeated throughout the work' (Pierre Boulez).

played by the cor anglais, is 'repeated many times, always by the cor anglais, "immutable" on a variable orchestral foundation without ever "progressing" nor leading to a development' (Michel Chion).

Following this 'slow and melancholy march of clouds, finishing in a grey gloom, gently tinged with white' (Debussy) is *Fêtes*, in which 'the movement, the dance-like rhythm of the atmosphere with 'sudden bursts of light' and 'the section representing a cortège passing through the festivities, merges into the midst of them' (Debussy). This second *Nocturne* has three sections: the first, a kind of perpetual motion evoking the rhythm of the festival, is abruptly interrupted by a fanfare whose extraordinary approach via 'successive levels' (Harry Halbreich), from the muted trumpets to the orchestral tutti, makes up the second section. With the third section, the two antinomic episodes blend together in a stunning symbiosis, before it all dissolves into silence.

Finally, the third *Nocturne, Sirens*, in which Debussy evokes 'the sea and its vast rhythm', joins a female choir, vocalizing on the syllable 'A'. Of a more complex structure than the preceding nocturnes, the third is also 'one of the first attempts to integrate vocals into the orchestra by treating them almost instrumentally' (Jean Barraqué).

Historical references

Drafted as early as 1892, and then returned to two years later in a version for violin and orchestra, the three *Nocturnes* were rewritten, in the definitive version, between 1897 and 1899, and performed on 27 October 1901.

Debussy, Claude

Children's Corner, 1908

Chouchou's father having fun

A series of six little piano pieces,
Children's Corner *reveals*
Debussy as a miniaturist anglophile
brilliantly cultivating his taste for
mischievous diversion.

In writing *Children's Corner*, the author of *Pelléas* addresses himself in principle to children learning the piano through amusing pieces, sometimes a bit mocking, of a reasonable level of difficulty of execution.

Entitled *Doctor Gradus ad Parnassum* (moderately lively), the first of the pieces alludes, ironically, to the famous didactic collection by Muzio Clementi (1752–1832), the *Gradus ad Parnassum*. It is in C major, built on a regular rhythm with a smooth melody which slows down briefly in the middle, apparently to represent the desire of the younger player to escape from this chore.

The second movement, *Jimbo's Lullaby* (fairly moderate), is tinged with exoticism in the use of the pentatonic scale in the outer sections, while the middle part, a bit more animated, returns to the use of the seven-note scale. This 'homage' in the form of a lullaby (B flat major) to 'Chouchou's' fluffy elephant, also includes a very skilled variation on the theme of the popular song '*Dodo, l'enfant do*'.

Another 'homage' to a toy, the *Serenade of the Doll* (*allegretto ma non troppo*, light and graceful), which should actually be called *Serenade for the Doll*, playfully mocks, with

Spanish-like rhythms, the guitar tune too obviously inspired 'by a pretty listener'.

The fourth piece in D minor, moderately lively, is entitled *The Snow is dancing*. We find here, as in the third piece of *Estampes* for piano (*Jardins sous la pluie*), the Debussy who has admirably mastered composition work based on groups of semiquavers, creating the impression of an 'inspiration' based on the observation of nature.

In *The Little Shepherd*, marked very moderate, the composer exposes a melody whose flexible phrasing initially recalls *Prélude à l'après-midi d'un faune*; and then develops in a more lively rhythm (general key of A major).

The last piece of the collection, *Gollywog's Cake-Walk* (an *allegro giusto* in E flat major) evokes, in its lively and staccato jazz-like rhythm, the dance of a 'black doll'.

Historical references

With the exception of *Serenade for the Doll* which dates from 1906, *Children's Corner* was composed in 1908. Harold Bauer carried out the first performance for the public on 18 December 1908, at Paris's Cercle Musicale.

> Claude-Emma Debussy, called Chouchou, daughter of Emma Bardoc and Debussy and the dedicatee of *Children's Corner* ('with the tender apologies from the father for what is to follow') was a gifted child. Born on 30 November 1905, she died of diptheria just over a year after her father, on 16 July 1919.

Albéniz, Isaac

Iberia, for piano, 1909

The essence of Spain

In composing Iberia, *Albéniz chose the complex and subtle, rather than his usual simplicity.*

Interested in certain aspects of French impressionism, in the compositional discipline of the Schola cantorum, but even more sensitive to Lisztian virtuosity, to Domenico Scarlatti's art (the use of the *acciaccatura*), and to the *copla* of the *flamenco* tune, Albéniz, in *Iberia*, does not aim to burst apart a form, but rather achieves a synthesis which produces a 'brilliant, luminous, generous and radiant music' (Olivier Messiaen).

The work contains four books of three pieces. Built on the basis of two very similar themes and developed on the stylized rhythm of a *fandanguillo* (a popular Basque dance), the first piece of the first book, *Evocation*, has Debussyan coloration. The second, *El puerto*, on jerky rhythms, has the character of a *polo* (a dance tune from the South of Spain). In the darker and very 'orchestral' *Fête-Dieu à Seville*, Albéniz uses a *saeta* and seems to engage in a study of sensory relations between hearing and sight.

The second book, in which the author makes great use of *acciaccaturas*, begins with a piece called *Rondena* with flamenco rhythms (accompanying the melody of a

copla), which begins the following piece called *Almeria*. A *paso doble* theme with highly worked harmonies and a *marcha torera* theme alternate and mutually enrich each other in *Triana*.

With the pieces of the third book, *El Albaícin*, *El Polo* and *Lavapies*, which Debussy was very enthusiastic about, Albéniz really sparkles: he plays on the opposition of timbre reinvented on the piano (guitar, reeds, orchestral tutti) and replaces the key of B flat minor with Arab and Doric modes (*El Albaícin*), introduces modulations in remote tones (*El Polo*) and adds discords to discords (*Lavapies*).

Málaga, a piece greatly inspired by the flamenco style but innovative on a harmonic level, opens the last book. It is followed by *Jerez*, a long 'lyrical reverie' (Claude Rostand). Finally, *Eritana* brings the *Iberia* series, on the pulsating rhythms of a Sevillana, to its radiant and colourful conclusion.

Historical references

Composed between 1906 and 1908, the twelve pieces of *Iberia* were performed by Blanche Selva in Paris on 9 May 1906 (Book I), then in Saint-Jean-de-Luz on 11 September 1907 (Book II) and then again in Paris for the Princess Polignac on 2 January 1908 (Book III) and in the Salon d'automne, on 9 February 1909 (Book IV).

Ravel, Maurice

Gaspard de la Nuit, three poems for piano, 1909

Against the romantic piano

Gaspard de la Nuit *brings the passionate style created by the romantic piano to a level of artistry where the extra-musical literary aspects add a kind of exotic charm.*

Of a more typically Ravelian writing than *Miroirs* (1904–5), and close to impressionism, the three piano pieces entitled *Gaspard de la Nuit* are based on three prose poems which the author of *Daphnis et Chloé* extracted from a book by Aloysius Bertrand (1807–41) from which he borrowed its title and the title of the three poems: *Ondine, Le Gibet, Scarbo.* Linked to each other by a fairly obvious architechtonic thread (the work actually imitates the three movement sonata: *Ondine = allegro, Le Gibet = adagio, Scarbo = finale*) these three pieces draw their source material less from the unusual and the fantastical in which Bertrand's three fantasies are steeped, than from the numerous sound evocations that their text contains and which probably motivate Ravel's selection; the words 'Listen! Listen' make up the verbal leitmotiv of *Ondine*, where the poet makes allusion to 'sound lozenges', to a 'murmured song', etc. It is the 'bell which rings' and the 'skeleton of a hanged person' that are left to be examined, but mostly to be heard when we come to the end of *Le Gibet*.

To be played without dragging, in a melodic and blended manner, *Ondine* develops a moving but very clear melodic line, decorated with arpeggios elaborated according to Liszt's skilful technique of chords of rapidly played notes. This piece, also full of iridescent harmonies brilliantly resolved what Ravel called 'a technical problem'.

Abandoning virtuosity to arrive at something more 'modern' in the indeterminate nature of the harmony, *Le Gibet*, built on a rigorous *ostinato* (B flat major) to be played without a change of tempo, makes use of several piano registers: 'Its sound palette is of an almost orchestral quality' (H. H. Stuckenschmidt).

Scarbo, also rich in orchestral sounding timbre, marks a return to virtuosity, Ravel having expressed that he wanted this work to be of an even more difficult execution than Balakirev's *Islamey*. Here the emphasis is placed on the breaks of rhythm, but all the devices used reach the level of great art.

Historical references

Composed in the summer of 1908 in Levallois, *Gaspard de la Nuit* was played for the first time in public in Paris on 8 January 1909, by Ricardo Vines (1875–1943) who had introduced Ravel to Aloysius's works.

Schönberg, Arnold

Five Pieces for orchestra, 1909

Opus 16

The timbre making the melody

Schönberg's only orchestral work from his 'free', atonal period, Opus 16 *owes its very original colours to the technique of timbre-melody with which he was experimenting.*

Although the *Five Pieces* opus 16 calls for a very large orchestra, Schönberg chose, rather, to make use of an ensemble of soloists — a technique for which he owes a lot to Mahler. Doubling of instruments was avoided as much as possible, the timbres were differentiated and the orchestral mass only used in its entirety in a few instances. The produced effect is somewhat 'that of chamber music whose instrumental combinations change continually' (Charles Rosen). The very notion of orchestration is thus questioned, as the timbre abandons its surface function to become a structural component in its own right.

But the principle of highly differentiated instrumentation also makes the polyphonic textures introduced by Schönberg, which had become very complex by the abandonment of tonality, more readable: the counterpoint 'freed from tonal constraints is able to develop itself with an unprecedented richness', and the harmonic construction of the chords proceeds by 'the accumulation of diverging intervals' (Pierre Boulez).

The parallel abandonment of classical forms of development make these pieces as short (less than 15 minutes in total) as they are complex. The contradiction between duration and complexity is responsible for the extreme tension manifested by some of them, principally the first whose explosions of sound may even surpass those in Stravinsky's *Rite of Spring*. The contrast with the sophisticated sounds of the second, *andante*, is also particularly striking.

The work owes its fame to pieces three and five, with which Schönberg systematized his *Klangfarbenmelodie* (timbre melody) principle. In the third, *moderato*, this technique is applied to a *chord* of five notes, which is immutable, but changes timbre as soon as each of its three notes is played by a new instrument, the transition from one timbre to another having to be made as smoothly as possible. And in the fifth, *allegretto*, the principle is applied to a great melodic line, developing within a very complex polyphony and constantly going from one instrument to another.

Historical references

Composed very quickly, between 23 May and 11 August 1909, the *Five Pieces* opus 16 were performed in London on 3 September 1912.

> The principle of instrumentation of the *Five Pieces for orchestra* implies that 'each phrase is liable to receive an original orchestral colour' and, mostly, that it is 'characterized less by its harmonic content than by the instrumental combinations' (Charles Rosen).

Webern, Anton

Six Pieces for orchestra, 1909

Opus 6

The pleasure of sound

Webern's only work for full orchestra, the Six Pieces *opus 6 give themselves over, in a rarefied but seductive atmosphere, to an almost hedonistic exploration of sound.*

Like Schönberg for his *Five Pieces* opus 16, Webern required a very large orchestra for his *Six Pieces* and chose to use an ensemble of soloists according to Schönberg's *timbre melody* principle, which he discovered at the same time. However, while the sound space of the *Five Pieces* opus 16 was generally very full, that of the *Six Pieces* opus 6 was voluntarily scant. This rarefaction of the sound material — increased by the preponderant use of slow tempos — allows the almost continuous timbre melodies to appear more precise and distinct. From the very beginning of the first piece a very explicit example is given of this phenomenon: a motif played

by the flute is interrupted by the muted trumpets, coloured by two brief celesta chords. The contrast achieved between the flute and the trumpet is not meant to 'embellish' the phrase, but rather to 'give it meaning' (H. L. Matter).

This said, the extreme sonorous seduction of these pieces also comes from the uncommon instrumental formulas used here by Webern, like the opposition of a solo string instrument with the string ensemble, or the use of some instruments (flute, trumpet, harp, tuba) in unusually low registers. According to Pierre Boulez, this seduction results from the relative simplicity of the polyphony (a principal melodic 'line' accompanied by chords) and from the use of intervals which are joined sufficiently to create the impression of continuity, despite a writing based exclusively on a collection of brief motifs.

With the exception of the second, made very brilliant by trombone trill, all of the pieces of this opus are slow (the sound material is contemplated as if in slow motion) and short (generally no longer than 12 minutes). But the fourth piece (slow, a funeral march), a long *crescendo* beginning *pianissimo* and ending *fortissimo* with lots of percussion, is undeniably the 'climax' of the work; especially as the last bars give less the impression of having participated in a funeral march than of a progressive and jubilant explosion of sound.

Historical references

Composed in 1909, the *Six Pieces* opus 6 were performed in Vienna on 31 March 1913, and conducted by Schönberg who was also the dedicatee of the work.

The Five Pieces opus 10

More 'aphoristic' than the pieces of opus 6, and requiring instruments (guitar, mandolin, harmonium) rarely used in a symphonic work except by Mahler or Schönberg, the *Five Pieces for orchestra opus 10*, composed by Webern in 1913, having removed all the spectacular effects found in opus 6, are even more perfect. They undoubtedly constitute, with the *Bagatelles for string quartet opus 9*, the peak of Webern's pre-serial production.

Debussy, Claude

Images for orchestra, 1913

New sound visions

In their rhythmic fluidity and the attention they give to the timbre, the Images *for orchestra — and especially the second,* Iberia *— anticipate new distinctive features of sound.*

To have composed *Three Images* based on the 'colour' of a given country is surprising for Debussy, if we are to believe his unkind declarations about the use of folklore. But, it is true that his Scotland, evoked by the principal theme of *Gigues*, is very subtle, that the hispanicism of *Iberia*, although more blatant, is no less entirely imaginary, and that the popular song '*Nous n'irons plus au bois*', heard in *Rondes de printemps*, is not enough to endow this last *Image* with a specific 'Frenchness'. Debussy had said of these three pieces, 'I tried to create something *different* — in a sense *realities* — that which imbeciles call *impressionism*'; and these 'realities' could refer to the most commendable feature of *Images*, to their renewed, because clearer, vision of the sound material.

The order, for publication, of *Images* was meant to arrange the three pieces in this order: *Gigues, Iberia, Rondes de printemps*, with the two shorter pieces framing the longer one, itself divided into three movements. While this symmetry may be pleasing to the eye, it was less so for the ear, for *Rondes* seems pale next to *Iberia*. Pierre Boulez recommends playing the order: *Rondes de printemps, Gigues, Iberia*.

In comparison with the preceding orchestral works, the orchestration of *Images* is both more precise and more bare (the use of the xylophone in *Gigues* and *Iberia* is revealing in this sense), the harmony is more discordant, the form 'more fragmented in appearance, more unified in reality' (Harry Halbreich), and the constant proliferation of motifs is based on dramatically reduced intervals. While, up to *La Mer*, the emancipation of timbre ensued more from the modes of development invented by Debussy, it now tended to become an independent component of the musical discourse. This phenomena is particularly evident in the splendid coda of *Gigues* and the second movement of *Iberia*.

It is in its entirety that this second *Image*, longer than the two others as it contains three movements ('Par les rues et par les chemins', 'Les Parfums de la nuit', 'Le Matin d'un jour de fête'), is significant. In its art of transitions, as expressed in the extraordinary transition, by successive overlappings, from the second movement to the third; and in the fluidity of its tempos by avoiding establishing regular beats, this *Image* foreshadows the contemporary music notion of continuous time.

Historical references

The *Images* were composed between 1906 and 1912. Finished respectively in December 1908 and May 1909, *Iberia* and *Rondes de printemps* were performed in February and March 1910. Started in 1909, *Gigues*, whose orchestration was completed by André Caplet in 1912, was performed in January 1913, at the first performance of the entire triptych.

Berg, Alban

Three pieces for orchestra, 1914

Opus 6

An anticipation of an opera

Berg's Three Pieces *opus 6 propose an orchestral dramatic art which successively reflects the use of sound, musical connotations and formal complexity.*

As Berg remarked, the *Three Pieces* opus 6 are not 'detached' pieces. In order to reinforce the unity of his work, he created several thematic references from one piece to another.

But the work is striking initially in its extreme sound density. And, while we must see in its use of a gigantic orchestral complement the influences of Schönberg's *Three Pieces* opus 16, Berg's opus 6 establishes itself in the tradition of Mahler's works, as the ideas of the two composers are drawn towards each other.

The first piece, *Praeludium*, in an almost mythical gesture, tries to 'represent music'

The sequence of these pieces is like that of a symphony in four movements, where the first piece, *Praeludium* (Prelude) represents the first movement, *Reigen* (Round) the second, representing both the scherzo and the slow movement, and the third piece, *Marsch* (March), as the finale.

Berg dedicated his opus 6 to Schönberg for his 40th birthday, and also to respond to the criticisms that the 'irritated master' had made of his earlier works.

(Dominique Jameux). With an art of transition which is confounding, the beginning of the piece allows for the transition from the *noise* (tom-tom, drum, cymbals) to the *sound* (entry of the bassoon) via the kettledrums (which are percussion with determined pitch); then within sound itself, the transition from the *note* (still the bassoon) to the *chord* (whose six notes, following a coloration technique borrowed from Schönberg, are played by different instruments); and finally from the *sound* to *melody* (by the progressive construction of the theme). The music can thus develop and progressively attain its highest point of tension and then return progressively, but differently, to its beginning, the last bars being an approximate inversion of the first. One can also hear, in these four minutes of music 'the reduction of a single note' and see in this piece 'a prelude fulfilling its maximum potential' (Étienne Barilier).

Of very sophisticated writing and mixing its binary triple time rhythm which is of a constantly varied waltz, the second piece, *Reigen*, appears to want to finish with the 'comfortable' mood of salon music, as the waltz represents here 'a world both evil and good' (D. Jameux).

With the final *march*, Berg claims to have written the most complex piece yet created. The delights of formal construction are pushed to a degree rarely attained, and few musical works achieve such a sense of vertigo. An effort of almost hysterical proportions, this third piece however, does not really resolve itself until his next work, the opera *Wozzeck*.

Historical references

Composed in 1913–14, opus 6 was not performed in its entirety until 1930.

Falla, Manuel de

Nights in the Gardens of Spain, 1916

The setting for the song

Linked to Spanish folklore and to French music of Spanish inspiration (Ravel, Debussy), the Nights in the Gardens of Spain *also established itself in the turn-of-the-century impressionist movement.*

Manuel de Falla seems to have always been loath to use pre-established forms: he never made use of the symphony, nor the sonata, nor the quartet, and his *Concerto* for harpsichord, hardly resembles concerto.

Noches en los jardines de España (*Nights in the Gardens of Spain*), a composition originally written for solo piano, is no exception. It is made up of three 'Symphonic Impressions' (the composer's own sub-title) for piano and orchestra which deserve to be interpreted, not like a concerto, but like a kind of impressionistic orchestra-piano duet, in that it makes musical reference — not only in its titles — to nature.

In the first piece, an *allegro tranquillo e misterioso* entitled 'En el Generalife', the

sound image of a calm Andalusian night, suddenly restless in parts, then calm again, is established over two melodic themes played respectively by the orchestra and the piano. The second theme, inspired by a *zorongo* (a musical style derived from the flamenco), emphasizes the paler colour of the first based on the undulating rhythm of a *jaleo*, but these two very similar themes are so indistinguishable to the ear that we often hear 'En el Generalife' as a single series of free variations on its initial *canto*.

Built on several rhythms with indistinct contours, the 'Danza lejana' (*allegretto guisto*) follows the first theme with a second, defined by Falla himself as a consequence of the second theme of 'En el Generalife' and which, also included in the finale, could perhaps constitute what Suzanne Demarquez called 'a brief tribute to the cyclical form'.

Less marked by the impressionist aesthetic than the two preceding pieces (its tonal rigour leaves no room for modulations), the finale, 'En los jardines de la Sierra de Córdoba' (*vivo*), is constructed in the form of a *copla* with an *estribillo* (refrain), with the same structure as a classical rondo. It brings out, for the first time, the high tones of a percussion, hitherto limited to the kettledrums, but not very effective in evoking, particularly on a Cordoban fandango rhythm, the din of a nocturnal celebration dissipated by the arrival of the dawn.

> Less well-known, but of a clearly more 'advanced' writing, the very sonorous and purified *Concerto for Harpsichord* (or piano), *flute, oboe, clarinet, violin and cello* (1923–26) is among the most remarkable by Manuel de Falla. It is, in fact, a chamber music piece written at the request of Wanda Landowska (1879–1959) to whom it is dedicated and who performed it in Barcelona on 5 November 1926.

Historical references

Falla composed his *Nights* in Paris and in Barcelona, between 1909 and 1915. The premiere took place on 9 April 1916 in Madrid.

Schönberg, Arnold

Five Pieces for piano, 1923

Opus 23

The series of 12

The Five Pieces *opus 23 mark Schönberg's transition to the 'method of composition with 12 notes'. The fifth piece is, in fact, the first dodecaphonic serial piece to be written.*

Schönberg's serial period was inaugurated by these *Five Pieces* for piano which constitute, above all, an attempt to restore order, as opposed to his preceding 'free' atonal period. In fact, atonality, 'as well as being a liberating force, also constituted, in Schönberg's eyes, a dangerous ferment of anarchy' (Francis Bayer). For, while the only rule was that any note could maintain, with any other note, any relation other than tonal, the promised liberation was at great risk of becoming the 'liberty of indifference', and the anticipated 'isotropic interval' would become in the long run 'nothing

---

The pianistic work

Arnold Schönberg composed a total of five piano collections: *Three Pieces* opus 11 (1909), *Six Little Pieces* opus 19 (1911), *Five Pieces* opus 23 (1920–3), *Suite* opus 25 (1921–3) and another *Two Pieces* opus 33, respectively written between 1929 and 1932. In none of these works did Schönberg really evolve the sound conception of the keyboard. His pianistic style was perhaps 'one of the last examples of the "great piano", as it was conceived of by the best composers from Schumann to Brahms' (Pierre Boulez).

---

more than an amorphous space' (F.Bayer). It was, therefore, to endow music with a new unifying principle that Schönberg elaborated his serial order, and it was the discovery of this new order that was achieved with the help of the *Five Pieces*, opus 23.

Although not yet serial, the first four pieces of this collection obeyed nonetheless two principles — 'the unity of the musical material and the unity of the motif variations' (Charles Rosen) — which were to be revealed as crucial components of serialism. The principle of unity of the material, originally spread over the whole chromatic space, becomes that of the series of 12 notes; and the principle of motif transformation, once systematized, creates many principles of derivation, making it possible to obtain all series from the basis of an initial (base) series.

The first piece, *sehr langsam* (very slow) is remarkable in the way it uses a material principally composed of minor seconds and thirds, and in the way it combines the two melodies which run through it, with the help of all the techniques of variation. Similarly, the third piece, *langsam* (slow) displays an even greater concern for economy as it is based on a single motif of five notes.

Entirely composed — for the first time — on a series of 12 notes (see p. 231), the fifth and last piece of opus 23, *Walzer* (Waltz) is therefore *historic*, even though the use it makes of the series is still fairly cautious. It is all the more significant in that, unlike the preceding pieces, the motif which engenders this series is not treated melodically; in other words, melodic development and serial structure are not compatible. And this revolution — as Charles Rosen noted — will prove to have enormous consequences.

Varèse, Edgar

Ionization for percussion, 1933

Sound reorganized

The first Western work for solo percussion, Ionization *offers primarily 'an organization of notes determined according to a new sound scale' (M. Choquer).*

Written for about forty instruments which, except for two sirens and a piano all belong to the percussion family (woods, metals and skins), *Ionization* has only three instruments which produce definite pitches. It also is usually considered to be the first work organized on the basis of 'indeterminate' notes. But although in his complete rejection of temperament and in his concern for always reconsidering the sound phenomena, Varèse did not subject the 'organized notes' of *Ionization* to any traditional scale, they did not avoid all classification. On the contrary, a recent analysis reveals that the composition established 'classifications very clearly discernible to the ear' which were based on the register of the instruments and their 'inertia' (Marc Choquer). Further-

more, Varèse made use of this classification system as the principle of rhythmic variation, with the rule being that the speed of a rhythm is inversely proportional to the inertia of the instrument on which it is played. Thus, 'the first rhythm played on the military drum when it is associated with the tarole and the clear drum (weaker inertias) finds itself accelerated and slightly shortened; when next associated with the solo tarole the rhythm becomes even shorter and faster. In brief, 'the instrument in play is the matrix for the intended musical process' (M. Choquer).

After a first part which puts the main rhythmic elements of the work in place, these approximately five minutes of music respect a fairly simple structure alternating 'divisions' and 'groupings' — divisions correspond to the segments of rhythmic proliferation by 'ionization', and the groupings are created by 'rhythmic unisons' (Robert Craft). In the last section of the work, in a slow tempo, three instruments with determinate pitches (glockenspiel, bells, piano) are introduced which, although principally used for 'blocks', are no less capable of resulting in a melodic figure repeated several times. But this figure is aimed mainly at 'the fusion of rhythms and timbres progressively gelling in a complex resonance' (M. Choquer), for it is true that the last bars of *Ionization* create less the impression of an ending than of an immobilization of the sound material.

A precursor

Having always considered the musical phenomenon in terms of its acoustic qualities Varèse became interested very early on in the first attempts of electro-acoustic music. He wrote *Déserts* (1950–4) for orchestra and magnetic tape, and *Poème électronique* (1958) for tape alone. He is seen today primarily as an undeniable precursor to the most recent trends of young music.

Historical references

Composed in Paris between 1929 and 1931, *Ionization* was first performed in 1933 in New York.

Bartók, Béla

Music for strings, percussion and celesta, 1937

A skilful handling of timbres

Refining to an extreme level the use of struck sounds, based on an unprecedented instrumental device, this composition is the formal peak of Bartók's works.

Elaborated with the help of a harmonic writing system which allows for a great expansion of tonal functions (abolished by serialism), the *Music for strings* presents what Claude Rostand called 'an external kinship' with the serialism of Schönberg and the Vienna School.

The instrumental music makes use of two string quintets, sometimes playing together (first movement), sometimes apart (second, third, and fourth movements), a full percussion (two drums, cymbals, large drum, tom-tom, kettledrums with pedals), a celesta, a xylophone, a harp and a piano.

From the first to the last movement, the slow-fast-slow-fast alternance models its structure on the church sonata of the 17th century.

The celesta is a percussion instrument invented in 1868 by Victor Mustel. Equipped with a keyboard, it resembles a harmonium. Its hammers, covered in felt like those of a piano, hit against metal strips. Before Bartók, the fairly curt but crystalline resonance of this instrument had been brought into prominence by Tchaikovsky (*Nutcracker*, 'Dance of the sugar-plum fairy'), Ravel (*Ma mère l'Oye*, a passage entitled 'Laideronette') and Mahler (at the end of *Song of the Earth* and in the last bars of the *Kindertotenlieder*).

A very sombre theme of an almost atonal melodic nature, is played *pianissimo* by the violas at the beginning of the *andante tranquillo* (first movement). It soon generates a fugue built around 'a large *crescendo-decrescendo* arch' (Hermo Lendvai). At the peak of this arch, the successive entries of the fugue's subject are inverted in such a way that the second part of the movement is the mirror-image of the first.

Issuing from a sonata-form, the second movement (*allegro*) uses a theme of popular inspiration related to the main theme of the first movement. Bartók extracts from this theme 'prodigious effects of wild dynamism' (Pierre Citron).

The third movement (*adagio*) which may well be the most remarkable, is a nocturne of sorts. It respects the structural principle of the arch-form which, in this case, creates a division in five sections (A–B–C–B–A). Of all these episodes with very original timbre combinations, the most amazing is section A, a rhythmic episode with kettledrum *glissandi*. Each section is linked to the others by motifs of the subject of the initial fugue (first movement).

Constructed as a rondo in order to better detect the popular melodic and rhythmic aspects, the last movement (*allegro molto*) re-establishes the key of A major which was actually the imperceptible base key of the first movement. Just before the end of the piece, the subject of the fugue (up until now expressed in a chromatic form) reappears in a diatonic form.

Historical references

Bartók composed the *Music for strings* in 1936. It had been commissioned by Paul Sacher, head of Basel's Chamber Orchestra, and who gave the first performance for the public on 21 January 1937.

Messiaen, Olivier

Oiseaux exotiques for piano and small orchestra, 1956

High-flying counterpoint

Combining sound transpositions of bird songs with Greek and Hindu rhythms, this work produces a polyphony of great virtuosity.

Written for solo piano, two flutes, one oboe, four clarinets, one bassoon, two horns, one trumpet, one glockenspiel, one xylophone, and five percussionists, the *Oiseaux exotiques* owe their lively colour to this unusual formation — in which strings are absent.

This opposition between a solo instrument and a small orchestra also determines the form of the work, alternating five piano cadenzas with eight segments for the orchestra, only two of which, the great central *tutti* and the great final *tutti*, use the entire instrumental ensemble. The six other sections serve as introductions, interludes or codas. Two of them are blatantly descriptive: 'Orage, Tonnere sur la forêt amazonienne' and 'Quatre hurlements du tétras

cupidon, suivis de L'Orage' (which is the reverse of the first).

The progression of the work depends on 'an arbitrary arrangement of 48 bird songs from different continents' (Harry Halbreich) and the *realism* displayed by the piece (the convened birds are faithfully reproduced) is, however, no less *imaginary* (for their assembly transgresses geographical boundaries). More precisely, these 48 birds, brought together for the sole purposes of the piece, mainly come from North America, but also from India, South America, China, Malaysia and the Canary Islands. And their names have an undeniably exotic ring to them: the red cardinal of Virginia, the liothrix of China, the shama of India, the white-crested garulaxe of the Himalayas.

However, the ornithological material does not account for the entire work, for in the two great orchestral *tuttis* the percussion parts also play Greek and Hindu rhythms, the first varying in an almost mechanical way and the second remaining unchanged. Messaien explained: 'This strict obstinacy of rhythms in changing or remaining the same is in constant opposition with the extreme freedom of the bird song melodies and allow for the increased enrichment of the counterpoint produced'.

Historical references

Commissioned by Pierre Boulez for the Domaine musical concerts, this work was written between October 1955 and January 1956, and first performed on 10 March 1956 with Yvonne Loriod on piano.

Other orchestral pieces by Olivier Messiaen: *Les Offrandes oubliées* (1930), *L'Ascension* (1932), *Turangalîla Symphonie* (1946–8), *Réveil des oiseaux* (1953), *Chronochromie* (1960), *Sept Haïkaï*, Japanese sketches (1962), *Couleurs de la Cité celeste* (1963), *Et exspecto resurrectionem mortuorum* (1964), *Des canyons aux étoiles* (1971–4).

Xenakis, Iannis

Pithoprakta for 50 instruments, 1957

A theory of distinct 'clouds'

By using, with Pithoprakta *(his second work), the calculation of probabilities to treat sound masses as 'clouds', Xenakis invented 'Stochastic' music.*

Pithoprakta — meaning action caused by probabilities — uses fifty instruments each playing a different part, which include 46 strings, two trombones, one wood-block and one xylophone. The work — according to a technique introduced in *Metastasis* (1954) — makes a systematic and generalized use of *glissandi* (continuous sounds), but it confronts these with an equally rigorous and static use of *pizzicati* (discontinuous sounds). In other words, '*Pithoprakta* confronts the notions of continuity and discontinuity, and all the transitions from one to the other' (Daniel Durney).

More precisely, thanks to a general method of formalization which appeals to the theory of probability, and for this reason called 'stochastic', Xenakis succeeds in distinguishing here very different types of sound amalgams. These are, principally, the '*cloud*' of sounds (an amalgam of sound points statistically configurated — where each point is as short a sound as possible), the *mass* of sounds (a statistical amalgam of glissé sounds whose duration and intervals of pitch is variable), the *block* of sounds (which is an immobile mass, or amalgam of held sounds) and finally the *nebula*, or galaxy, which is an interweaving of clouds, masses and blocks.

While these calculations are rather complex, the work which results from them, issues from 'sound climates' organized mathematically, and follows a fairly simple progression in five highly differentiated sections which are all the more distinct for being separated by rests lasting from one to four bars.

The first section is entirely made up of *clouds*, and their initially indeterminate sounds (the string instruments are struck on their bodies) become increasingly determinate (the strings now playing *pizzicati*).

The second section, offering at first an intermediate sound state between the *cloud* and the mass, achieved by the *glissandi* playing of *pizzicati*, then crumbles a block into a cloud, and finishes in a very rarefied space.

The third section is a nebula slowed down into a block-cloud by the emergence of the strings.

Following the play of points of the fourth section, the fifth finally transforms masses into clouds, clouds into blocks and blocks into a single sound which closes the work.

New types of sounds

'My first endeavour was to introduce into music global phenomena issuing from a large number of isolated sound events. There existed two limited and fundamental types; firstly disjointed sound occurrences like the string *pizzicati*, and secondly the continually varying occurrences like the *glissandi*' (Xenakis).

Historical references

Written in 1955–6, *Pithoprakta* was first performed on 8 March 1957 under the direction of Hermann Scherchen, to whom it was dedicated.

Stockhausen, Karlheinz

Gruppen for three orchestras, 1958

Spatialized time

The emancipation of musical time, brought about by Stockhausen in Gruppen, *led to a stereophonic explosion of the orchestra and marked the beginning of modern spatial music.*

While the title *Gruppen* primarily designates the division of the orchestra into three instrumental groups, it also takes into account the writing principle used for this work which the composer called *Gruppenform* (group form).

This form uses a new segmentation of the musical discourse which no longer sees the note as the unifying element, but rather the group of sounds which must be given enough definition to be distinguishable. Each group is determined 'by its dimensions, its form, its density and mostly by its own sound quality which results from the particular treatment given to the different parameters of sound which make it up' (F.

In the 1950s and 60s, Stockhausen was undoubtedly the most inventive composer of his generation. He explored many aspects of musical research which are reflected in his *aleatory music* (Klavierstück XI, 1956), *spatial music* (Carré for choirs and four orchestras, 1960), the *coming together* of instrumental and electronic music (Kontakte, 1960), and the *'live' transformation* of instrumental music by electronics (Mikrophonie I, 1964, Mixtur, 1964, Mantra, 1970), and more.

Bayer). This method which allows for the enrichment of the orchestral palette, as a 'group' is just as likely to be made up of a very short, isolated note, as to form a complex sound with a density so great that the perception of it becomes statistical.

The 'effective spatialization' of the writing processes carried out in *Gruppen* is the result of a contemplation, not of space, but of the parameter of *time*. Guided by the desire to make all sound parameters as important as pitch, Stockhausen came to consider the notion of musical *time*, and, with *Gruppen*, realized the need to confront, within this same work, different times. Because such a simultaneity would not be possible unless each different tempo was led by a different conductor, he gave each of them a separate instrumental group.

The three orchestras placed at the left, in front and at the right of the audience, and including, respectively, 36, 37 and 36 instruments, had very similar formations, for this similarity allowed one sound to travel from one orchestra to another. But in addition to the possible transfers, exchanges and echoes, this device also made it easier to detect various 'group forms' presented, and to play up the opposition between isolated notes and sound aggregates. From this point of view, a passage played by the brass would be particularly successful, for the transfers of sound were added to by the use of mutes giving the impression of distance.

Historical references

Composed between 1955 and 1957, *Gruppen* was first performed on 24 March 1958 in Cologne, under the codirection of the composer, Bruno Maderna and Pierre Boulez.

Dutilleux, Henri

Métaboles for orchestra, 1965

New principles of variation

In order to renew the symphonic material, the Métaboles *adopted a principle of transformation which allowed for the progressive movement from one orchestral figure to another.*

Written for a large orchestra including an imposing percussion section, the *Métaboles* contain five pieces linked without interruption and which cannot, as the composer swears, 'give rise to fragmentary executions'. For, despite their distinct characterization, these five pieces nonetheless follow a group structure.

For example, while the first four have a particular orchestral colour, due to the respective predominance of woods, strings brass and percussion, the fifth finally brings together the entire orchestra in a sound synthesis. Furthermore, and in accordance with the title of the work — a metabole is

An exceptional figure

Considered by some — perhaps because of his ultimately very reasonable modernity — to be one of the greatest living composers, but accused of academicism by the others, Henri Dutilleux is, in any event, an exceptional figure in contemporary music. Because he wrote slowly, his repertoire is fairly limited, but includes a *Piano Sonata* (1948), two *Symphonies* (1951 and 1959), *Tout un monde lointain* for violin and orchestra (1970), *Cinq figures de résonances* for two pianos (1970–6), a string quartet *Ainsi la nuit* (1976), *Timbres, Espace, Mouvement* for orchestra (1977) and, very recently, a *Violin Concerto*.

a rhetorical device which consistently varies the same idea — each piece implies the following one. For each piece, 'the initial figure — melodic, rhythmic, harmonic or simply instrumental — undergoes a series of transformations. At a certain stage in their evolution — towards the end of each piece — the distortion is so pronounced that it creates a new figure which appears just beneath the symphonic texture. This is the figure that primes the following piece, and so on until the last piece, where the initial figure of the work stands out again in the coda, in a long ascensional movement' (H. Dutilleux). The coherence of the work, already assured by this linking device, is further strengthened by a unifying principle based on the use of a pivotal note (E) and of a special interval (the augmented fourth).

The first piece, 'Incantatoire', owes its mood of an incarnation to the repetition of a short and lashing theme. The second 'Linéaire', for solo strings, develops a very rich polyphony whose strict division of lines continues to grow, reaching 27 true sections. While the third, 'Obsessional', is serial, if not in spirit, then at least in its beginning material (a series of 12 notes), the fourth, 'Torpide', which is athematic and makes use of numerous percussion instruments with indeterminate notes, 'is entirely centred on the metamorphoses of a six-note chord' (Daniel Humbert). And finally, the fifth movement, 'Flamboyant', which is extremely virtuosic and recapitulates the entire work, finishes with an immense orchestral *tutti* on the single note E, which precedes a chord mixing true fourths with augmented fourths.

Historical references

Commissioned in 1959 by the Cleveland Orchestra, *Métaboles* was first performed on 14 January 1965.

Boulez, Pierre

Responses for instrumental ensemble, soloists and electro-acoustic devices, 1984

Theatre of metamorphoses (*J. Ricardou*)

A mixed music which combines instrumental sound with its electronic transformations, Responses *sets out, in a very seductive play of sound, the continuous replies of is protagonists.*

Responses, which can only be realized in a large rectangular or square room, is made up of three 'distinct instances' (D. Jameux). At the centre of the space, on a podium, is an instrumental ensemble of 24 musicians, made up of woods, brass and strings. Distributed at equal distances around the room, are six soloists playing exclusively resonant instruments: a piano, a piano with electric organ, a cymbalum, a vibraphone, and a xylophone which is joined by a glockenspiel. An electro-accoustic piece completes the group.

This contingent firstly arranges six tape-recorders, placed close to the soloists, in which the prerecorded tapes of synthetic sounds — a kind of background noise which Boulez called a 'wallpaper' — are triggered automatically by the sound intensity created by the soloists.

But the role of this device is mainly to transform the sounds of the six soloists, and their sound metamorphoses result, in a sense, in the extension, the multiplication of their natural resonances. There are three types of transformations brought about: harmonic, rhythmic and spatial. More precisely, the electronic device is capable of instantly changing the harmonic structure of a sound emitted by an instrument; of producing, based on an instrumental motif,

and thanks to a system of multiple echoes, very complex rhythms achieved by the superimposition; and finally, of making the synthetic sounds thus produced travel according to an enlarged type of stereophony with six loudspeakers distributed among the soloists.

The responses flow from one soloist to another, and from instrumental sound to electronic sounds. The entry of the soloists is the most spectacular: six huge arpeggiato chords amplified, travel throughout the whole space, while others retain the first electronic transformations. With the actual coda of the work, finally, chords played again by the soloists alone, becoming less and less frequent, are gradually overcome by silence 'until no sound response is given' (D. Jameux).

Historical references

A first version of *Responses* was performed on 18 October 1981 by the *Ensemble intercontemporain*. The work was subsequently performed in two other versions, each time increased, in 1982 and then in 1984.

Responses, which is still not finished today, benefitted from the technological support of IRCAM, and in particular of the *machine 4X* invented by the Italian engineer Giuseppe di Giugno. Mainly known for his instrumental and vocal works, such as *Le Marteau sans Maître* for alto voice and six instruments (1955), and *Pli selon pli*, in the style of Mallarmé, for soprano and orchestra (1957–62), Pierre Boulez has always been interested in the relationship between music and electronics. This interest is testified to by 'attempts', before *Responses*, which included *Poésie pour pouvoir* for orchestra and magnetic tape (1958).

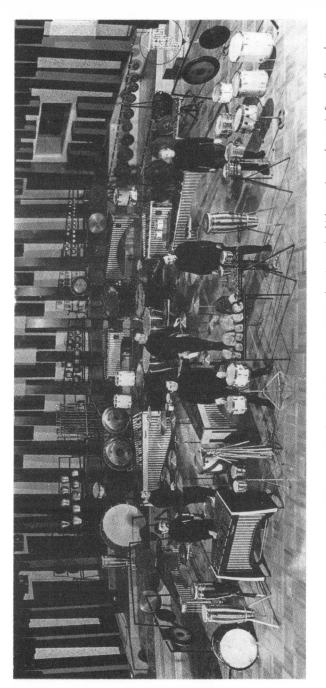

The Strasbourg Percussions Founded in 1961, at Pierre Boulez's instigation, l'Ensemble de musique contemporaine des Percussions de Strasbourg brought together six players: Jean-Paul Batigne, Gabriel Bouchet (joined the group in 1963). Olivier Dejours (a member since 1975), Jean-Paul Finkbeiner, Claude Ricou and Georges van Gucht.

Having slightly more than 400 instruments at their disposal (about three tonnes of equipment), which were in popular use in Europe (large drum, kettledrums, cymbals, glockenspiel, etc ...), or of African origin (underarm drum, sanza ...), or Afro-Cuban (bongos, congas ...), or Asiatic (gongs, bells, vibraphones, etc ...), these musicians gave rise to and created a large number of works for solo percussions as well as many pieces written for percussion and wind instruments.

CHRONOLOGY OF COMPOSERS

Year			
90			
80			
70			
60			
1950			
40			
30			
20			
10			
1900			
90			
80			
70			
60			
1850			
40			
30			
20			
10			
1800			
90			
80			
70			
60			
1750			
40			
30			
20			
10			
1700			
90			
80			
70			
60			
1650			

AUSTRIA AND GERMANY

J.S. Bach 1685 — 1750
Handel 1685 — 1759
Haydn 1732 — 1809
Mozart 1756 — 1791
Beethoven 1770 — 1827
Weber 1786 — 1826
Schubert 1797 — 1828
Mendelssohn 1809 — 1847
Schumann 1810 — 1856
Wagner 1813 — 1883
Bruckner 1824 — 1896
J. Strauss (fils) 1825 — 1899
Brahms 1833 — 1897
Mahler 1860 — 1911
R. Strauss 1864 — 1949
Schönberg 1874 — 1951
Webern 1883 — 1945
Berg 1885 — 1935
Stockhausen 1928 —

This chronology, which only includes composers of instrumental works, brings out two major musical regions of the 18th and 19th centuries: France and Austria/Germany. Nonetheless, we must not forget that Italy, while not being highly represented here, gave us many of the greatest composers of lyrical music of the 19th century.

SPAIN

Albéniz 1860 — 1903
Falla 1876 — 1946

UNITED STATES

Ives 1874 — 1954
Varèse 1883 — 1965
Gershwin 1898 — 1937
Carter 1908 —
Cage 1912 —

CENTRAL EUROPE

Chopin 1810 — 1849
Liszt 1811 — 1886
Dvořák 1841 — 1904
Janáček 1854 — 1928
Bartók 1881 — 1945
Ligeti 1923 —

In all the cultural areas represented here, the end of the 19th and the beginning of the 20th century include a huge number of composers of instrumental works. This is due less to a generational phenomenon than to the explosive proliferation of musical forms inherited from the 18th and 19th centuries.

FRANCE

1803 Berlioz 1869
1822 Franck 1890
1823 Lalo 1892
1835 Saint-Saëns 1921
1838 Bizet 1875
1841 Chabrier 1894
1845 Fauré 1924
1855 Chausson 1899
1862 Debussy 1918
1865 Dukas 1935
1866 Satie 1925
1869 Roussel 1937
1875 Ravel 1937
1892 Honegger (Swiss) 1955
1892 Milhaud 1974
1908 Messiaen
1916 Dutilleux
1922 Xenakis
1925 Boulez

ITALY

1653 Corelli 1713
1678 Vivaldi 1741
1685 D. Scarlatti 1757
1792 Rossini 1868
1813 Verdi 1901
1925 Berio

RUSSIA

1839 Mussorgsky 1881
1840 Tchaikovsky 1893
1844 Rimsky-Korsakov 1908
1872 Skryabin 1915
1873 Rachmaninov 1943
1882 Stravinsky 1971
1891 Prokofiev 1953
1906 Shostakovich 1975

SCANDINAVIAN COUNTRIES

1843 Grieg 1907
1865 Sibelius 1957

Glossary

acciaccatura (Italian *acciaccare*, 'to crush') A process of ornamentation, widely used by the harpsichordists of the 18th century (notably Scarlatti) which consists in simultaneously striking a keyboard note (called the principal note) and the note next to it, the latter being released soon after.

appoggiatura (Italian *appoggiare*, 'to lean') A grace note, harmonically unrelated to the chord in which it is played to produce a relatively distinct discord.

arpeggio (Italian *arpe*, 'harp') A chord in which the notes are rapidly played one after the other (from low to high or vice versa) instead of being played simultaneously (plaqué).

atonality A term which describes all music which does not respect the laws of the Occidental tonal system. Atonality uses the whole range of the chromatic (qv) scale's resources. The notion applies both to music which is not tonal (modal) and to music containing passages whose tonality is not precisely determinable (extension of Wagnerian chromaticism, and Debussyan harmonic 'layering') and finally to music suspending, non-systematically but deliberately, all tonal functions (this initiative goes back to Schönberg with his *Quartet No.2* opus 10). And music which is organized nontonally (see **dodecaphonic**) is a fortiori atonal.

attack 1. The very beginning of a piece of music. 2. The means of starting to emit a sound on an instrument.

basso continuo A continuous instrumental part (organ, harpsichord or lute usually doubled by a bass viol, a cello or a bassoon) meant to support, from the 17th century, within the framework of an accompanied monody, the principal vocal or instrumental melodic line. Only the bass is indicated and it is therefore up to the interpreter to 'realize' it by completing the harmony, either according to a planned musical system (figured bass) or to an impromptu use (non-figured bass). The basso continuo disappeared completely in 1775.

basso ostinato see **ostinato**.

beat A regular rhythmic pulse.

cadence A harmonic (or plagal, or perfect) cadence is a sequence of chords which acts as the formal conclusion to a musical phrase.

cadenza (Italian, *'cadence'* – a virtuoso passage) A flourish, in principle improvised by the soloist during the first, second (fairly rare) or third movement of a concerto, allowing the soloist to shine (the orchestra remaining silent).

cantilena In the field of instrumental music, a cantilena is a work or a part of a work built to highlight a melody which is essentially smooth and tuneful.

choral(e) see introductory text p. 19.

chord The superimposition of a minimum of three sounds emitted simultaneously. Associated mainly with harmony, it was, in the classical era, based on a distribution in thirds and was classified as 'concordant' chords (the most concordant was the perfect chord, eg C,E,G) or discordant ones (eg sevenths). More recently it 'has become a sound medley, chosen for its potential for tension or relaxation, according to the registers it occupies and the intervals which it puts into play' (Pierre Boulez).

chromatic 1. An adjective which describes an interval separating two notes with the same name (where one is altered or both are differently altered, eg C — C sharp, G flat — G sharp). 2. A term designating 'by extension, a composition or a part of a composition in which many ... sequences of chromatic intervals intervene' (Roland de Candé). Opposite of **diatonic**.

coda (Italian, *'tail'*) A section usually added to the structure of a given musical form, which closes a particular part of a work by announcing its imminent conclusion or by effectively representing the end.

concordance see **discord**.

continuo see **basso continuo**.

counter-melody (French, *'contre-chant'*) A secondary melodic line which is audible at the same time as the principal melodic line.

counterpoint A stylistic technique of combining several melodic lines (or voices) according to strict rules. These lines, which derive one from the other, still retain their own internal logic (melodic colour, rhythm ...) and are therefore bound to be heard simultaneously. Counterpoint, as it refers to the simultaneous progression of different lines, is considered to be a horizontal musical dimension. Fugue is the most elaborate form of counterpoint.

cyclic (form): The structure of a musical composition based on a 'generator' (base) theme, or cyclic theme, one or more elements of which are heard periodically in different movements of the work, in such a way as to reinforce the structural unity of the work. The expression 'cyclic form' comes from Vincent d'Indy who felt that Beethoven was the inventor of this structure and considered César Franck to be the first to consciously use it.

degree A term given to the successive notes of a scale. Eg in the scale of C major (C,D,E,F,G,A,B,C,D), the tonic C is the first degree, D is the second, etc.

development 1. The second part of an 'academic fugue' (see introductory text, p. 65), after the exposition, consisting mainly of a series of modulations. Between each modulation a brief free contrapuntal divertimento episode occurs. 2. The second section of the sonata-form within which the themes of the exposition break apart and come back together in various tonalities (see diagram p. 118).

diatonic 1. An adjective describing an interval separating two adjacent notes with different names (eg D–E, B–C). 2. A term for a scale made up of a sequence of notes all with different names (C, D, E, F ...) and separated by unequal intervals of tones and semitones. Opposite of **chromatic**.

discord An interval or chord which, in the framework of a given historical period or musical culture, establishes a relationship with adjacent notes that is considered 'illogical' (harmonic destabilization) and creates an audible impression of tension.

In the classical era, a chord that was considered pleasing to the ear (concord) had to follow a discord to provide its resolution. Modern harmony, on the other hand, frequently uses complex dissonant chords (discords), which today are no longer perceived as such.

dodecaphonic (music) A word invented by René Leibowitz in 1949 to designate the atonal system of musical writing which Schönberg introduced in 1923. This system, which is not based on the diatonic scale uses the 12 notes of the chromatic scale. It is particularly significant for having abolished the distinction between concordance and dissonance (see **serial**).

dominant A term given, in the classical era, to the fifth degree of the diatonic scale. For example, in the scale of C major, the dominant is G. This degree takes on the 'principal structural role, acting either as a support or as a starting point towards the conclusive tonic' (Jacques Chailley).

duration A period of time during which a note or a rest is held.

dynamics Gradations of intensity. Until Mozart, it was left mostly to the interpreter's initiative. This musical element has since been more and more set by the writing itself.

equal temperament see text p. 84.

exposition 1. The first part of an 'academic fugue' (see introductory text p. 65) which expounds the subject (or theme) in the principal key, and presents, in a second voice, the response (transposition of the subject in the key of the dominant) and then reintroduces the subject in a third voice, and finally the response in a fourth. 2. The first section of the sonata-form in which the thematic material of a structured movement is presented (see diagram p. 118).

figured bass see **basso continuo**.

fourth In the diatonic scale, this is an interval of four degrees (eg C–F).

fugato A passage in fugal style without being a fugue in its strictest sense (see introductory text p. 65).

fugue see introductory text p. 65.

glissandi An instrumental technique of going progressively from one note to another by sliding, without stopping on any intermediate note, the bow of a violin, the slide of a trombone, and so on. On the piano, it involves running the fingers rapidly and lightly over the white keys.

harmony A group of rules governing the formation and the sequence of chords. Harmony, as 'the temporal succession of sonorous "masses" made up of all the notes simultaneously emitted by different voices', is considered a vertical musical dimension.

harmonics 1. These are secondary tones emitted due to the vibration (or resonance) of a musical instrument simultaneously with the principal (fundamental) tone. The pitch of the fundamental, more clearly perceived because of its considerably stronger intensity, is attributed to the tone of the instrument in question. The acoustic distribution of the principal tones, and of their harmonics, is what characterizes the timbre of musical tones. 2. When applied to a means of playing particular to bow instruments, harmonics are the sounds produced by the partial vibration of the strings.

indeterminate This is said of a sound produced by certain percussion instruments, such as the bass drum, the triangle, etc, whose pitch cannot be determined. Among the percussion instruments which, on the other hand, generate determinate sounds are the kettledrums, bells, xylophones and vibraphones.

inflection A sign placed before a note to modify its pitch either by raising it a semitone (sharp) or by lowering it a semitone (flat), or by re-establishing its original pitch (natural) which had previously been raised or lowered.

instrumentation A musical composition which involves writing for each instrument in the orchestra in a way that brings out the technical potential of their sound qualities. As distinct from orchestration.

intensity A degree of force or power of a sound fundamentally linked to the amplitude of the air vibrations. The intensity of sound goes from the weakest to the strongest, referred to in music as from *pianissimo* to *fortissimo*.

intrada The introductory piece of an instrumental suite, comparable to the initial movement of a French overture, in that they are both solemn.

interval The distance between two notes. Simple intervals: second, third, fourth, etc up to and including the octave. Compound intervals: 9th, 10th, 11th, etc.

legato (Italian, 'bound together') The opposite of *staccato*, it is a manner of playing in which the notes follow smoothly from one another.

leitmotiv (German, 'leading motive') A theme which represents an idea, a person or a situation and constantly recurs, sometimes modified, to evoke that idea, person or situation by actually 'suggesting the transformations' (Jacques Chailley). This use of theme was at its height with Wagnerian dramaturgy.

lied-form A tripartite form (here the word 'form' signifies internal structure) based on the succession of two themes and the repeat of the first. This structure is generally that of the slow movement of a sonata, a concerto or a symphony (see diagram p. 118).

melody The musical organization of pitches, the succession of which is perceived as a coherent linear structure.

melody of tone colours (German, *Klangfarbenmelodie*) A process defined by Schönberg (*Treatise on Harmony*, 1911) which he introduced in 1909, consisting of a succession of different tone colours (timbre), which produce a coherent whole, analogous (in principle) to that of a pitch melody. As a result, the more one wants a tone-colour melody to be heard, the less its respective pitches should vary.

metre A term used in music, by analogy with versification, to designate a particular rhythmic formula.

minuet A French dance in triple-time of peasant origin (16th century), but very much in fashion in the court of the 17th century (Lully's minuets). It was integrated into the instrumental suite, before becoming a constituent element of symphonies (Stamitz, Haydn) and of sonatas. It also went from being a moderate movement to an increasingly rapid movement, foreshadowing, from that point, the scherzo of Beethoven and his successors.

mode A way of ordering the intervals of a scale (tones, semitones), within a given musical system. While there are many types; ancient modes, exotic modes (Hindu, Chinese), popular modes (tsigane, etc), tonal music only admits two: major and minor.

modulation The transition from one key to another, while respecting the rules of classical harmony.

monodic The term used, as opposed to polyphonic, to characterize either a solo song or a vocal or instrumental composition, made up essentially of an accomplished principal melodic line.

motif A group of notes, less numerous than those that make up a theme. The distinction between these two notions is often difficult to establish.

orchestration 1. The art of scoring music involving the formation of a blend of timbres by associating different instruments in which the tonal groups maximize the sounds of the orchestra in terms of the sought after overall effect. 2. The adaptation of a work for orchestra, which was originally composed for many or one soloist(s).

ornament A note or small group of notes written or improvised, which are added to a melodic line to embellish it. Examples include the *acciaccatura*, *appoggiature*, *gruppetto*, *tremolo*, *trille*, etc.

ostinato (Italian, '*obstinate*') A melodic or rhythmic formula in which a relatively long sequence of notes is repeated persistently. The basso ostinato, or ground bass, is a particular type of ostinate which is the basis of the chaconne and the passacaille forms.

parameter An expression sometimes used for each of the four constituent elements of sound (pitch, intensity, duration, timbre).

pause A conventional graphic sign placed above or below a note or a rest to tell the player to prolong this note or rest as long as desired.

phrasing The punctuation of the musical discourse, its subdivision into phrases, segments of phrases, etc, done by an interpreter across the continuous passages and pauses.

pitch One of the parameters of sound linked to the notion (used in acoustics) of the vibrations emitted by the striking, rubbing, etc, of an instrument. As the

number of vibrations increases the higher the pitch, as it decreases the lower the pitch.

pizzicato (Italian, '*pinched*') A means of emitting a sound on bow instruments by plucking with the finger.

polyphony In a general sense this work can be applied to all music composed for many voices or instruments. But it is much more often used to designate a combination of 'voices' (melodic lines) produced simultaneously and conserving some degree of autonomy from each other, as is required in the counterpoint technique.

polyrhythms The superimposition of two or more rhythmic phrases often of different forms (one based on the binary, the other on the ternary) played simultaneously.

polytonality The superimposition, in a musical composition, of melodies or harmonies belonging to different keys.

programme (music) Music associated with the depiction of images produced by real events or psychic phenomena, which the composer wants to illustrate.

realization The completion of a score by writing in, or by improvising on an instrument, the summary notation of a basso continuo, whether it is figured or not (see **basso continuo**).

recapitulation The third section of the sonata-form, after the exposition and development. It brings the first and the second themes of the exposition into the principal key of the piece (see diagram p. 118).

recitative A passage executed by an instrument in a declamatory style (by analogy with the recitative of vocal music, a type of declamation which approaches spoken language).

resolution see **discord**.

rondo In instrumental music this word indicates a lively musical form defined 'by the alternance of a principal phrase — the refrain — with secondary parts that are different each time — the verses' (André Hodeir). In the classical era the sonata, the symphony and the concerto often used a rondo for the final movement.

rhythm 1. A sequence of durations organized 'according to perceptible proportions' (Jacques Chailley). 2. Music being the 'art of time' par excellence, the rhythm can, more generally, govern and order each of its dimensions (relationships between the different parts of a work, harmonic modifications, changes of timbre or of intensity, etc).

saeta A religious melody of a lyric nature, most often improvised from a Gregorian melodic base which is heard in Spain during the processions of Holy Week.

scale 1. A series of notes arranged in conjoint degrees, where the distribution is based either on the mode or on the key in consideration. Scales which obey the laws of tonality are called diatonic (major or minor). 2. Chromatic scale: succession of intervals of twelve semitones (C, C sharp, D, D sharp, E, F, etc).

scherzo (Italian, '*jest*', '*joke*') A rapid and lively movement of a musical work derived from the minuet and structured in two parts. The first (the scherzo proper) is reintroduced after the second, which is called the trio and observes an ABA pattern. For Beethoven and the composers of the 19th century, the scherzo tends to act as a substitute for the minuet in the string quartet, the sonata and the symphony. Chopin wrote scherzos which were independent piano works.

second In the diatonic scale, an interval of two degrees (eg C–D).

serialism A method of composition in which a musical work is generated from a unique series of a predetermined number of notes. This series is governed by their order of appearance and the notes are not subject to any hierarchy as they are all of equal value. The series, as defined by Schönberg in 1923, is 'dodecaphonic', because it uses all the 12 semitones of the chromatic scale. Once the original order has been established, the Schönbergian series underwent various transformations: inversion: a horizontal mirror-image, ie, upside down), recurrence: (a vertical mirror-image, ie, backwards) and recurrence of inversion (see p. 231). And, as each of these four forms (the original series, its inversion, its recurrence and the recurrences of the inversion) can, themselves, be transposed on to the 12 semitones of the chromatic scale,

one series can lead to 48 different arrangements. This method of writing works equally well melodically as with chords. Initially applied only to pitch, the Schönbergian series was expanded in the 1950s to other parameters of sound (duration, intensity, timbre) (see **series**).

series see diagram on following page.

sonata see introductory text p. 117.

sonata-form A musical construction, originating in the classical era, governing an isolated movement of a work or even the entire work. It takes on different aspects according to the movement it is applied to. It is most strictly defined with regard to the first movement of classico-romantic works; it contains three main sections: exposition (generally repeated), development, recapitulation (optionally followed by a coda). (See diagram p. 118.) According to Charles Rosen, when a second movement (or slow movement) respects the sonata-form, it usually does not include a development; when a third movement is in sonata-form (minuet) the ABA form respects the order of exposition, development, recapitulation. Finally, if it is applied to a fourth movement, the sonata-form returns, in a less strict construction, to the shape that it had in the first movement.

staccato (Italian, '*detached*') A method of playing which detaches each note from adjacent notes. The opposite of *legato*.

stretto (Italian, *stretto*, 'tightening') The part of a fugue which precedes its conclusion; it is formed by a series of contrapuntal entries of the subject and of the response, coming closer and closer together.

tempo An approximate indication of speed of execution: (*adagio*, slow; *allegro*, fast; *allegro moderato*, moderate fast; etc) or a precise metronomic measure. In the first case, the speed is almost always based, in part, on the mood to be created by the interpreter.

theme A relatively-long musical phrase, usually melodic, which frequently serves as the basis for the development of a composition or part of a composition. Reappearing throughout the piece, it may or may not occur in variations. The theme must, in principle, be distinguished from

Series

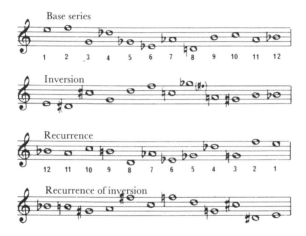

The original series of twelve notes which Schönberg composed to create his Fifth Piano Piece, opus 23 *(see p. 215).*

Base series

1 2 3 4 5 6 7 8 9 10 11 12

Inversion

Recurrence

12 11 10 9 8 7 6 5 4 3 2 1

Recurrence of inversion

The main transformations of the series (see **serialism** *p. 230) in Schönberg's opus 25.*

the motif which is shorter; in a fugue, the theme is called the subject.

third In the diatonic scale, an interval of three degrees (eg C–E).

timbre (French, '*Tone-colour*') The term for one of the constituent elements of sound, acoustically defined as 'the way in which the principal tone is superimposed by various accompanying harmonies' (Jacques Chailley). In a musical work, the timbre facilitates the identification of the nature of the source of a tone: violin, trumpet, etc) (see also **Melody of tone colours**).

tone 1. The greatest distance between two adjacent degrees on the diatonic scale (there is one tone between C + D, D + E, etc). A tone can be divided into two semitones (C — C sharp, C sharp — D) of

different types (one chromatic, the other diatonic) which make up the smallest intervals of the diatonic scale. 2. A synonym for tonality (improper use).

tonality (Key) 1. A term which describes all music which rests on a hierarchy of pitch, and privileges certain among these. The notes privileged in this way and in particular the tonic, are thus perceived as poles of attraction to which all others are subjugated. This hierarchy gave rise, in the classical era to the establishment of very complex organizational rules, but it is in fact only necessary for one pitch to be repeated more often than another in a musical passage, to create a 'tonal impression'. As a result, only the strictly egalitarian arrangement of tones in a given musical scale, such as that of dodecaphonic music, was able to suppress the perception of that effect. 2. More specifically, this term refers to the classical tonal organization; that which obeys a 'specific harmonic system based on the perfect chord and on rules of succession and attraction between dicordant and concordant chords ... according to the "tension-relaxation" balance which characterizes the classical cadence' (Michel Chion). 3. Applied to a work, tonality is determined by the principal tone. (Thus Mozart's *Symphony No.41 'Jupiter'*, is written in the tonality (or key) of C major).

tonic In the tonal (or modal) system, it is the first note (or first degree) of the scale in question. This note gives its name to the key: a tonic of C means the key of C (also called the 'key-note').

trill This is a manner of execution, initially ornamental which consists of a rapid and progressively accelerated striking of a given note and its conjoint note, usually the upper one.

trio see **scherzo**.

tutti (Italian, '*all*') 1. On a musical score, it is a sign indicating that all the instruments must play. 2. A passage played by the whole orchestra.

variation see introductory text, p. 195.

voice see **counterpoint**.

Index

Note: Entries in **bold type** refer to item headings on the pages referred to in the book.